"Judith Johnson brings dec_____ ..p..ience working with the dying and their loved ones to this extraordinary, much-needed book about how to confront our mortality with open-hearted curiosity and mindful awareness. Intelligent, wise, and gracefully written, her work deserves a place on your shelf beside Ernest Becker's *The Denial of Death* and Sogyal Rinpoche's *The Tibetan Book of Living and Dying*. I could not recommend it more highly." —Mark Matousek, author of *When You Are Falling, Dive: Lessons in the Art of Living*

"Inspired by the death of her own mother, Judith Johnson reveals how the personal can touch the universal. With refreshing honesty, she exposes cultural taboos and helps us to examine limiting core beliefs and discover how to transform our relationship to death. Her book is at once practical, encouraging, and reassuring for those wishing to be a compassionate companion to people facing illness and death." —Frank Ostaseski, founder and director of Metta Institute and author of *The Five Invitations*

"Judith Johnson offers important guidelines for dealing with death and dying, and she urges us all to prepare ourselves and assist others in a caring and intelligent way. You can sense how her heart has been educated by experience as she explores many facets of dying in the contemporary world." —Thomas Moore, author of *Care of the Soul*

"As a guide to those seeking to consciously grow, serve, and thrive as elders, I find *Making Peace with Death and Dying* a comprehensive, powerful, and vitally important resource. Judith Johnson's book is unique in its exploration of virtually every facet of death and dying in the contemporary world. It paints a vivid picture of how the strong cultural denial of dying and death disempowers and disables us from preparing in so many important ways for one of life's most natural, and important, experiences. And it contrasts this with a rapidly emerging (yet grounded in many of the world's spiritual traditions) understanding of how to meet death with compassion, acceptance, trust, and even curiosity. A significant section of this book is devoted to reflections, exercises, and poignant stories which help you explore your relationship to your mortality. These are in support of the book's invitation to befriend life's final passage and the smaller endings throughout life as opportunities for growth, compassion, and true embracing of each precious experience of transitory mortal life." —Ron Pevny, director of the Center for Conscious Eldering and author of *Conscious Living, Conscious Aging*

"In this deeply felt book, Judith Johnson shares the lessons she has learned on dying and living following the death of her beloved mother. Her journey of discovery encompasses not only the practical aspects of caring for loved ones at the end of life, but also the cultural, historical, and most importantly, spiritual aspects of our relationship with death and dying. This book is an invitation to radically transform how we live by examining our understanding of death, a project which is crucial for our society." —Leslie J. Blackhall, MD, MTS, Tussi and John Kluge Chair for Palliative Medicine, University of Virginia School of Medicine

"*Making Peace with Death and Dying* is everything you ever wanted to know about dying and the death culture. Yes, that is an exaggeration, BUT this book is comprehensive, honest, woven with personal stories, and very well done. Don't let the title scare you. It is very much about living." —Barbara Karnes, RN, author of *The Final Act of Living*

"Judith Johnson has written a heartfelt appeal for us to free ourselves from the death taboo that continues to haunt our culture. She also provides many helpful practices to assist us in developing a healthy relationship with death and dying—our own and others. This book springs out of the author's strong spiritual commitment to her dying mother. It makes a valuable contribution to the emerging literature on holistic approaches to the profound and inescapable realm of death." —Ralph White, cofounder of New York Open Center and author of *The Jeweled Highway: On the Quest for a Life of Meaning*

making peace with death and dying

A Practical Guide to Liberating Ourselves from the Death Taboo

Judith Johnson

Monkfish Book Publishing Company
Rhinebeck, New York

Paperback ISBN: 978-1-948626-53-8
eBook ISBN: 978-1-948626-54-5

Library of Congress Cataloging-in-Publication Data

Names: Johnson, Judith (Judith Ann), 1948- author.
Title: Making peace with death and dying : a practical guide to liberating
   ourselves from the death taboo / Judith Johnson.
Description: Rhinebeck, New York : Monkfish Book Publishing Company, [2022]
   | Includes bibliographical references.
Identifiers: LCCN 2021038750 (print) | LCCN 2021038751 (ebook) | ISBN
   9781948626538 (paperback) | ISBN 9781948626545 (ebook)
Subjects: LCSH: Death--Social aspects--United States. | Grief--Social
   aspects--United States.
Classification: LCC HQ1073.5.U6 J64 2022 (print) | LCC HQ1073.5.U6
   (ebook) | DDC 306.90973--dc23
LC record available at https://lccn.loc.gov/2021038750
LC ebook record available at https://lccn.loc.gov/2021038751

Book and cover design by Colin Rolfe
Front cover image by Sandra Seitamaa

Monkfish Book Publishing Company
22 East Market Street, Suite 304
Rhinebeck, NY 12572
(845) 876-4861
monkfishpublishing.com

For my beloved brother Bob,
for being my touchstone of family
and a great blessing in my life.

contents

Part One:
The Changing Face of Death in America

Part Two:
Transforming Your Relationship to Death and Dying

fulfilling a deathbed promise to my mother

Toward the end of my mother's dying process, I was sitting beside her holding her hand—just being with her. Suddenly, she grabbed my wrist, gave me that eye-piercing look that only mothers can give, and made me promise to write about what we had learned about living and dying under the American Death Taboo. She didn't call it that, but that's how I have come to think of it. This book is the fulfillment of my deathbed promise to my mother.

Before I share with you some of the tender and magnificent lessons my mom and I learned about dying, death, and grieving, I want to say a few words about the exercises in this book. They are designed to engage you in actively exploring your own relationship with death in order to achieve greater inner peace by freeing yourself from the Death Taboo. Breaking free of the insidious effects of our Death Taboo requires more than the mere intellectual process of reading a book. Personal liberation necessitates deeper inner exploration. There are forty exercises. You may want to do some or all of them with others with whom you can share your respective points of view and open up dialogue on these important matters. Also, consider writing your answers in a journal. The act of writing can assist you in probing for deeper answers, and the recording of your responses can be useful for future reference.

This first exercise is intended to give you a reference point for where you are in your relationship to your own mortality as you began reading this book.

I encourage you to participate in as many of the exercises in this book as possible, as each one is intended to assist you in evolving your own relationship to death and dying.

Exercise 1: My Worst-Case Scenario

Be brave. Go to that place inside of you where your worst fears about your own death reside. Please do not edit your thoughts. Let them all into your awareness. Let them flow freely and be sure to check all dimensions of the possible experience: physical, mental, emotional, medical, spiritual, social, financial, legal, etc.

On one side of a blank sheet of paper, describe in detail how you imagine your own death. What exactly do you see happening?

On the other side of the paper, draw a picture of what you see. If you have some crayons or colored pencils, use them. If not, a pen or pencil will do. Include as much detail as possible of what you see occurring at the time of your death.

When you have completed your picture, you might want to share it with others if you are doing this exercise together.

Mom's given name was Grace, but she earned the nickname "Cake" when I was about sixteen. My brother had noticed that on the rare occasions that we had cake for dessert, Mom had a certain ritual about cutting the cake. My dad would receive a normal restaurant-sized slice, and my brother, who was thin, would get an extra-large piece. Then my mother would glance wistfully at me and my sister, who shared a propensity to gain weight at the mere sight of sweets, and she would give us each the slenderest of slices. She always cut cakes at an angle, causing her to straighten the edge of the cake out before the next slice, and she would clean the knife on the edge of the milk-glass cake stand, leaving piles of crumbled cake. Her own slice was modest. Coincidentally, my sister and I would be excused from dish duty on cake nights, and the next day Mom would diet on cottage cheese. All the cake debris would have mysteriously vanished. One night, observing this ritual, my brother started to say, "We should call you Cake Eater," but he edited out the second word, and so she became forever after known to us as "Cake."

For the most part, I adored my mother. She was feisty, funny, independent-minded, wise, smart, very kind, and devoted to her children's well-being—we were very lucky. She was my greatest teacher in the territory of dying, death, and grieving. We shared a home during the final nine years of her life. It was one of the hardest yet tenderest and most magnificent journeys of my life so far. As Cake's physical capabilities declined, I became her errand runner and chauffeur to the hairdresser and doctors' appointments. I became her ears to capture the conversations that she faked her way through, only catching about half the words. I became her eyes because macular degeneration was taking away her eyesight. And I took it upon myself to be the one who bore witness to her experiences and, whenever possible, to comfort her and lift her spirits because sometimes her physical, mental, and emotional aches and pains made her part of the journey more challenging than she could bear. In other words, I actively loved her.

Cake and I were best friends during the final years of her life. I was extremely grateful and blessed to find that her mind and sense of humor were as sharp as tacks until the very end. However, we ran into our fair share of major and minor skirmishes about our personal boundaries and our preferences regarding seemingly mundane things like how to load a dishwasher. We weren't saints, but each of us did the best we could.

As time went on, we evolved our rhythm of learning to see what the day would bring in terms of the normal and unique challenges an aging person faces. And then she fell. In an instant the stakes became very high as we were transported into a tender and terrifying journey together during the last six months of her life.

On the balmy and beautiful Sunday of her final Memorial Day weekend, Cake fell backwards down a flight of stairs. I was a mere five yards away and out of sight when I heard her cry out a millisecond before her head hit the cabinet at the bottom of the stairs, and she landed in a thumping heap on the floor. In that instant, every cell of my body screamed with terror as I ran to find out if she had survived and, if so, how broken she was. Blood was spurting from her head and elbow to the rhythm of her heartbeat. Calm, as she had always been in a crisis, the RN in her directed me to elevate her head, compress the wounds, and call 911. I didn't seem to have enough arms, and for twelve long minutes until the EMTs arrived, the rest of the world disappeared as I held Cake and felt more helpless than ever before. And my love for her was magnified more deeply than I had ever loved anyone before. My life as I had known it was disappearing from view as I became consumed by fear, shock, and my new responsibilities as a 24/7 caregiver and patient advocate in territory I had never seen before.

Yes, it was horrible. But there was also tenderness and a deepening intimacy that opened up between us that was the sweetest connection with another person I had ever known. I was terrified of the responsibility, but I thank God that the depth of my love for her made me very brave.

There were times when Cake's needs felt like a bottomless pit and an endless parade of critical events. Sometimes I didn't know what day it was and often I didn't get out of my pajamas. I lost all momentum in my personal endeavors and became isolated from my friends. In spite of how much I loved my mother, I felt overwhelmed and trapped.

I didn't realize that, as a caregiver, I needed care too. Family support was very limited, and it seemed as though it was Cake and me against the world. When I reached out to friends for comfort, they seemed to only hear my anger and frustration with the situation. They didn't recognize that I needed them to love me enough to allow me to show this part of myself to them and have them love me anyway and love me through it. Instead, they withdrew, and I felt abandoned.

With that said, the deepening love and tenderness that Cake and I shared far outweighed the price I paid by putting my own needs and life on the back burner. In spite of the frequent life-and-death emergencies that blindsided us day after day and never feeling that I really had a clue how or what to do, we lived in love's embrace each and every day. I discovered that the bond of love between us was stronger than the trials and tribulations of Cake's dying. That was a great comfort to me—to know that I was capable of that kind of loving. We were like dance partners bound by love and circumstance, sometimes following and sometimes leading each other through to the end.

I would be less than honest if I didn't confess to getting a good look at my own dark side as well. Sometimes I wasn't very nice to Cake—or myself, for that matter. My own frustrations, impatience, and other less-than-lovely qualities got the best of me. But then a switch happened. I was bringing her to the hospital one day when we locked horns about where to park and what door to enter. Disconnected from each other by our attachment to our respective points of view, our loving bond severed in an instant and was replaced by a palpable, cold hatred of each other. I wanted to slam her in her wheelchair against the wall, and her fantasy of what to do with me was no kinder. We carried on because we had to, but we shut each other out for several hours. I was shocked by how easy it was to be so unkind and how tenuous the ties of love can be if we neglect them. I recognized how easy it was to squelch what little dignity and autonomy my mother had left by simply overriding her input because I thought I had a better solution to the problem at hand or because it was more expeditious for me. It was moments like this that tested our love and my commitment and intention to be a good and loving caregiver. Thankfully, we both made the choice that it was more important to be loving than to be right.

With 20/20 hindsight, I now recognize what a privilege and a gift our time together was while bearing witness to one another's deepest truth. We stopped putting on a happy face for each other when we were struggling and allowed our authenticity to be seen— our wonderful qualities and those darker parts of ourselves that had plenty of room for improvement. We learned to love and accept each other in the fullness of our beings without condition through it all. We allowed *nothing* to be more important than loving each other.

We both learned we were better at giving than receiving love, but each of us broke through what stood in our way of letting another human being really know us and love us and care deeply for us. Thanks to Cake and the experience we shared, I have no doubt that I am both wildly lovable and capable of very profound loving as well. It's ironic that something as feared and scary as the death and dying of a loved one can teach you about love. I think that is one of death's greatest gifts for those who face it with open hearts together.

the seven life and death lessons my mother taught me

Here are some of the lessons for which I am most grateful.

1. It's okay to be afraid. In the beginning, I judged my fears as wrong. In time, I came to appreciate that fear goes with the territory of death and dying. It is perfectly normal to be fearful about your own death or that of a loved one. Every fiber of our being has been acculturated to survival and to fear of the unfamiliar. Our fear is very real and very normal. We can't move past it until we first acknowledge it and realize that it is just one of several possibilities of how to view the situation. Fear can either stop us in our tracks or be used as a steppingstone to learn and grow and strengthen ourselves and our relationships with each other. The choice is ours to make.

2. Let nothing be more important than loving each other. Indeed, caregiving my mother was a total disruption of how I had been living my life. Yet, in hindsight I now see what a blessing it was to be thrown into a situation that forced us both to intertwine our lives so completely. It called our love into action. While ostensibly she was dying and I was caregiving, what we were really doing was profoundly demonstrating our love for each other.

When someone I care about is feeling blue, I've become better at taking the time to be there with them in whatever way seems appropriate. I have become accustomed to letting bad news interfere with my plans rather than buying into my own excuses about how I don't have the time or energy to rise to the occasion. I make the time to share my heart with them in whatever way I can. I've learned that if I want more loving in my life, I need to be available to the opportunities that present themselves—regardless of how seemingly pleasant or unpleasant the context. Even when I don't know what to say or do, I've noticed that just letting someone know I care can matter a lot to them and can liberate me from potential regrets later on for not reaching out.

When my mother was dying, there was one family member she kept asking to see because there was unfinished business between them. Four times Cake asked. On one of those occasions, she was in intensive care with a 50/50 chance of making it through the night. Each time I called this person and shared Cake's request, she showed up four days later with an entourage that minimized the opportunity for Cake to have one-on-one time with her. The resolution never occurred between them, but Cake made peace with the situation in her own heart before dying. It's so important for us to pay attention and to be brave in responding to the needs of others—especially when time is running out.

3. Everyone who is dying needs a loving advocate. When someone is critically ill or simply frail, his or her energy is needed just to cope and to heal if that is an option. There may be all kinds of specialists being called in to consult on the case, and all too often, no one is looking at the whole picture or has up-to-date information from everyone on the case. I was so busy and overwhelmed with my new role as Cake's caregiver that it took me a long time to realize this and to see that I needed to keep track and connect the dots and advocate for her concerns and overall well-being. In my mother's case, for example, she kept getting nosocomial (hospital-acquired) infections. Each infection brought on yet another antibiotic with another set of side effects that would make her susceptible to yet another opportunistic infection, and another antibiotic would be prescribed and so on. It wasn't quite popular knowledge yet that most of these infections were being spread by lack of handwashing by hospital personnel going from one patient to another. If you or a loved one is hospitalized, pay attention to whether or not people wash their hands before touching you or your loved one. And feel free to speak up and ask them to wash their hands. Sometimes, people are in a rush and cutting corners. Don't let them do that with you.

I used to spend seven to ten hours a day with Cake when she was hospitalized, trying to keep track of everything that they were doing to her. I was busy all the time. I couldn't even begin to account for what was going on when I wasn't there! It wasn't until after it was all over that I realized I should have kept a notebook handy and that the specialists were each myopically focused on treating her symptoms in their particular field, and nobody was putting it all together.

4. Death is not a popular topic among doctors. The medical model for terminal disease and death is a work-in-progress. Doctors take an oath to preserve life. Sometimes they perceive a patient's death or the need to refer the patient to hospice care as a personal failure. Expect most doctors to do everything they can think of to keep their patient going, and don't expect them to broach the subjects of palliative care or death.

Between hospitalizations, my mother made a lot of visits to the ER. It was there that one brave and wonderful doctor finally took me aside and told me that there was really nothing further medically that could be done for Cake and suggested that we consider hospice care. This was the first anyone had mentioned hospice and my mother in the same thought. I burst into tears, and he held and comforted me until I was over the shock of hearing what no one wants to hear—that your loved one is, indeed, going down a slippery slope toward death. I will always be grateful to him for telling me the truth, so we could adjust our expectations, perspective, and plans accordingly.

5. It's wise to avoid judging one another. Here is my favorite expression: W*e are all doing the best we can, and this is what it looks like.* Each of us has a complex assortment of skills, abilities, fears, traits, and preferences. Compassion comes forward when we realize that how we think another "should" behave is of no significance, for indeed, if we walked in his or her shoes, we would likely behave no differently. Particularly in stressful times, compassion for one another goes a very long way.

6. When someone you love is dying, it is his or her dying— not yours. No matter how smart you are or how certain you feel that your own ideas of what should or should not be done are the "right" way, your job is not to lead the way but to follow the lead of the one who is dying. Encourage the dying person to make his or her own choices. If he or she wants to be alone, give space. If food is refused, don't force the issue. If the person wants to make changes in his or her will, it's not up to you to decide whether or not that is a good idea. Be supportive in making that happen. If the dying one wants to talk about dying, listen. Your job is to support the dying, not to direct the process.

7. Don't leave yourself with any regrets. Whether you are the one who is dying, or you are a loved one of the dying person, pay attention inwardly to see if you are aware of any unfinished business between you. Is there something that needs to be said or done to communicate your love, forgiveness, or gratitude that would enhance the quality of your relationships or possibly heal a past hurt or misunderstanding? Be bold and speak up, being careful to do so with sensitivity and kindness to the others involved. If you can clear the air or fill it with the sweetness of love's presence, doing so can be a great blessing for all involved.

Although Cake's body, and the person she was, left this world in 2006, not a day passes without my being aware of how much better a person I am for having been her daughter and for stepping up in service to her at the end of her life. I am constantly renewed and strengthened by her memory and the knowledge of how well we loved each other. I'm very proud of us. So far in my life, she was the one who really saw me. She bore witness to my beauty and my ugliness but never withdrew her love and caring for my well-being. Her love made me stretch into the best I had in me. The pain of my losing her pales in comparison to the memory of our love and friendship and the fact that I know I did the very best I could.

Death is not optional, but love is. Each one of us chooses the quality of our relationships a thousand times each day. Those of us who choose to make nothing more important than loving each other are truly blessed.

part one

the changing face of death in America

chapter 1

the American death taboo

*"*A civilization that denies death ends by denying life.*"*

—Octavio Paz

D EATH IS A GREAT TABOO in Western society. Our culture of death is saturated with beliefs and behaviors characterized by great fear and sadness. It is not uncommon to distance oneself from the dying. We are almost instinctively afraid that what they are doing is contagious somehow. Yet not all cultures and belief systems view death in this way. The purpose of Part One of this book is to take a good look at this taboo and how it influences our ways of living and dying—and to summarize major trends in the movement to transform our culture of death.

It is important to understand the ways that we have been both consciously and unconsciously influenced by the Death Taboo and emotionally disabled from handling death in a healthy way. It is my hope that this understanding will motivate you to maximize your own freedom and to help others to liberate themselves from the many far-reaching tentacles of the Death Taboo.

Exercise 2: How Do I Really Feel About Death and Dying?

Please provide candid answers to the following questions. Simply allow the prompts to reveal to you any conscious and unconscious ways that anxieties and fears about death manifest in you and/or your life.

1. My first reaction when I hear that someone has died is usually _____.

2. The way(s) my reaction differs if the person is a stranger versus someone who I love is _____.

3. The following statement(s) best describe my beliefs about death:
   - It is a tragedy.
   - It shouldn't happen.
   - Death is normal.
   - Death gives meaning to life.
   - Death renders life meaningless.
   - I don't know what I believe about death.

4. Other beliefs I have about death and dying include _____.

5. The things I am most afraid of about my own death are _____.

6. The fact that I will die affects how I live my life in the following way(s) _____.

a childhood memory of death

When I was eight, my Uncle Eddie died. He was my favorite uncle because he made me feel so special. I don't remember how my mother prepared me for his funeral, but I have a visceral memory of experiencing foreboding as I sat beside her in the car driving to his funeral several hours away from our home. I still carry a strong recollection of standing beside his casket feeling deeply disturbed that his hands were folded in such a way that his left index finger was hidden from view. In life, that fingernail had wrapped around the top of his finger, and it always reminded me of a parrot's tongue. Uncle Eddie was my first dead person, and he was rendered just like any other dead person by the way they hid that signature fingernail. I was obsessed with the need to rearrange his hands, but I was afraid to touch him. Somehow, I knew you weren't supposed to touch a dead person. I also didn't like the fact that they had put lipstick and powder on him—he would have hated that! I recall being bewildered by the fact that I didn't know how to say goodbye without hugging him.

the process of acculturation

Each culture and subculture has its own particular guidance that seeps through the pores of its members, shaping their thinking, feelings, and behavior. Mostly, we learn through observation, repetition, and the reactions of others, especially if we step out of line. A culture functions by interpreting experiences, regulating behaviors, and generating social norms and taboos that guide us in what is considered proper and acceptable and what is frowned upon. In the US, for example, we eat hot dogs and hamburgers on the Fourth of July and turkey for Thanksgiving. We are happy when a baby is born, and we cry when someone we love dies.

In addition to the national culture, there are numerous

subcultures that contribute to our ways of thinking and being as well. For example, any three Americans—say, an Irish-Catholic baby boomer, a teen punk-rocker, and a Holocaust survivor—will have significantly different views on life and death. While each will be affected by the overarching cultural norms pervading society, their subculture norms and personal experiences will also color their beliefs and behaviors about death.

The process of acculturation has a profound and subtle impact on our individual and collective lives. It programs our expectations without regard for logic. For example, I was raised Catholic, and I remember it being unthinkable for a woman to enter church without a covering on her head, but men were expected to remove their hats before entering. That seemed odd to me, but I obeyed for fear of what would happen if I did not. Unless and until we individually or collectively consider the efficacy of a particular cultural norm, it runs on autopilot shaping our thoughts, feelings, and behaviors. History has shown us that many cultural norms subsequently evolve or are replaced by others. Such is now the case with the culture of death in America.

the culture of death

A culture of death is a mindset that consciously and unconsciously informs and regulates how a group of people relate to dying, death, and grieving. In the American culture of death, we are taught to keep death in the dark and to hold it at arm's length. "Don't think about it." "Don't talk about it." "Just don't go there." It's taboo. Why would we advise anyone to avoid preparing mentally, emotionally, physically, and spiritually for an inescapable, huge event of uncertain timing?

Yet, that is precisely what we do. Death sits like an elephant in the room that we all pretend not to see. Most of us behave like children, squeezing our eyes shut behind our hands, as though what we were looking at has disappeared because we aren't seeing it. Yet, we know it's there. The greatest misfortune of this way of relating to death is that it requires a conspiracy of silence that isolates us from each other, cutting off the sharing of our wisdom, fears, vulnerabilities, compassion, comfort, loving kindness, and caring when these expressions are most needed.

One of the vivid memories I carry that motivated me to write this book is of a man who used to visit his terminally ill wife across the hall from Cake's hospital room. We became more aware of this woman one day when I was reading to my mother and got up to close the door, concerned that the volume of my voice as I read to my hearing-challenged mother might disturb others. The woman called out urgently, "Please don't close the door—I'm enjoying this story." From then on, I read to them both.

At about 4:00 p.m. each day, this woman's husband and only visitor came for about twenty minutes. I never sensed animosity between them, but I could instinctually feel his awkward discomfort and her emotional hunger across the unutterable gulf between them. He would sit far across the room from her, fidgeting with his hat, only able to speak superficially about things like the weather. I imagined what a comfort it would have been to her if he could only have moved his chair beside her bed and silently held her hand. This man symbolizes to me the millions of people who live under the spell of the Death Taboo, not knowing what to say or do when a loved one is dying. Not knowing how to tenderly, intimately, and vulnerably be with the dying person in the face of death, too many of us sit beside one another in emotional isolation in the deafening silence of the Death Taboo. And it's not our fault—this is how we have been trained to behave. What an awful and non-refundable price we pay!

In Chapter 4, we will look at some of the wonderful things that are happening to create a healthier culture of death in America. But first, it is helpful to understand how this Death Taboo came into being and the ramifications of living under its influence.

chapter 2

the five deep taproots of the American culture of death

I N HIS 2008 BOOK, *On Human Nature*, Pulitzer Prize-winning sociobiologist Edward O. Wilson calls the American culture of death "a bizarre combination of Stone Age emotions, medieval beliefs, and godlike technology." Our culture has deep and tenacious roots that are being loosened as more and more Americans challenge the fundamental beliefs and values that have dominated our relationship to dying, death, and grieving. The five major taproots of our culture of death are as follows:

1. Polarized thinking. One of the lynchpins that holds the Death Taboo in place is a style of thinking whereby people, things, and experiences are compared to one another. We rank their value based upon their relative desirability. Unfortunately, this has a way of shortchanging us from learning how to appreciate and cope with all dimensions of life's realities. For example, we tell ourselves that life is good, and death is bad, yet these two aspects of the human journey are inextricably joined together. Each moment, they are occurring simultaneously. When we see life as good and desirable and death as bad and to be avoided, we turn away from death and fail to develop the necessary capabilities to effectively meet the challenges of life's end and the many disappointments and lesser deaths of daily life. Breaking free of polarized thinking is the focal point of the first key to making a graceful exit from this world and is the topic of Chapter 6.

2. The Black Plague. The European cultural roots of early, non-indigenous Americans bore a memory of the Black Plague, which caused people to fear that death was lurking all about them. Multiple outbreaks of the bubonic plague had ravaged Europe. According to Philip Fairleader, author of *The Late Middle Ages*, what was called the "Black Death" of 1348 killed almost half of Europe's population in just four years! Outbreaks continued to recur in Europe until the nineteenth century, striking fear in the hearts of all who survived. Prior to that, death had been seen as a normal part of life, but thereafter it became something to fear throughout one's life.

Many of the stark, black-and-white images we see today of skeletons, skulls and crossbones, and the Grim Reaper date back to this time. Originally, these images were intended to be worn by individuals in the hope that death would pass over them, thinking they were already dead. But these same images have endured for over six centuries as our dominant cultural perception of death, and they continue to reinforce the pervasive fear of death in our society.

3. The birth of the funeral industry. The third major contribution to the Death Taboo came with the advent of the funeral industry in the aftermath of the Civil War. At the time, the primary emphasis in treating the dying was to ease their symptoms. Most deaths occurred at home just days after the onset of an illness with family members caring for their dying loved one. Burial arrangements were also made by family and neighbors. The viewing of the dead typically took place in the parlor room of the family home, followed by burial on family property. As communities grew, common cemeteries also emerged.

During the Civil War, when soldiers died far from home, embalming gained legitimacy as a desirable method to preserve the integrity of their bodies while being shipped home. After the war, the cross-country journey and public viewing of Abraham Lincoln's body was another critical turning point in building acceptance of embalming.

Thus the US funeral industry emerged in tandem with the increasing acceptance of embalming, and the parlor room was moved from the family home to the newly emerging funeral homes. Furniture makers gained a second source of income building coffins. The role of the undertaker became a new profession. The undertaker literally undertook all logistical arrangements for the dead. This included transport, viewing, funeral arrangements, and burial—all previously handled by family and neighbors.

By the early twentieth century, embalming had assumed a central place in American burial practices, and funeral homes provided the expertise for tending to the dead. Previously an organic, intimate process of families and loved ones, tending to the death of a loved one was the norm. It was replaced by delegating responsibility to professionals and then relying upon them for guidance.

4. The institutionalization of medical care. Advances in science, technology, and industry brought about sweeping changes, resulting in an increased life expectancy due to improvements in sanitation in living and working conditions. The medical industry focused on offering hope of recovery to the sick rather than simply having their symptoms eased by the local doctor. Death was no longer the fait accompli of illness as lifesaving and life-prolonging discoveries contributed to lengthening lives.

As with the advent of the funeral industry, the rise of the medical industry replaced the practice of families caring for the sick in their homes by moving the afflicted to the hospital in hopes of curing their disease and prolonging their life. The cultural norm of death occurring at home only days after the onset of illness, with loved ones gathered in prayer and caring, was replaced by increasingly sophisticated medical technologies employed by professionals in institutional settings.

This medicalization of care for the sick and dying brought with it a subtle shift whereby those who were dying were depersonalized into bodies in need of medical attention. The enthusiasm of doctors regarding saving their patients also brought with it a triage mentality that gave less attention to those patients whose disease failed to respond to treatment. Death was equated with medical failure. Many healthcare professionals became increasingly uncomfortable addressing end-of-life concerns with patients and families.

We are now living in a time when many of us have come to fear facing a prolonged death characterized by overtreatment and procedures that are invasive and debilitating. The cure is often worse than the diagnosed disease itself. Many families drain their life savings seeking a cure for a terminally ill family member because they are unable to accept death as a reasonable option. Unrealistic hopes also result in delays in taking advantage of the services of hospice and palliative care programs. Some equate the choice to use the services of these programs with giving up hope rather than making a well-considered choice to acknowledge and adjust to the imminence of death.

5. The institutionalization of the sick and elderly. In the 1930s, the elderly began to be moved out of their homes as well when President Franklin Roosevelt passed the Social Security Act that provided funding to support services and nursing homes for the elderly. As a result, the number of private nursing homes grew steadily since the 1940s. Just as what happened with the sick and dying, elderly people were moved out of their homes into institutional settings, and family care was replaced by professional caregiving.

The combined impact of these five factors left most Americans unfamiliar with and ill-equipped to cope with the realities of death and dying. Where loved ones used to rely on one another to provide care and comfort, we learned to rely on the authority and expertise of doctors, professional caregivers, nursing homes, and the funeral industry to tell us what to do. This depersonalization made death and dying a more abstract experience for loved ones. A new normal has emerged with loved ones often feeling and acting like awkward spectators more than loving, hands-on caregivers to the dying. Typically, only one family member, usually a woman, steps up to be the primary caregiver and liaison to the medical professionals. She keeps the rest of the busy family informed, and the aging or dying loved one is isolated in an institutional setting.

Before the intergenerational family broke down, death was a family affair—a normal part of life—with multiple generations living under one roof or in one community and tending to a dying loved one as a domestic experience. Now, hectic lives and geographic dispersion, coupled with high-tech medical capabilities and the rise of the funeral industry, tastefully conceal death from everyday life. Sadly, our progress has brought with it a stripping away of the intimacy we used to have with each other as we faced our deaths and served as a comfort to one another. For many, caring for the dying, attending funerals, and other shared death rituals have come to be perceived as burdensome, inconvenient interruptions in our busy lives. Death has been removed from our sight in daily life by focusing our attention merely on the making of efficient choices while delegating the messy and dirty work of tending to our loved one's care to institutional workers.

This has come at a heavy price for the majority of Americans as our isolation from the death experience has increased our discomfort with it. Children are often shielded from death until their adult years when they find themselves not having a clue what to say or do when someone they care about dies. They are initiated instead into the Death Taboo's conspiracy of silence. Death has become something to be afraid of, something to feel awkward about, and something to avoid. Yet try as we might to avoid thinking or communicating about death, it lurks about us as a foreboding presence.

chapter 3

ten costs and consequences of the death taboo

T HE DEATH TABOO INFLUENCES BOTH our living and our dying. Here are the ten major costs and consequences of living in a death-denying culture:

1. Living in fear. What has come to be called "death anxiety" is the underbelly of the Death Taboo. It is a pervasive sense of distress about death and dying that lingers in the background of our minds. For some, it can be an obsession that stands in the way of experiencing life. Again, it is important to recognize that it is not our fault that we deny death. That is how we have been trained to respond to it. The fear of death is at once culturally pervasive yet deeply private. Fear places our focus on the future and away from the present, rendering us unable to take appropriate action in the present. Most of us can't quite wrap our brains around the fact that we are going to die, so we avoid the topic altogether. For many, death is an abstract and intellectual concept that has not yet been integrated into how we live. We haven't made peace with our own mortality. The fear of death is complex and lives in both our conscious and unconscious minds. Here are the major reflections of our fear of death:

- The unknown nature and timing of death
- Concerns about pain and suffering
- Being physically and emotionally isolated at the end of life

- The loss of loved ones
- The mystery of what happens after death
- Having a loved one predecease us
- Dying in a sterile hospital environment possibly being tended to by over-worked, underpaid strangers while wanting to be at home surrounded by your loved ones
- Being hooked up to machines—being kept alive when you are ready to die
- Living under the fear of nuclear destruction and acts of terrorism
- Being a burden, dependent on loved ones and caregivers
- Getting old and losing mental and bodily functions
- Being forgotten or feeling irrelevant or inconsequential
- Facing regrets

"I do not fear death. I had been dead for billions and billions of years before I was born and had not suffered the slightest inconvenience from it."

—*Mark Twain*

Whether dealing with a mild and often unconscious anxiety about death or a debilitating fear, how we think, feel, and behave in our daily lives is affected by how we perceive and relate to death. Both anxiety and fear are triggered by stress, and while simply avoiding stress factors can yield temporary and short-term benefits, it is necessary to get at the root of the fear to truly liberate ourselves from it.

Is fear the only way to react to death? No. The dynamics of fear stand in the way of accepting our mortality and evolving a healthy relationship with death and dying. To get to the bottom of our fear requires looking at the assumptions we make about death, which we will do in Chapter 7.

The Death Taboo is on autopilot, constantly influencing our thoughts, behaviors, and attitudes toward dying, death, and grieving. As if trying to hold a beach ball under the water, the denial of death expends an enormous amount of our energy that could be put to far better use if we learned how to have a healthy response to death instead. As explained by John-Roger, a spiritual teacher and educator:

> When you deny something, you are actually giving energy to it. You know it's real, or you wouldn't be denying it. When you deny something, you actually affirm its existence. That thing will use the energy you give it and grow to a level that you can't handle. Don't deny it; acknowledge its existence and work to bring it to a level you can handle.

Debbie Ford, an American self-help author, has a mnemonic for the word "denial": *Don't Even Notice I Am Lying*. Our dominant cultural response to dying, death, and grieving is to be afraid. Coupled with the fact that our instinctive response to fear is to fight against the object of our fear, to flee from it, or to freeze, we find ourselves dealing with death very much like the three monkeys who see no, hear no, speak no evil. Originally, the three monkeys were a proverbial reminder to be of good mind, speech, and action. Similarly, the Death Taboo teaches us to look the other way and refuse to acknowledge what we perceive to be the ultimate evil: death. We have learned to suppress our true feelings and fears—our very humanity—thinking this is a way to cope with that we have deemed unacceptable. Yet this doesn't cope with the situation at all.

"Everyone is so afraid, but the real Sufis just laugh: nothing tyrannizes their hearts. What strikes the oyster shell does not damage the pearl."

—*Jalāl ad-Dīn Rumi*

2. Being ill-informed, unprepared, and ill-equipped for death. Can you imagine going on a long trip or moving to a new home and not packing before departure, or arriving at the airport for an overseas flight not knowing that you would need a passport or photo ID? Boys and girls in scouting troops are taught to "be prepared," but for some reason we exempt ourselves from being prepared for death. As a result, we find ourselves, as I did, called upon to care for a dying loved one with no idea what we should or could be doing to help. What is normal? What are the options? Who should be making decisions? What questions should I ask of whom? Caught off guard, we are thrown into crisis mode, which is never the best state of mind for making important decisions.

Typically, we avoid even the most basic elements of end-of-life planning, such as having a healthcare proxy and a will. Too uncomfortable to think about or talk about it, we don't take the time to figure out what arrangements we would want to have made on our behalf in the event of our death. Afraid of upsetting someone by broaching the subject, we isolate ourselves and don't share our thoughts, fears, and preferences with loved ones or our doctors. As a result, we leave our grieving loved ones to second-guess our wishes without our input. End-of-life planning offers us the opportunity to influence the quality of life's end and to minimize the confusion, stress, and suffering that results when we fail to put our affairs in order. Chapter 14 will help make this task easier if you haven't already put your affairs in order. Those of you who have already done so might discover that you put your affairs in order with an emphasis on legal and financial concerns but omitted a heartfelt dimension that expresses your more personal wishes.

We tend to live with unrealistic expectations about life and death. We behave as though everyone is supposed to die really old and worn out. Yet according to the US Center for Disease Control:

- 27.6 percent of us die before the age of 65
- 16.5 percent of us die between the ages of 65 and 74
- 25.3 percent of us die between the ages of 75 and 84
- 31.0 percent after the age of 85

These statistics shatter the illusion that only a few people die when they are young and that only old people need to be concerned about putting their affairs in order.

It is not only those who die that are affected by death. Each individual who dies is someone's child, mother or father, sister or brother, grandma or grandpa, wife or husband, dear friend, lover, colleague, or adversary. We are all connected to each other in the web of humanity.

Each year, 2.8 million Americans die. Yet we behave as if death shouldn't happen. By denying the reality of death and dying, we disable ourselves from appropriately preparing physically, mentally, emotionally, spiritually, socially, medically, financially, and legally. We have the tools, but we pretend it is better not to use them because they make it too real. We tell ourselves that we have so many other more important things to do. Lacking the capacity to accept the reality of death prohibits us from dealing with it in the most fundamental of ways. How futile and hurtful to be taught to avoid what is a normal part of the human experience.

For many, life passes by in an uninterrupted race against time with more things to do than hours in the day, weeks, or years at hand. If we are not careful, life consumes us, leaving very little opportunity to explore how life is being lived or to attend to those things that we do not regard as urgent priorities.

Since, according to the Center for Disease Control, the vast majority of Americans will die as a result of illness, most people have the time to slow down at the end of life and to reflect upon their journey. Loved ones are also typically called to self-reflection when someone is nearing life's end. Unfortunately, the timing of this examination provides the dying person only a small window of opportunity, and the self-examination is pursued during heightened stress. Too many find themselves running out of time to make any desired changes or to communicate what has been left unsaid. *Making Peace with Death and Dying* is designed to free you from your own anxieties around death and to empower you to fearlessly meet death on your own terms.

We are taught that life is good, and death is bad. Therefore, it is counterintuitive to seek a deeper understanding of the wisdom of death's presence in our lives, the issues it raises, and the profound decisions that will someday need to be made. Instead, we avoid death like the plague, unable to cope with its reality. Ironically, death is as normal as birth and life. All three are essential parts of the life cycle of a human being.

The Death Taboo sabotages and suppresses our ability to evolve a personal perspective on death. By breaking the silence within ourselves on this topic, we set the foundation for making decisions that are in alignment with our deepest beliefs and values about living and dying.

It is in claiming these values and beliefs that we are best able to meet death on our own terms with greater self-determination about such things as our end-of-life healthcare, the disposition of our body and belongings, and the kind of end-of-life ritual that would be appropriate for us. It also supports us in coping with the death of our loved ones by making it acceptable and normal to talk about our experiences, thoughts, and fears about death.

3. Seeking the "Fountain of Youth" rather than fully embracing all phases of life. The American culture of death is greatly influenced by the value placed on youth and achievement. Within the context of our propensity for polarized thinking, it is easy to see why aging, dying, and death are, relatively speaking, perceived as failures. The elderly and the mere subject of death are grim reminders of our existential vulnerability and our inability to control life and death. We institutionalize and marginalize the aging and dying and often don't make the time to keep our relationships with them alive. By placing polarized value judgments on youth and aging, we deny ourselves the opportunity to comprehend the inherent blessings and challenges of every phase of life.

4. Emotional isolation. Honoring the taboo around death requires pushing down our true feelings and, in many ways, becoming strangers to ourselves and each other. This emotional isolation creates pointless suffering. Most of us have no idea how to talk about death. Many of us, especially terminally ill patients, put a smile on our faces and silently suffer through our concerns in emotional isolation. Rather than entering into the vulnerability and comfort of intimacy with our loved ones, we are more likely to suffer through the experience frightened, alone, and ill-prepared.

Sometimes we tell ourselves that we are protecting our loved one by not sharing the truth of our fears over disappointing medical test results. We avoid the vulnerability and intimacy with ourselves and each other of knowing, exploring, and sharing our concerns about death and dying. When we need each other the most, we withhold our love not knowing what to say or do. Our lack of experience and comfort around death leaves us with limited tolerance for, or acceptance of, the raw emotions of grief and loss and the fact that these feelings arrive long before the death actually occurs.

Chapters 7 and 8 are designed to assist in developing greater familiarity with your own deepest beliefs and fears about death and learning how to lead with your tender and vulnerable heart to develop greater intimacy with loved ones facing death.

5. Disconnect between our wishes and reality. The following facts shed additional light on how much of a disconnect exists between what we say we want to experience regarding death and dying and what our actual experiences are—which begs the question of "why?"

According to CBS's 2010 *60 Minutes* report, "The Cost of Dying," only 10 percent of us will die suddenly due to an accident, heart attack, or another unexpected event. Nine out of ten of us will die at the end of a progressive disease. And the vast majority of Americans say they want to die at home yet 75 percent die in a hospital or nursing home and one in five spends their last days in an ICU. It's no wonder a 2018 article by the American Medical Association reports that a quarter of all Medicare spending is for our care during the last year of life. "The Cost of Dying" also reported that in 2009, Medicare paid $55 billion just for doctor and hospital bills for the last two months of patients' lives. That's more than the budget for the Department of Homeland Security or the Department of Education. And it's been estimated that 20 percent to 30 percent of these medical expenses may have had no meaningful impact on extending life. Most of the bills were paid for by the Federal Government with few or no questions asked.

Another anomaly is that 80 percent of people say that, if seriously ill, they would want to talk to their doctor about end-of-life care, yet a mere 7 percent report having had an end-of-life conversation with their doctor, according to a California Health Foundation Study, *Attitudes and Experiences with Death and Dying.* It is interesting to note that it wasn't until 2016 that the Medicare reimbursement policy changed to provide coverage for such conversations. Until then, doctors were not financially incentivized to have these important conversations with their patients. As Atul Gawande, surgeon and public health researcher, says in *Being Mortal: Medicine and*

What Matters in the End, "If end-of-life discussions were an experimental drug, the FDA would approve it."

Doctors, like the rest of us, have been acculturated into the conspiracy of silence about death. How often does this cause the patient to endure the pain of more drugs and procedures, which simply delay the inevitable need to face death while offering little hope for improvement?

6. Postponing and avoiding end-of-life planning. One of the most detrimental outcomes of our avoidance of death and dying is that we tend to sidestep making practical plans for the end of life. We delude ourselves by believing that we have plenty of time. Many superstitiously believe that if we put our affairs in order, our readiness will somehow bring about our demise. Yet in reality, not exploring and communicating our preferences for end-of-life care or appointing a healthcare proxy or granting a power of attorney and filing a will leaves us vulnerable to potentially devastating consequences. Current estimates agree that approximately one in three US adults completes any type of advance directive for end-of-life care. Similarly, only 32 percent of Americans in the Caring.com 2020 Estate Planning and Wills Survey have a will, including less than half of those over age fifty-five. This not only causes tremendous heartache and confusion for loved ones, but unnecessary legal, accounting, and funeral expenses incurred as a direct result of families and loved ones not knowing the wishes of the dying or deceased.

Consider the following possibilities:

- What if your worst nightmare is being on life support when there is no hope of a cure—but you never told anyone?
- What if your loved ones are put in the position of having to second-guess your wishes, and the one who takes charge has beliefs that yield choices vastly different from those you would make for yourself?

- What if your money and personal effects get tied up in the courts for years because you have no will, or your loved ones could only find a very old copy of a will you left behind? Legal fees for a simple will are inconsequential compared to the costs associated with finalizing an estate where there is no will or a poorly written one.

These situations often go on for years. My aunt, for example, had written a simple will leaving her entire estate of approximately $30,000 to her church. Because we were unable to find an original copy of this will, it took four years, and her church only received a pittance after legal expenses were paid.

Another dimension of end-of-life planning that the majority of Americans avoid is the planning of their funeral or memorial service. Most people purchasing funeral services are woefully ignorant of all the alternative ways of saying their goodbyes. Typically, bereft loved ones rely on the guidance of funeral directors and clergy who may not have even known the deceased. My friend Lisa told me how she fought against the urge to scream out "Blah Blah Blah" during her grandfather's dry, generic funeral service because it neither reflected him nor his beliefs. Many of us end up spending beyond our means for fear of being perceived as not doing enough to honor the deceased. The National Funeral Directors Association reports that the average funeral in the US, excluding a cemetery plot and grave, is approximately $9,000.

When we deny the realities of our mortality, we leave a mess behind for others to deal with. Chapter 14 simplifies the basics of putting your affairs in order from a place of authenticity with ease and grace.

7. Denial of the power of grief. Another ramification of the Death Taboo is that no one teaches us how to cope with grief. For some, our hearts are broken asunder by uncontainable sorrow, and we find ourselves overwhelmed and isolated as the world goes on all around us. Others are unable to surrender to their grief and attempt to carry on as usual without acknowledging and processing their mental anguish and deep sense of loss. We are trained to respond to death by seeking to be in control and not allowing life to appear too messy. Rather than being swallowed up by grief when a loved one dies, we are encouraged to get on with our lives as quickly as possible. Yet anyone who has suffered the loss of a loved one knows that grief has no regard for these guidelines. Grief has a mind of its own and will have its way with the griever, one way or another. We are forever changed by our grief and must evolve a new sense of normalcy.

I was speaking to a friend who shuddered recalling the 4:00 a.m. call she received forty years ago when her twenty-year-old son was killed in a car accident seven hours away. For her, it was as though it happened yesterday. For forty years now, this trauma has been replayed in her heart and mind without the benefit of any grief counseling to help her integrate this experience into her life. She has gone on to live a full and productive life, but that particular wound remains an unhealed trauma that she carries with her every single day. Chapters 10 and 11 offer some useful techniques for integrating our grief into a way of moving forward that is less debilitating than what my dear friend experiences every time she recalls the loss of her son.

We each have our own way of grieving, and each death touches us in its own unique way. However, can you imagine being expected to "get over" the death of someone you love deeply in four days? That's the average bereavement leave given by American businesses when the deceased is an immediate family member, according to the Grief Recovery Institute's 2003 groundbreaking study, *The "Hidden" Annual Costs of Grief in America's Workplace*. Recognizing that debilitating emotional pain may be due to a wide range of life events such as a miscarriage or pet loss, The Grief Recovery Institute has done in-depth research into the financial impact of grief in the workplace.

The truth is there is no quick fix for "getting over" a death in either our business or private life. It takes time to find our new normal and to restore our ability to function effectively.

It can be challenging for a grieving employee to acknowledge his or her vulnerability and personal needs for fear of job loss. However, denying our grief in order to carry on as expected is dangerous. When we suppress our grief, it expresses itself in other ways such as depression, anger, addiction, substance abuse, and physical illness. The reality is that grief is typically a devastating experience best healed with time, patience, compassion, loving kindness, and reduced expectations of productivity.

The love that connects us is powerful, profound, and—for most of us—our most treasured possession. When someone we love dies, it is quite normal to be devastated and dysfunctional. Just as our physical resources are diverted to the healing process after a serious illness or injury, so are our mental and emotional energies redirected to the grieving process or the avoidance of this natural process, whether we like it or not. Grief is an equal opportunity employer, whether you are a CEO or an assembly line worker. When you are grieving, you are a human being with a broken heart.

While there are somewhat predictable patterns to grief, each of us will have our own unique journey through the grieving process. For those interacting with the grieving, there is no more effective medicine than love in action—a smile, a helping hand, a note of sympathy, picking up the slack at home or work with compassion, an invitation to lunch or to go for a walk together. Let your heart be your guide. Grief has a life of its own and cannot be neatly compartmentalized on your calendar.

Grief is normal, but our lack of preparation for coping with grief when it arrives in our lives is a cultural failure. As will be discussed in the next chapter, there are more and more wonderful resources available to assist us with our grief. However, many people are resistant to using these services because they are still under the spell of the Death Taboo that tells them they are expected to carry on and get over it. As a result, many suffer shame, guilt, and depression when faced with the reality that their grief does not go away or conform to external expectations.

Grief doesn't start after someone has died. It is the anticipation of loss that ushers in the grieving process both for the one who is nearing death and for loved ones. For an employer to provide bereavement leave after the death has occurred is often far too little, far too late.

8. The costs of death and grief in the workplace. American businesses pay a hefty price for our inability to relate to dying, death, and grieving in a realistic and compassionate manner. The two major categories of expense are attributed to caregiving and grieving. In 2006, *The MetLife Caregiving Cost Study: Productivity Losses to US Business* estimated that the annual cost to American businesses of full-time employed caregivers was $33.6 billion. This includes costs associated with absenteeism, workday interruptions, crises in care, supervision, unpaid leave, and increased turnover. The Grief Recovery Institute has estimated the cost to US businesses of such grief-inducing experiences as the death of loved ones or a close friend, divorce, family crises, financial losses, pet losses, and other major life events at more than $113 billion annually in lost productivity, lost business, and poor performance. In his 2017 blog, "Complicated Grief," Stephen Moeller, a grief recovery specialist defines grief as "the normal and natural reaction to any change from what is familiar in life." The Grief Recovery Institute estimates that 1 in 4 employees is grieving at any given time.

It is important to consider the fact that these costs do not capture the additional impact of one employee's loss on fellow workers. Stretched beyond their limits, those with caregiving responsibilities at home or suffering a major loss cannot maintain their previous levels of productivity, and fellow workers must either willingly or resentfully pick up the slack. The Grief Recovery Institute's study captured the experiences of 25,000 participants who provided the following insights into the impact of their grieving on their ability to work: 85 percent of management level decision makers indicated that their decision-making ranked from "very poor" to "fair" in the weeks or months following the grief incident that affected them. Similarly, 90 percent of those in Blue Collar and other physical jobs indicated a much higher incidence of physical injuries due to reduced concentration in the weeks or months following the grief incident.

When study participants were asked if their reduced ability to concentrate affected them for any period of time beyond any allowed bereavement time in the case of the death of a loved one, 75 percent indicated that reduced capacity affected them significantly beyond the allowed leave. Asked to estimate the amount of lost days that they believed were the direct and immediate result of their reduced focus, 50 percent reported at least thirty lost days in which their value to the company or business was dramatically reduced. Furthermore, reduced productivity may well have contained significant negative consequences in the form of poor decision-making, poor supervisory skills, reduced sales ability, and increased workplace accidents and injuries. An additional 20 percent reported being affected for substantially longer than thirty days. Whether at home or work, the bottom line is that when your heart is broken, your mind doesn't function well, and the healing process takes more time than we are typically willing to accept.

9. The impact of the Death Taboo on the medical model. Prior to the introduction and ongoing integration of palliative care and hospice into the medical model, the death of a patient was viewed as a failure by the doctors and medical staff. To this day, many doctors continue to be reluctant to refer a patient to palliative care because they consider it a form of giving up on their ability to "save" their patient. On a deep level, many doctors equate such a referral with professional failure to uphold the Hippocratic oath and an indication of incompetence. In reality, there are just two things they just can't seem to fix: aging and dying.

The 2009 thanatology textbook *The Last Dance* tells the story of a contemporary hospital where the word "death" is forbidden among the hospital staff. They inform colleagues of a patient's death by asking, "Guess who's not going to shop at Walmart anymore?" Given this state of consciousness, it is easy to understand the quest for medical interventions to forestall death. Doctors continue to have difficulty telling patients and their loved ones that there is nothing further to be done medically.

How does this state of consciousness affect the death experience of a patient? A twelve-year-old girl named Lucy Grogan who died of leukemia in 2006 wrote a letter to her doctor from her deathbed. She asked him to promise that in the future when he looked at a dying child, he would see her love as well as her sick body. An environment sterilized for the bodies of the sick and dying must take care not to sanitize away the expression of love, fear, and other natural human emotions.

In too many hospitals and nursing homes, the Death Taboo leaves terminal patients to figure out what to do for themselves. I remember back in the 1980s when so many gay men were dying. My friend Rick told me that half his address book had been wiped out over the course of one year. He attended one or two funerals weekly. Living in a society with such a powerful Death Taboo left this community unsupported to deal with the prevalence of death among them.

I also remember being in a hospital visiting my friend Steve, who was dying. His friend Mark was down the hall, and although I didn't know Mark, I paid him a visit as a kindness and favor to Steve. When I first looked in his room, I saw an emaciated, noodle-like man covered in sarcomas with a dinner tray towering over his supine body, just out of reach. I watched as he tried to reach his hand up to feel what was on the tray, but his arm kept falling back onto the bed, banging against his boney leg, and causing him to wince. I asked if I could come in and if he'd like some help. He was grateful and directed me in raising the head of his bed and lowering the tray. Eating was the last thing in the world he wanted to do, he said. In fact, the smell of the food made him nauseous, but he had promised his friends that he would bulk up to make himself stronger so he could live on, and he didn't want to let them down. He was so busy fighting death, which came several days later, that I wonder if he ever made peace with it before he died.

Back then, just about everyone was zip-lipped, unconscious, and repressed where death was concerned. Getting better was the only acceptable option no matter how close to death the patient was. Loved ones would cheer patients on and urge them to fight for their life even when death would have been a blessing. Today, many of us continue to enter the room of a dying loved one, putting a perky smile on our face and saying something like, "Your color looks good today," rather than allowing authentic emotions to show for fear that one of us would not be able to handle it. Thankfully, the comfort and wisdom of palliative care and hospice are beginning to teach us a more realistic and compassionate way of relating to each other in the presence of death and dying.

With doctors and their patients both reluctant to discuss death, needed conversations are still more likely to be avoided than pursued by either party. A few years ago, my dear eighty-nine-year-old friend Roy was in the hospital dying, and his doctor kept fudging through conversations with his family about what Roy needed. The doctor would suggest possible tests that could be done or new specialists to bring in to consult on Roy's case. We all knew Roy was dying. One of his daughters finally blurted out to the doctor, "Don't you think it would be a good idea for you to refer Roy to hospice?" As though insulted by the suggestion that his services were not going to further help Roy, he said, "Well, of course, if that's what you want to do." How sad that he could not support the family in making such a critical decision.

Our doctors usually know the probable course a terminal disease will take but are more inclined to treat immediate symptoms rather than to educate us about the bigger picture. Decline and death remain difficult topics of discussion. In contrast to this, I fondly remember two of my mother's doctors who shared the truth as they knew it with me. The first was the Emergency Room doctor I mentioned earlier who was the first to be candid with me about the fact that my mother was not going to get any better and broached the subject of hospice for the first time. The other was her cardiologist who never tried to give me false hope. He explained that she was on a slippery slope toward death and could be expected to have periods of rapid decline followed by plateaus, but that she simply would not get any better. This truth made it far easier for us to be realistic and to treasure the time we had left together.

Most hospital patients, relying on doctors to advise them of their healthcare options, fail to take into consideration the vested interests of the doctors and hospitals and their inherent reluctance to face the end of medical options. As a result, many terminal patients are given false hope by a frenzy of tests and procedures that do little more than protect against potential lawsuits and provide financial benefit to the doctors, hospitals, and insurance and drug companies. Unfortunately, they also delay needed honesty about the patient's prognosis while denying the patient the opportunity to transition into the process of dying.

Hope needs to find a more realistic place in the dying part of our lives. The not-so-hidden message of the medical model now is that hope ends where medical alternatives to preserve life run out. Yet, for those of us who view dying as an essential part of life's journey, there is hope beyond medicine, hope that says, "I hope my loved one dies peacefully and with no regrets." Or: "I hope I am able to be a comfort to my loved one as he or she comes to life's end. I hope I have the courage to be honest, authentic, and responsive to his or her needs."

10. Diversion of our focus away from the deep spiritual mysteries and wisdom of life and death. Spiritually, many people have a difficult time reconciling belief in God with the reality of death as part of the human journey. Some carry a judgment against God as having set up this whole thing called life the wrong way. Consider the ramifications of creating such a small god that it must fit into the box of human understanding. Where is the awe in a world without the mystical? For, indeed, what is more profound and mystical than the depth of tenderness, intimacy, love, and vulnerability we can share in the face of death?

When all is said and done, is it not the loving and caring we have shared that we hold most dear at life's end? Being authentic and intimate with each other in the presence of death is a great gift. To be able to serve a loved one facing death from a place of personal strength rather than fear gives us the satisfaction of knowing we did our best after they are gone. This can soften our grief. Unfortunately, for those blinded by their fears of death and dying, the natural instinct is to run and hide and make excuses for not being available.

In the spiritual tradition that I follow, I have learned that, just as there are laws of the physical universe, there are rules governing spiritual consciousness as well. The degree to which we are aware of the presence of the divine in our lives is governed by these laws. As we become able to comprehend and align ourselves with them, we gain access to the treasures they guard. If we slam the door of our mind shut, we forbid ourselves entry into these mysteries. The five laws of spirit are acceptance, cooperation, understanding, loving, and enthusiasm, and they represent a passageway to mental and emotional freedom. When we do not work in cooperation with these laws, our consciousness typically operates in a reactive mode to external conditions. We perceive ourselves to be victims or winners in the game of life. Seeing death as wrong or bad is a perfect example. Acceptance of death—the acknowledgment of its presence without judgment or rejection—enables us to cooperate with the experience rather than trying to escape it.

Here is another spiritual conundrum—if, from your point of view, God is fallible, then who is in charge in your worldview? Isn't such a god too small? Alternatively, if you were to surmise that perhaps God wasn't making a mistake after all, then there must be some divine wisdom to the reality of death. By fearing and avoiding death, we block our access to the process of exploring the divine wisdom, mysteries, and blessings that are part of death. This is one of the most damaging consequences of the Death Taboo and will be explored in Chapter 11.

Other cultures educate their members about the reality of death and the processes of dying and grieving. Ours has abdicated responsibility in these matters and fumbles with the consequences. Until now, we have been left to figure it out for ourselves, relying on doctors and funeral directors to tell us what to do once we are face-to-face with death and overwhelmed by its presence. We haven't known what to say, what to do, how to cope, or how to grieve. Most of us simply let the experts lead us around by the nose—too stunned to take charge of the situation ourselves. We have paid a huge price for upholding the Death Taboo both personally and as a society. Shadowboxing with death expends a lot of energy that could be put to better use learning skills to deal with the uncertainty, sadness, and loss that surrounds death, skills that would allow us to find our own authentic response to its inevitability.

The good news is that cultures are always evolving as new challenges, opportunities, and fundamental changes impinge upon them. Sometimes, norms and taboos remain in effect long after their utility and originating cause have passed away. Such is the case with the Death Taboo at the core of the American culture of death. Not only has it outlived its usefulness, but it is an example of a cultural norm that does not support the health and well-being of its members. Just as what is considered to be "normal" in a dysfunctional family fails to serve the highest good of the family members, so too can cultural norms provide a disservice to members of a given society. Living in a culture that fails to embrace the full depth and breadth of the human experience leaves its members ill-equipped for reality. Wouldn't we be better served by learning how to meet death with compassion, acceptance, capability, existential preparedness, and far less anxiety and fear?

Clearly, there is room for improvement in how we relate to death both as individuals and as a society. The good news is the work that needs to be done is well underway, as will be discussed in Chapter 4. The fundamental challenge is to change our underlying consciousness about death—how we hold this concept in our minds and how we teach future generations to relate to death. Replacing the old with healthier new ways of thinking about and dealing with death is the focus of Part Two of this book, which provides a roadmap to lightening up our individual consciousness about, and engagement with, death. Who knew death could be an uplifting and enriching topic!

Exercise 3: How Does the Death Taboo Manifest in My Life?

For each of the ten consequences of the Death Taboo listed below, ask yourself how you see it reflected in the way you are living your life and how you relate to your mortality. Also consider how you experience this issue being prevalent in your family, community, and society. Ask yourself if you are experiencing any of the following:

1. Living in fear
2. Being ill-informed, unprepared, and ill-equipped for death
3. Seeking the fountain of youth rather than fully embracing all phases of life

4. Emotional isolation
5. Disconnect between our wishes and reality
6. Postponing and avoiding end-of-life planning
7. Denial of the power of grief
8. The costs of death and grief in the workplace
9. The impact of the Death Taboo on the medical model
10. Diversion of our focus away from the deep spiritual mysteries and wisdom of life and death

———————

chapter 4

putting a new face on death

*"*We don't really talk about death and I feel we can integrate
it in our lives not in a morbid way, but so it gives
meaning to everything else.*"*

—Arianna Huffington

THE US CULTURE OF DEATH is getting a facelift. Let's take a
look at some of the wonderful things that are happening to
create a healthier culture of death and dying and how these changes
have come about. We are experiencing a cultural awakening to greater awareness and courage in facing our own death and the deaths of
those we love. We are indeed living in exciting times where death
is concerned! In fact, there is a virtual revolution going on in how
we relate to our mortality. The American culture of death is getting
a much needed overhaul. The time is ripe for you to do your part
by taking a good look at the old and emerging cultures of death to
reassess your individual point of view and to join in the shaping of
this new face of death. Although transforming the culture of death
in America may seem like a lofty idea, it is happening one person at
a time. In the following model, see if you can identify where you are
in relationship to this revolution.

Everett Rogers' diffusion of innovation theory

Rogers' theory provides a great context in which to view the changes that are occurring in our culture of death. Represented by a simple bell curve, this theory portrays the typical rate of progression of any innovation being introduced to society as the five groups identified by Rogers adapt to the change. Innovators initiate the process and have the highest propensity to adopt the innovation. Next are Early Adopters and the Early Majority with slower rates of adapting to the change.

Like a giant game of whisper-down-the-lane, Rogers' theory depicts how social innovation takes hold. It begins with Innovators who define issues and propose solutions. Momentum mounts when they share their point of view with Early Adopters who jump on board and subsequently enthuse the Early Majority until the innovation becomes a fairly normal part of how we function. On the descending side of the bell curve are the two groups with the highest rate of resistance to the change. They are the Late Majority and the Laggards. Think of the advent of cell phones, the use of the words "hashtag" or "emoji."

In terms of transforming our culture of death in America, we are still in the early stages of change with a healthy population of Innovators, Early Adopters, and some Early Majority participants now coming aboard. What has been missing and causes *Making Peace with Death and Dying* to be so timely is its presentation of clear and effective transformational tools that allow us to, individually and collectively, dismantle the impact of the Death Taboo on our lives. This work must be done one person at a time in the privacy of our own minds as we upgrade our internal, all too often autopilot thoughts and fears about death and dying.

The transformation of our culture of death is creating enormous changes in our lives. For example, the concept of hospice and palliative care was first introduced into the US in 1963. By 1974, the first US hospice was built, and by 1986, the Medicare Hospice Benefit was made permanent by Congress. Since then, hospices and palliative care programs have started throughout the country. The Early Majority group is just now becoming advocates for palliative care.

the single-most profound change:
hospice and palliative care

The term "hospice" comes from the root word "hospitality," and according to the National Hospice and Palliative Care Organization, the use of this word can be traced back to medieval times. Back then, the term "hospice" referred to a place of shelter and rest for travelers on a long journey. Physician Dame Cicely Saunders opened the first hospice that specialized in care for dying patients in 1967 in London.

Both hospice and palliative care provide treatment for pain and symptoms being experienced by the patient. While hospice care is specifically for the dying, palliative care refers to providing treatment for pain and symptoms to anyone at any stage of a serious illness. Hospice services come into play when it is determined that no further curative treatments are available or desired by the patient for his or her underlying disease. Palliative care is available along with curative treatments. In other words, palliative care is not dependent on a patient's prognosis. In both cases, the patient's nonphysical needs are addressed as well.

An internet search is a good way to find a hospice or palliative care program in your area. Hospices generally serve specific geographic areas such as a county or city. Each one is largely funded and regulated by Medicare and other health insurance providers. If you are looking for a local hospice, check with your County Office for the Aging.

Hospice services have evolved from a volunteer-led movement to a significant part of our healthcare system. Palliative care programs tend to be affiliated with hospitals and other medical treatment facilities. The increasing popularity of hospice and palliative care programs raise a challenge to the traditional medical model that focuses almost entirely on providing curative treatment for physical diseases.

Hospice services are now reaching the Early Majority of Americans. A 2013 study in the *Journal of the American Medical Association* estimated that the percentage of Medicare patients who died in the hospital declined from 33 percent to 25 percent between 2000 and 2009. Those who died while receiving hospice care nearly doubled from 22 percent to 43 percent during the same period. Unfortunately, many of the hospice referrals continue to occur only in the last three days of life.

There remains a prevalent, often unspoken, concern among many that entertaining the possibility of using hospice services means giving up all hope of improving the patient's condition. This still serves as a major barrier inhibiting many people from availing themselves or their loved ones of hospice services. The truth is that studies consistently report that patients who receive hospice care live longer and more comfortably than those who do not.

My mother and I had the great good fortune of receiving hospice services for six months. I was delighted to find that care for the caregiver is built into the hospice program. I mentioned earlier that an ER doctor tenderly broached the subject of hospice with me. At that point, Cake had been in and out of the hospital and had had about six urgent trips to the ER before this doctor spoke to me to say that there was nothing further to do medically for her and suggested bringing in hospice. I'm so grateful to him—and to us—for being realistic about her condition. We knew she was dying. I don't think either of us had any idea what hospice would be other than comfort care for her physical symptoms.

At first, I was overwhelmed by all the dimensions of hospice care. I was afraid of being pushed out of my primary caregiver role as I had been when my mother had previously been admitted to the hospital.

Once I began to trust that the hospice workers were there to help me rather than to displace me, I relaxed into the experience, which I can only equate to what I imagine it would be like to be abducted by angels. These were our personal favorite things about hospice:

- Hospice is designed to care for all dimensions of the dying and his or her caregivers. They actually care about your mental, emotional, spiritual, financial, legal, and social well-being, as well as your physical comfort. And they provide grief support after your loved one dies.

- The music program was a great surprise to us. Before lack of funding eliminated this from our local hospice program, a delightful young woman came several times with her guitar and small harp to do music therapy with Cake. I was ignorantly condescending and tolerant when she first arrived, not wanting anyone to mess with my mommy, but once she started, I instantly changed my tune and couldn't wait for her to come again. She played my mother's favorite songs, the ones that touched her heart and transported her back to beloved times in her life. It was cathartic and precious for her (and for me, eavesdropping out of sight).

- Hospice monitored and paid for Cake's medications and delivered them to the door immediately.

- They checked in privately with my mother to make sure that she was getting her needs met and to see if she had anything incomplete in her life that she wanted to finish. As it turned out, it was one of the hospice nurses who facilitated my mother being able to finally meet with the family member she kept asking to see.

- I was no longer alone trying to figure it all out and to orchestrate making sure my mother's needs were being met. I had a team of experts who helped me and 24/7 access to a nurse on duty just a phone call away who was willing to come to my mother's bedside in case of an emergency. I never felt like I was being perceived as a burden or that I was being judged for calling and needing support.

- We had our own personal hospice team who were well-trained and experienced with the intricacies of death and dying. I no longer had to fumble through in my ignorance. I could always ask, or they would anticipate our needs and let us know what to expect and how best to respond.

———————

It is my hope that the philosophy of hospice and palliative care eventually become incorporated in our entire medical system. What this would look like is shifting away from such a myopic focus on the physical body and treating us as multidimensional human beings with personalities, thoughts, emotions, and financial concerns, as well as spiritual and religious beliefs.

As palliative care is integrated into the preexisting medical model, the Death Taboo is weakened through the introduction of a softer, gentler, and accepting way of relating to suffering and death. Doctors, medical staff, patients, and their loved ones are learning how to embrace the normalcy of death and the need to honor thoughts and emotions around dying.

Palliative care has only been recognized as a medical specialty in the US since 2006 and is now being taught in medical schools and training programs for nurses. They, in turn, are being called upon to serve as role models of compassion and human dignity in dealing with patients who are suffering and/or dying rather than as previously trained to emotionally distance themselves and function only as clinicians. A change in consciousness of this magnitude takes time.

historical highlights of our changing culture of death

Before we imagine our future possibilities, let's take a closer look at the magnitude of change that has already come about in our culture of death as we rise up the bell curve of Everett Rogers' Diffusion of Innovation Theory. As you will see from the following overview of the history of change in our culture of death, Innovators and Early Adopters of change have infiltrated our systems of medicine, law, professional education, media, and literature for the general public. Now it is time for us to become active adoptees of change, one person at a time. If you are reading this book, you are an Early Bird to this movement on the left side of Everett Rogers' chart and are helping to create the momentum for this historical change.

In the late 1800s, the primary emphasis of medical care in the US was on easing symptoms. Most deaths occurred at home only a few days after the onset of a serious illness. From 1900 to the 1950s the focus of healthcare shifted from easing suffering to curing disease. Our average life span increased due to the growth of science and industry and improvements in sanitation, living, and working conditions. Lifesaving and life-prolonging discoveries, such as CPR, antibiotics, pain medications, and advances in anesthesia also added to our health and longevity. Scientific advances led to the medicalization of care at the end of life. The care of the elderly, sick, and dying moved out of our homes into nursing homes, hospitals, and other healthcare facilities. Patients whose disease failed to respond to treatments were given less priority. Death of a patient was equated with medical failure. Funeral arrangements were also removed from the home as the funeral industry established its expertise in handling after-death arrangements. These forms of isolation from the death experience have increased our discomfort with the dying process and death itself.

The door to this evolution of our relationship to mortality cracked open in 1959 as the result of the publication of Herman

Feifel's groundbreaking book, *The Meaning of Death,* which ignited interest in this topic among academics and has since become a classic. Since then, enormous changes have been made in the areas of legislation, palliative care, and education of medical personnel and the public to shift how Americans deal with death and dying. Here are some of the pivotal changes that have been transforming our culture of death.

From the late 1960s through the 1970s:

- The concept of hospice was introduced as specialized care for the dying first in England and then in the US supported by federal funds.
- The term "brain death" was introduced by a faculty committee at Harvard.
- Elizabeth Kübler-Ross's book *On Death and Dying* identified the five stages of grief through which terminally ill patients typically progress.
- The field of bioethics was introduced.

From the 1980s through the 1990s:

- The American Academy of Hospice and Palliative Medicine (AAHPM) was launched.
- The George Soros and Robert Wood Johnson Foundations joined forces to change America's death-denying culture by funding programs in professional education, institutional change, and public engagement.
- The Patient Self-Determination Act was passed to encourage us all to decide in advance of need about the types and extent of medical care we want to accept or refuse if we later become unable to make those decisions for ourselves due to illness.
- TV broadcast of *Before I Die,* hosted by journalist Tim

Russert, began a media campaign to build public awareness of end-of-life issues.

And in the past twenty years:

- Bill Moyers' *On Our Own Terms* aired on public TV and
  drew over 20 million viewers (nearly 60 percent higher
  than the PBS prime-time average), and *The Cost of Dying*
  was aired on *60 Minutes*.
- Ongoing national patient education programs seek to
  motivate Americans to legally document end-of-life
  wishes.
- The American Board of Medical Specialties recognized hospice and palliative medicine as a medical specialty.
- The concept of the Death Café was introduced in England
  and there have now been over 12,904 Death Cafés offered
  in seventy-nine countries.

an abundance of new books about life's end

Throughout the past half-century and into the present as well, the
writings of Elizabeth Kübler-Ross and others from the bedside of
the dying have continued to give voice to concerns about how people relate to death and the quality of consciousness and care offered
the dying and grieving. There are now numerous books about the
quality of end-of-life care, the needs of the dying and their caregivers, the grieving process, and how-to books about putting your
affairs in order and creating a memorial service that celebrates the
life of the deceased. Unfortunately, the majority of these books only
reach readers in crisis—those facing their own imminent death or
those who are loved ones of the dying.

When I was thrown into the crisis with my mother, the last thing
I had time to do was read a book or consult a website to educate us

about the issues and options we were facing. I just dove in headfirst and doggy-paddled my way through it all, armed only with my relative ignorance, my tenacity, and my deep love for my mother. My experience has motivated me to reach out now to others to encourage them to learn about end-of-life issues and to heal their own relationship with death while still in the prime of their life rather than in a state of emergency.

Tibetan Buddhist teachings on death and impermanence

The influx of Buddhist teachings into the Western world is a ramification of China's exile of His Holiness the Dalai Lama from Tibet that dispersed Tibetan monks around the world since 1959. Buddhist teachings about death and dying are helping many of us to evolve our relationship with death.

Prior to the influx of Eastern philosophies to the West, our worldview was largely Judeo-Christian—nearly everyone believed in God and sourced understanding of the purpose of life from Abrahamic roots. When Eastern thought arrived on our shores, it had a profound impact by merely introducing us to a very different way of looking at life. This is especially true in terms of our thinking about death, so much so that it deserves to be acknowledged here as some of the good news that is transforming our culture of death.

Essentially, the Buddhist view of death is framed in terms of human consciousness, while the Western view focuses on the physical body. In the West, death is a taboo subject. It is seen as something "wrong" and not to be discussed. In contrast, Buddhists view awareness of our impermanence as essential to our everyday thoughts and behaviors and the fundamental ground for living a happy life. Buddhist teachers have done a tremendous job of contributing to our reframing of death in the West.

While I am not a practicing Buddhist, I find the Tibetan Buddhist teachings on death to be a source of great wisdom and potential liberation, particularly for those still under the influence of the Death Taboo in the West. Sogyal Rinpoche, author of *The Tibetan Book of Living and Dying*, has a particular skill in drawing out the universal messages of these teachings and making them understandable to the Western mind without losing any of their authenticity, purity, and power. What follows here is a summary of the teachings on death and impermanence drawn from four of Sogyal Rinpoche's lectures: *Transcending All Fear of Death; The Essence of The Tibetan Book of Living and Dying (Parts One and Two);* and *Reflecting on Death.*

According to Sogyal Rinpoche, reflections on death and impermanence are the very cornerstone of all spiritual paths. Among Christian contemplatives, for example, there is an expression "*memento mori*": "Remember that you will die." Buddhist teachings encourage awareness of the fact that we could die at any moment. This helps us to maintain awareness of the preciousness of life and encourages us to sort out our priorities.

From a Buddhist perspective, the root cause of all our suffering is the fact that we do not take enough time to come to know ourselves—our true nature, our enlightened Buddha mind. Beyond our ordinary everyday mind is our true mind, which radiates the qualities of tremendous light or brilliance (wisdom) and great warmth (love and compassion). Sogyal Rinpoche uses the analogy of the sky to contrast this state of enlightenment to our everyday mind. Our daily thoughts, feelings, and actions are like temporary clouds that come and go in an endless sky that, like the enlightened mind, is beyond birth and death.

Coming to know our true nature requires overcoming our ordinary mind and moving past our ego. In our day-to-day lives, we are absorbed and distracted by our thoughts, feelings, and activities. It is easy to allow ignorance, negative emotions, and actions to obscure our true nature, much the same way that clouds block our awareness of the endless sky. We all have the potential to connect beyond our ordinary minds to deeper states of profound wisdom, love, and compassion. It is this state of mind that is said to endure past death. Tibetan Buddhists believe that if we do not come to glimpse our true nature in life, we will not be prepared to recognize it and enter into it at death.

This transformation of mind is not only essential preparation for death, but like cleaning the smudges off your eyeglasses, it allows us to see more clearly in life in such a way that our very perceptions transform, and circumstances will appear differently. Whether or not we are able to see clearly, it is important to remember that even when our ordinary mind is cloudy, the sky-like nature of mind is still there. Weather is only on the surface. Deep in the sky-like nature of our minds it is pure.

In many Western spiritual traditions, we use the expression, "Let go and let God." Similarly, the Buddhists teach that the essential path to personal transformation and freedom comes from learning to stop grasping after permanence, for indeed, everything is in a constant state of change. The message of impermanence is that the main cause of suffering is attachment. Since what we grasp for is impermanent, grasping is an act of futility.

We have to learn to let go. We don't have to change—simply change our minds and recognize that, as Sogyal Rinpoche says, "Impermanence is the very nature and fabric of life . . . We associate impermanence with losing and death, but when we really understand it, it is the most secure thing. You lose the clouds, but you gain the sky. The most permanent thing is impermanence." When we realize this, we are made stronger spiritually.

Our fear of death, according to Sogyal Rinpoche, is the fear of life, of facing ourselves. Looking into death is actually facing ourselves, because sooner or later we have to come to terms with ourselves. That is why we tend to think of death only when we are dying. However, to look at yourself and your life at death is too little, too late where personal transformation is concerned. That is why Tibetan Buddhist teachings stress that we should always contemplate death and impermanence as a way of breaking through to our true nature.

Rainer Maria Rilke likened our deepest fears to dragons guarding our greatest treasure. Milarepa, a revered tenth-century Tibetan poet and sage, said it this way:

> All worldly pursuits have but the one unavoidable end, which is sorrow: acquisitions end in dispersion; buildings in destruction; meetings in separation; births, in death. Knowing this, one should, from the very first, renounce acquisition and heaping up, and building, and meeting; and faithful to the commands of an eminent guru, set about realizing the Truth (which has no birth or death).

We discover that this understanding about impermanence is really our greatest friend. It drives us to ask such questions as:

- If everything dies and changes, then what is really true?
- Is there something behind the appearances?
- Is there something boundless and infinitely spacious in which the dance of change and impermanence takes place?
- Is there something, in fact, we can depend on that does survive what we call death?

When we allow these questions to occupy us and we reflect upon them, we slowly find ourselves making a profound shift in the way we view everything. With continued contemplation and practice in letting go, we come to uncover in ourselves something we cannot name or describe or conceptualize, which is something that lies behind all the changes and deaths of the world. Our myopic focus upon our desires, what we are grasping for, and that which we are trying to avoid, begins to dissolve and fall away. As this happens, we catch repeated and glowing glimpses of the vast implications behind the truth of impermanence. In his lecture, *Transcending All Fear of Death*, Sogyal Rinpoche describes this transformation saying:

> It is as if all our lives we have been flying in an airplane through dark clouds and turbulence when suddenly the plane soars above these into the clear boundless skies. Inspired and exhilarated by this new dimension of freedom, we come to uncover a depth of peace, joy and confidence in ourselves that fills us with wonder and gradually breeds in us a certainty that there is in us something that nothing destroys, that nothing alters, and that cannot die.

Sogyal Rinpoche further describes:

> . . . as the new awareness becomes vivid and almost unbroken, there occurs a personal and utterly non-conceptual revelation of what we are, why we are here, and how we should act which amounts in the end to nothing less than a new life, new birth—almost a resurrection . . . You discover something in yourself that does not die.

He also speaks of death using the analogy of "being on a train platform waiting for a train and knowing that you must take that train but don't know when it is coming and having great anxiety because your bags are not packed." We do not prepare for death or live thoughtfully because we think we will live forever. We know we will die someday, but we prefer not to absorb that thought and to pretend instead that we have an unlimited lease on life.

We become lazy in how we live our lives. As Rinpoche describes:

The particular kind of laziness in the West is an active one. We do everything and anything to avoid ourselves. We fill our lives with so many activities that there is not really a chance for the truth of ourselves to be revealed. There is no gap. Yet we live with an abiding anxiety since we have not faced ourselves or our death. There is deep anxiety because death represents our ultimate fear.

Learning to live in the immediacy of death helps us to sort out our priorities and to realize what is truly important in life. We learn that there is really not much time to waste. Death helps us to look into our life in a deeper way. We come to realize that only two things really matter when we die—how we have lived and the state of consciousness we have achieved by the time we die. When we take care of those most important things, then we can relax. Milarepa said it this way, "My religion is not to be ashamed of myself when I die."

An unenlightened mind sees death as defeat—a tragedy. Buddhist teachings suggest death is really an extraordinary opportunity for transformation and personal liberation. When we die, it is only the end of one cycle. Those who hold tight to their current life expression don't allow for their liberation to take place. Those who do allow it not only surrender to the death of their bodies but they allow their ordinary mind to die with all its delusions as well. Milarepa described it this way: "In horror of death, I took to the mountains. Meditating again and again on the uncertainty of the hour of death, I captured the fortress of the deathless unending nature of mind. Now all fear of death is done and gone."

Tibetan Buddhist teachings provide three pieces of advice for the moment of death which also serve practitioners well in how to live their lives:

- Let go of all grasping, attachments, and aversions.
- Keep your heart and mind pure.
- Unite your mind with the wisdom mind of the Buddha.

Those practicing these techniques in life who are really able to let go inside themselves, find they are able to cope better with outer stress and are less bothered by what transpires in their lives. When we integrate this view as part of our being through meditation and through action then we can meet death fearlessly. By practicing getting into the high ground of our consciousness during life through meditation and contemplation, we prepare ourselves for the moment of death.

There is also advice given for those who help the dying. Essentially, we are called upon to simply be there to maintain a consciousness of unconditional loving, free of attachments. Love is not expressed by grasping after the life of the dying one. This kind of attachment, Sogyal Rinpoche teaches, is actually what spoils love. To truly realize love for one another, we have to let go. When a loved one is dying, we can best serve them by giving them our acceptance and blessing to die and by surrounding them with our love.

Imagine how different it would be to live in a society that believes that the purpose of life is to achieve enlightenment. In this context, life is seen as an impermanent state of being. Death is not viewed as the end of life but merely the end of the body we inhabit in this life. As such, death is not a primary source of fear. Rather, it is believed to lead to a rebirth and continuation of the process of seeking an enlightened state of consciousness and further opportunities to be of service to others.

the conversation about death goes public

The conversation about death went public in America with the advent of the Death Café in London in 2011. The purpose of the Death Café is to increase awareness of death with a view to helping people make the most of their lives. People, often strangers, gather to share refreshments and talk about death. I have attended a number of Death Cafés and have been struck by the candor with which total strangers share their deepest beliefs, fears, preferences, and feelings about death and dying. These same people often admit to not having any such conversations with their loved ones—it seems the Death Taboo still holds many in its grip in the privacy of our homes.

While great strides have been made in transforming our relationship to mortality, we are still primarily addressing the symptoms of the Death Taboo rather than the root cause of our dis-ease around death. *Making Peace with Death and Dying* responds to the fundamental unmet need for an effective tool to intentionally deconstruct the autopilot influences of the Death Taboo. To cultivate a healthier relationship with death for us as individuals and as a society, this work is intended to move the conversation about death into action in our lives.

two demographic trends feeding the momentum of change

Momentum is clearly building to free ourselves from the Death Taboo. It is interesting to note that this acceleration is fueled by two major demographic trends that are simultaneously calling for a greater depth of personal meaning in the experiences of living and dying.

The first of these trends is that 76 million Baby Boomers, known for their redefinition of traditional values, are now becoming Elder Boomers. They are rethinking death while in the process of saying final goodbyes to their parents. In addition, they are seeing their peers being diagnosed with major illnesses and dying. Death is a greater presence in their lives.

The second group having a profound impact on how we view death is the 88 million Americans (27 percent of us) who self-identify as "Spiritual But Not Religious." Typically, these individuals seek a deeper understanding of life's meaning and want more personalized life rituals. For example, they are much more likely to personalize their wedding ceremony and to want a memorial service that includes a celebration of the life of the deceased.

Another demographic fact that bears mentioning is the number of Americans who are providing care to someone who is ill, disabled, or aged. The 2015 *Caregiving in the U.S. Report* by the National Alliance for Caregiving and AARP reported that 43.5 million Americans are caregiving. In most cases, these are women with full- or part-time jobs and families as well. No matter how much we love the ones we care for, the responsibilities of caregiving are enormous and add a great deal of stress to the caregiver's life and family. As noted earlier, census data shows that only 10 percent of us will die suddenly due to an accident, heart attack, or other unexpected life event. The remaining 90 percent deal with progressive diseases. As a result of the many life-sustaining medical treatments available, we are likely to find ourselves dependent on others for a longer period of time. With families geographically dispersed, one family member living close to the dying tends to take on caregiving responsibilities. Other family members are shielded from the reality.

What is being called "death-delayed experience" refers to the fact that more of us are isolated from death until adulthood. This has served to increase our discomfort with death and the dying process. Being unfamiliar with the death and dying experience often results in profound emotional responses to the death of a loved one.

other significant changes

Other fairly recent developments in our culture of death include:

- the introduction of thanatology courses on college campuses

- cremation and memorial services becoming acceptable alternatives to burial and traditional funeral services
- green funerals bringing environmental consciousness to the funeral industry
- caregiver trainings now incorporating spiritual and mental health components
- new websites showing up daily to educate Americans about dying, death, and bereavement

Personalized memorial services provide the opportunity to acknowledge the essence of loved ones and to focus attention on celebrating their entire life rather than only grieving their death. Here are some examples of the kinds of thoughtful gestures people are using to memorialize their loved ones:

- Meri gave everyone little flashlights at her father's funeral because anyone who knew him marveled that he was never without one.
- I gave close friends a Christmas tree ornament with a picture of my mother waving goodbye that really captured her spirit.
- Sarah's friends toured her gardens before her service and, at her request, many of them subsequently transplanted her "babies" to their own gardens to live on in her memory.

These simple, thoughtful acts of caring and remembering inspire others to find ways to honor their loved ones. This is how the transformation is taking place. A similar change happened in the 1980s and 1990s when couples, many of them Baby Boomers, moved outside the boundaries of traditional wedding ceremonies to create more personalized services that truly reflected their unique values, beliefs, and life circumstances. Now, Baby Boomers and the

Spiritual but Not Religious are leading the way to enliven our rituals for honoring the deceased.

reconsidering the really big questions

The uncanny consistency of reports of near-death experiences has also provoked a re-evaluation of how we regard death and its nature. Neurosurgeon Eben Alexander's *New York Times* bestseller, *Proof of Heaven*, has helped to challenge the dominant notion that death of the body is the end of life and that human consciousness dies along with the body at what we commonly call the "time of death." A fundamental redefinition of the term "death" is underway. In fact, we used to think about these things with far greater simplicity—birth, life, death. Now the lines are getting blurred, and we are asking such questions as:

- When exactly is a person born?
- When does death occur?
- What exactly is it that is birthed?
- What passes away when someone dies?
- Is there indeed some part of us that never ends?

What do you think? What do you think death actually is? What do you think the significance of death is?

the Western view of death: a work in progress

Although those on the front lines of transforming our culture of death have paved the way for sweeping changes to take place in how we relate to our mortality, the majority of Americans remain under the influence of the Death Taboo. While dramatic changes are already underway in how we relate to death and dying, changes in behavior must take hold one person at a time. The process of finding freedom in relationship to death offers us the opportunity for profound liberation. In essence, it is a matter of bringing more love, courage, compassion, and authenticity to the foreground, while moving fears and anxiety about death to the background. For an individual, change is usually precipitated by a disturbing or empowering encounter with the death of a loved one or a public event of the magnitude of 9/11.

This is a good place to mention "neuroplasticity," also known as "cortical remapping," which will be discussed further in Chapter 6. This term refers to the recent scientific discovery of the brain's ability to change and adapt as a result of our experiences. Prior to the 1960s, it was believed that changes in the brain only took place during infancy and childhood, and thereafter the adult brain's structure was permanent. Researchers now know that the brain continues to create new neural pathways and alters existing ones to accommodate new learning and experiences. In other words, we have the ability to question and change our way of thinking and being for better or worse. The powerful implications of this fundamental capacity are captured in the following old Chinese proverb:

Sow a thought and reap an act;
Sow an act and reap a habit;
Sow a habit and reap a character;
Sow a character and reap a destiny.

Proverbs 23:7 captured this sentiment as well: "As a man thinks in his heart, so is he." This is true for us as individuals as well as for groups and societies at large. Repetitive thoughts form neural pathways as neurons that fire together get wired together. These pathways in our brains are like superhighways—the autopilot route. The good news is that we have the ability to change our synaptic wiring. It's important to periodically review our deepest beliefs and be willing to challenge them in order to keep our brains active and to not be lulled into a false sense of security. Otherwise, the thoughts we persist in become so familiar that we often take them for granted and misidentify them as the truth because of their familiarity. Our thoughts and beliefs become the building blocks and assumptions that serve as the foundation for a point of view that, unchallenged, will invisibly run on autopilot and shape our future thinking. Simply said—when we change our thinking, we change our experience.

In the case of the culture of death and dying, the brain's neuroplasticity is being called upon to consciously rethink the implications of the Death Taboo and its alternatives. Indeed, when it comes to something as personal as our own death or that of a loved one, it behooves us to recognize that, while many of our beliefs come from others, we have the freedom to think for ourselves about what is right for us. Our ability to change our perspective and to make different choices empowers us to change the quality of our experiences. As with any social transformation, shifting our relationship to death from one of fear and silence to acceptance, authenticity, and loving kindness is following a fairly predictable pattern of evolution, as noted in Everett Rogers Diffusion of Innovation Theory described in the beginning of this section.

I like to imagine what our lives would be like if we were taught to connect to a deep sense of self and to live our lives from that place. For example:

- What if we actually talked to each other in a curious and inquisitive way about such existential matters as the meaning of life and death?
- What if the cultural message were not to fear death but rather to develop a healthy curiosity about death, to accept its reality, and to prepare in advance of need?
- What if there were no external pressures to conform to a particular point of view? What would it be like if we

were encouraged to deeply think about and voice our own beliefs so that a collective conversation and response could truly reflect the individuals involved?

- What if we functioned as though everyone's voice and well-being really mattered?
- What if the American culture of death focused on being existentially mature and practically prepared?

When was the last time you talked with yourself or someone else about deep questions like these? Let's engage in this conversation. This next exercise gives you the opportunity to take stock of how you are now relating to death.

———

Exercise 4: How Do I Avoid Thinking About or Dealing with Death?

Rank each of the following statements in terms of how true it is for you on a scale of "Very True," "Somewhat True," or "Not True at All." After ranking the statements, spend a few minutes thinking about your responses. You may want to record and explore your thoughts in a journal or have a conversation with a friend about your point of view and explore theirs as well. Use this exercise to begin to open up the conversation about death among your own family and friends.

1. When I am with someone who is dying, I don't want the conversation to go below the surface.
2. I don't have an up-to-date healthcare proxy.
3. It is important to me to look as young as possible.
4. I don't ever want to get old.
5. I am afraid that if I put my affairs in order that will somehow

make me die sooner than if I continue to avoid putting my affairs in order.

6. I have lost at least one loved one or pet and never gotten over it.

7. When I think something has gone wrong in my life, I usually blame myself or someone else.

8. When someone I know and care about experiences the death of a loved one, I never know what to say.

9. I keep saying I want to put my affairs in order, but never get around to it.

10. I don't think there is any urgency for me to put my affairs in order.

11. I'm too young to die.

12. There is no way I would feel comfortable talking to my family about my end-of-life preferences.

---

chapter 5

developing existential maturity

"Normally we do not like to think about death. We would rather think about life. Why reflect on death? When you start preparing for death you soon realize that you must look into your life now... and come to face the truth of yourself. Death is like a mirror in which the true meaning of life is reflected."

—*Sogyal Rinpoche*

preparation in advance of need

WHEN AN ATHLETE IS PLANNING to run in a race, there is much preparation of body, mind, and soul. Yet knowing that we will all die, we tend to ignore that fact until receiving the urgent phone call that causes us to sprint out the door to a loved one's side at a moment's notice—ready or not. Or it might be a call that tells us we have a terminal diagnosis, and our entire future changes in an instant. Who among us will have the physical, mental, emotional, and spiritual stamina required to heed that call? What exactly can we do now to be better able to handle that call when it comes?

As you know by now, my motivation for writing this book was essentially to help others avoid many of the traumas I faced with my mother's death due to my ignorance and lack of experience in the territory of death and our society's Death Taboo. In the blink of an eye, life as you know it can disappear from view when a terminal diagnosis or phone call about a fatal accident puts your death or that of a loved one in the foreground of your life. Until now, the Death Taboo has prevented us from acclimating ourselves to the realities of death and dying in advance of need. When it comes, we run on sheer adrenaline, tenacity, and the love and support of others, if we are lucky. This all boils down to a matter of personal choice. Which would you prefer: to hide from the reality of death and dying, or to face your own death or that of a loved one with your eyes wide open, keeping well-informed and prepared for the challenges you will face?

Now that you know how to identify the Death Taboo in action along with its costs and consequences for us as individuals and collectively, you are free to make some changes in your relationship with death. This might seem strange at first. However, consider how an athlete mentally prepares for a competition by visually going through the event triumphantly. Similarly, it helps to create a positive image of your own death—a kind of "ideal scene." Reinforcing such an image can create new neural pathways to replace the existing conscious and unconscious fear patterns that have likely dominated your relationship to death. The process of finding the freedom, courage, and strength to stand in your own truth in relationship to death is a personal journey well worth taking. So, as a declaration of freedom from the tentacles of the Death Taboo, here is an exercise to help you create an image of yourself victorious at the finish line of your life. See yourself like a runner who envisions him or herself to be the first across the finish line breaking through the red ribbon, arms aloft, spent, and victorious. It is time to replace any fearful images of death by creating a beautiful vision of your own death— peaceful, complete, loved, knowing that you have done your very best, ready to let go, and perhaps curious about what lies ahead.

Exercise 5: Envisioning Your Victorious Death

Gather together your favorite writing and drawing tools. Close your eyes and imagine that you are on your deathbed and there is a radiant smile on your face. You are not afraid. You know that you really gave your life your best. You feel peaceful and relaxed, regardless of any physical pain. Your beliefs are a comfort to you. Knowing that you are dying, you are curious and perhaps a little impatient to know what lies ahead. Those whom you most wish to be by your side are there with you. The music of your choice is softly playing in the background. A beautiful fragrance fills the air. Your consciousness is floating in and out. You are ready to let go of your life and loved ones. Look around at your surroundings. Where are you? Who is with you? What is going on in your mind? In your heart?

Remember, this is your fantasy, so make it good!

Now, open your eyes and draw or share what you have seen and heard. Include as many details as possible. If any negative images, thoughts, or fears came up during this exercise that interfered with your ability to perceive a beautiful death for yourself, make note of them on the back of your paper as you will have the opportunity to work with them later.

the journey from your worst fears to your ideal scene

It takes courage to break through our fear and silence, but the rewards are immense. When all is said and done, I believe there is nothing more important for us to do in our lives than to express our heartfelt love for each other in acts of kindness, consideration, and caring. In the many facets of death and dying—both our own death and that of those we love—we are presented with numerous opportunities to hone our skills in loving and comforting each other with greater compassion, ease, and grace. The challenge is to let our love be stronger than our fears, judgments, resentments, busyness, and concerns about being inconvenienced. But having been taught to relate to death with fear and silence, we need to exercise some new muscles so we can lavishly love one another in the face of death.

authenticity, intimacy, and existential maturity in the face of death

There is a lot of talk these days about being "authentic"—the real deal, not a phony. The truth of the matter is that sometimes people simply do not know who they are. Many of us have never been encouraged to get to know ourselves better and have fallen prey to external forces, pressures, and influences that further distance us from a profound connection to a sense of our own inner truth. Indeed, the challenges of daily life have a way of consuming us. Yet, it is in this personal truth that our authenticity lies. Without grounding ourselves in our truth, there can be little or no intimacy with ourselves or others. In *The Silent Life,* Thomas Merton wrote:

> Not all men are called to be hermits, but all men need enough silence and solitude in their lives to enable the deep inner voice of their own true self to be heard at least occasionally. When that inner voice is not heard, when man cannot attain to the spiritual peace that comes from being perfectly at one with his own true self, his life is always miserable and exhausting. For he cannot go on happily for long, unless he is in contact with the springs of spiritual life which are hidden in the depths of his own soul. If man is constantly exiled from

his own home, locked out of his own spiritual solitude,
he ceases to be a true person.

There is nothing like an impending death to call us into the deep
truth of who we know ourselves to be, what matters most to us,
and our priorities in the face of life's deadline. But why wait till
then? Nurturing your own spiritual solitude prepares you for death.
Otherwise, death arrives as an unsupported crisis. We can use the
reality of death as motivation to live our lives with greater authenticity now.

A new term, "existential maturity," has emerged in academic and
palliative care circles, taking the idea of authenticity a step further.
Existential maturity suggests that it is not only important to live
as a true reflection of one's deepest beliefs and values, but to hold
one's self accountable for doing so. If we wait until the end of our
life to do so, we only get a small window of opportunity to make any
desired changes, and the self-examination is pursued during the
heightened stress of a "deadline."

Awareness of the inevitability of death is one of the most powerful life experiences to call us into a reflection on our existential
maturity as well. While some spiritual and religious traditions
encourage followers to live a self-examined life, there is no such call
to accountability for a human being in our socio-cultural arena. The
death and dying of a loved one is the most influential opportunity
we have to do so.

For many, life passes by in an uninterrupted race against time
with more things to do than hours in the days, weeks, or years at
hand. We are consumed by our busy lives, leaving us with little
opportunity to explore how life is being lived. Where is there room
in your schedule to ask yourself such big questions as:

- What really matters to me deep in the core of my being?
- Am I proud of myself as a human being?

Questions such as these will be explored in Chapter 7 to deepen the awareness of your own truth as the bedrock upon which your life is lived. These will serve as the filters through which you face your death. Let your love speak louder than your fear in the face of death.

Love makes us more brave, intimate, and compassionate with each other, rather than letting fears isolate us and render us less able to be authentic and helpful. Simple, yet courageous, acts of loving kindness are capable of filling, surrounding, and comforting the dying right to the very end—creating a safe place for them to leave this world.

Since the timing of death is a mystery, it behooves us to lavishly love each other as though this very day could be our last together. Facing fears about death—the ultimate uncertainty and anticipated loss—helps us to live with greater gusto, taking time to see the beauty that surrounds us, rather than dwelling on what we think we lack. It gives us the courage and wisdom to express our love for each other and to communicate honestly, even when we don't know how. This is a knowing that comes from the heart, not from the mind.

Accepting the finality and inescapability of death frees us to become aware of the precious nature of life and the opportunities that might otherwise be lost to take the time to express our love and caring. It also serves to motivate us to upgrade our relationship with death by exploring our beliefs about life and death, having the difficult conversations with loved ones, and documenting and communicating end-of-life preferences in advance of need as an act of love for ourselves and consideration for those who would otherwise be called upon to second-guess our wishes. In relationship to death and dying, existential maturity refers to a kind of peaceful acceptance of mortality that eases the pain of the impermanent nature of human existence.

The process of developing existential maturity involves recognizing and diminishing what Tibetan Buddhist nun Pema Chodron calls the "ubiquitous anxiety" associated with a deep fear of death. It requires moving our fears and anxiety to the background while enabling our love, courage, compassion, and authenticity to come to the foreground. When we do this in relationship to our fears about death, a whole new world of intimacy with ourselves and our loved ones can open up.

Instead of being victimized by the Death Taboo, let's do what it takes to give ourselves and each other "good" death experiences. Part Two of this book, Transforming Your Relationship to Death and Dying, presents the nine keys to liberating yourself from the personal and collective fears and repressive behaviors that typify our dominant contemporary culture of death. Part Two gives you the understanding and tools you need to break free of your own conscious and unconscious issues around death.

part two

transforming your relationship
to death and dying

chapter 6

key #1:
lifting above right/wrong thinking

*"*Out beyond ideas of wrongdoing and rightdoing
there is a field. I'll meet you there.*"*

—Jalāl ad-Dīn Rumi

OUR MINDS AND BODIES HAVE been programmed to view life as good and death as bad. That's what's running on autopilot unless we challenge those assumptions. The first step in breaking free of the Death Taboo is to recognize the impact and significance of this and to do what it takes to reprogram yourself. In this chapter, we will explore:

- How Death Taboo programming works
- Unitive consciousness, which is the alternative to right/ wrong thinking
- Four practices to strengthen unitive consciousness so we can reframe our perspectives about death and dying

right/wrong thinking: the fundamental problem

There are two essential flaws in the Death Taboo. First, it is built upon the belief that life is good and death is bad. Second, it implies that life and death are polar opposites rather than inseparably intertwined. However, just because we think or believe something doesn't mean it is true. Sometimes it simply means we haven't questioned it.

We live in a world of extremes: love and hate, good and bad, happy and sad, right and wrong, life and death. We are taught to notice our relative preferences and to seek more of what we like and less of what we do not like. Viewing life and death in this way naturally lends itself to always making comparisons rather than simply experiencing something in and of itself. As a result, we perceive things from the reference point of our personal preferences. Even on the most basic level of choosing between two seemingly insignificant alternatives—"Do I want chocolate or vanilla ice cream?"—the selection implies a rightness about one and wrongness about the other. It is not simply "I prefer this one" but an implied "not that one." We are constantly posturing ourselves for and against what we encounter in our lives.

Relating to the people, circumstances, and events of our lives through right/wrong thinking yields patterns of attachment and aversion. We try to get more of what we desire and to avoid the pain and suffering we associate with getting what we do not want or prefer. This polarized thinking teaches us to know ourselves and each other by our characteristics, our preferences, and our relative judgments of these things as being good or bad, better or worse, richer or poorer, sick or healthy. We name and label people, places, things, and experiences. It is a sorting process that directs us to selectively pay attention to that which is in agreement with our point of view and to ignore, judge, resist, or reject that which is not. In so doing, we lose sight of that which joins us together as one. Right/wrong thinking is a kind of nearsightedness or short-sightedness—a contraction of our perceptual field and therefore a limitation of input and access.

Cynthia Bourgeault, a contemporary mystic and Episcopal priest, uses the metaphor of computer operating systems to describe our potential to upgrade the operating system of our consciousness.

She notes that our either/or, binary, polarizing way of processing information and experiences divides the world into subject and object. The alternative, Bourgeault suggests, is a way of looking at and experiencing the world that is beyond the limitations of the rational mind. It is a unitive and more cosmic, multidimensional way of perceiving. In unitive consciousness, we do not stand separate from what we perceive. Rather, we experience ourselves as being in alignment with something greater than our egoic self.

Some of us think of that "something greater" as our connection to family, loved ones, community, or humanity. For others, this concept is put into more spiritual language with terms such as "the divine," "oneness," "God," "the unknown," or "the unknowable." Whatever language is most comfortable for each of us is fine. It is not the term used but the concept being conveyed that is important here. On this note, if you are uncomfortable with my use of spiritual words such as "God," please substitute your own language and seek to connect to the meaning behind the words.

In *Encountering the Wisdom Jesus*, Bourgeault speaks of "metanoia" as learning to see through the eye of the heart. She suggests that the mission of Jesus is to encourage this compassionate and interconnected state of consciousness. This point is echoed in other spiritual traditions as well. For example, Thich Nhat Hanh, the Vietnamese Zen Buddhist monk, says: "We are here to awaken from the illusion of our separateness."

thinking about life and death

Preferring life is genetically adaptive, and we have been culturally conditioned to prefer life to death. On one level this makes wonderful sense—or else we'd have a lot more people jumping off bridges. The preference for life functions as a control mechanism. It is a powerful force within us. However, dualistic thinking such as "life is good, and death is bad" is the foundation upon which the American

Death Taboo rests. As long as death is viewed as bad in contrast to birth and life as good, the taboo will continue to make fear and avoidance our dominant responses to death.

In contrast, from a unitive point of view, death can be seen as simply another stage of the continuum of birth, life, and death. This does not eliminate the experience of our pain, suffering, and loss around death. Death is not separate from life—it is not its opposite, but rather its final part. Knowing this helps us to make peace with death by opening to the possibility of embracing each stage of life with the wisdom that all of life has value—right through our very last breath and beyond.

I think there is great wisdom in the Buddhist tradition that teaches us to live without attachments and aversions by embracing and experiencing the fullness of life without prejudice—not in a passive or masochistic way. Rather, we willingly allow ourselves to engage all of the human experience in order to build skill in handling the harder parts of life, to reach toward each other in those times, and to build trust in the existence of God or some grand design beyond what our human faculties can comprehend. We surrender to something greater than our personal preferences and encounter the reality of our impermanence and our oneness with and vulnerability to something ineffable.

There is indeed enormous sadness and disappointment in both life and death. Instead of resisting and avoiding death, we have the option of learning to move through it without drowning in it. I do not think God made a mistake by incorporating sadness and death in the human experience. When we trust that there is some wisdom and purpose to all of life, we are better able to consistently pursue balance and completeness rather than focusing on the fulfillment of our personal preferences as our path through life.

Accepting the full range of the human experience draws us together into a oneness—a community of understanding and of caring for one another. This acceptance calls us to a way of being in relationship to one another similar to the promises made in the traditional wedding vows. In our oneness, we are asked to love, honor, and cherish one another in good times and bad, in sickness and in health. It is this overarching loving and caring that awakens us and lifts us above our polarized thinking about life and death and our personal experiences along the way. A greeting card kind of love is a plastic pipe dream suggesting that love sustains at some delightful pitch effortlessly and endlessly. In reality, love is revealed through our actions. Real loving takes effort—it lives and breathes in the choices we make in our relationships and is the most precious treasure we can share.

wrapping our brains around our mortality

One of the great paradoxes of life is that each of us has a certain amount of time allotted to us. But there's a catch—we don't get to know what that is. Furthermore, living and dying are simultaneous experiences, not sequential ones. So, when we say that we are living or dying, we are focusing upon one aspect and not the other, thus blinding ourselves to the fullness of our existence.

There is no joy without hardship.
If not for death, would we appreciate life?
If not for hate, would we know the ultimate goal is love?
—*Elisabeth Kübler-Ross*

We are taught to deny the dying part. Obedient to the Death Taboo, most of us push the mere thought of death below the surface of our consciousness and avoid it at all costs. In so doing, we fail to cultivate our ability to relate to and experience this dimension of our lives. We tend to relate to our mortality with unconscious and blatant denial, as if death will never happen to us. As a society, we have developed the Death Taboo as a way of collectively living in denial, the consequences of which we have already discussed in Chapter 3.

The Death Taboo has given us the impression that death is something terrible that happens at the end of life, something we shouldn't think or talk about until then. The new consciousness of death that is emerging in our culture suggests we are capable of living more fully to the very last breath of our life when we make peace with our mortality. We are called to surrender into the awe of simultaneously living and dying every moment of every day, one breath at a time, through our last breath. The primary intention of this book is to assist you in making this important transformation in your consciousness and, in turn, helping others to do so as well.

We are wise not to postpone this transformation of consciousness until there is an acute dying situation at hand. With that said, much of the discussion of this book centers around the active dying process and the opportunities available to the person who is dying and to their loved ones to improve the quality of consciousness they exhibit as they meet death's presence. It seems that those who get the greatest value from their lives are the ones who learn to make peace with their mortality and go about their business of appreciating the preciousness of life. The old way of pretending that death doesn't exist didn't make it magically go away. It simply disabled us in dealing with it. Given the inescapable fact that each one of us will die, as will everyone we know—those we love and those we have turned our backs upon—it is time to learn how to make the best of this reality.

An internet image search of the word "death" shows how pervasive our society's belief is that death is a bad thing. What if this perspective is just an old thought form about death that is misleading us? For example, what if all the consistent reports of near-death experiences are actually true and there is beauty that lies ahead of this physical life that is incomprehensible to us? What if the point is not to avoid death but to use the inevitability of death as a source of motivation to live and embrace our life more fully—to see it as the precious, albeit time-limited wonder it is.

This next exercise allows you to visually encounter the Death Taboo juxtaposed to what those who have had near-death experiences have seen.

Exercise 6: Internet Word Search

Conduct an internet image search for the word "death." Take a good look at the images and record at least five to ten observations of what kinds of thoughts and feelings these images evoke for you.

Now, do an image search of the phrase "near death experience." Once again, take a good look at the images and record at least five to ten observations of what thoughts and feelings these images evoke for you.

Compare the images and your lists. Ask yourself:

- Which of these most closely represents my personal feelings about death?
- Which of these would I prefer to be true about death?

This is the challenge we face at the heart of the Death Taboo. Images of skulls, skeletons, and the Grim Reaper are the visual representation of how we have been brainwashed to think and feel about death, which is essentially to fear it. In contrast, images of near-death experiences consistently represent death as a beautiful, awesome experience in which we transition from this level of existence into another filled with light. Steve Jobs' sister, Mona Simpson, reported that his last six words were an enthusiastic "Oh wow! Oh wow! Oh wow!" How differently might we live and die if we were taught to relate to death in this way rather than as something scary and awful?

If you are someone who carries a lot of fear and anxiety about death, challenge yourself to be open to the possibilities that death is not as awful a destiny as our Death Taboo would have us believe. If your thoughts are filled with doom and gloom about the matter, consider what spiritual teachers John-Roger and Pauli Sanderson say about this in their book, *When Are You Coming Home?*:

> Think about what your attitude would be if you knew there is a place already prepared for you, a place that is your rightful home. It is a place kept safe and sacred for you until you are ready to accept that it exists and are ready to move toward it. You know you'll be welcomed there by the most loving being you can imagine. Wouldn't your attitude include elements of gratitude, enthusiasm, peace, and loving? Wouldn't you be so grateful to know you are coming home?

Those who remain under the influence of the Death Taboo will continue to avoid death by not thinking about it, not preparing for its eventuality, and not talking to each other about it. Those of us who use this first key of lifting above right/wrong thinking will radically change the quality of how we live and how we die.

neuroplasticity and conscious intention

Thank God for neuroplasticity! As powerful as our beliefs are, the good news is we can change them. As mentioned in Chapter 4, neuroscientists have discovered that repetitive thoughts form neural pathways as neurons that fire together get wired together. Thus, the more a particular thought or belief is activated and reinforced, the stronger these neural pathways become and the more automatically they become our go-to pattern of perception and behavior. When we change our beliefs, we have different thoughts, which in turn will result in different feelings, actions, and ways of experiencing our living and dying. This is a very new idea in our culture, by the way. Prefigured in the 1940s by the Indian Kriya Yoga guru Paramahansa Yogananda, it only reached consensus among neuroscientists in the 1990s. Prior to that it was believed that after early childhood our brains were physiologically static, unchanging organs throughout the rest of our lives. The concept of neuroplasticity has now replaced this view, saying that our neural pathways and synapses do indeed change in response to such things as changes in our understanding, thinking, behavior, environment, and experiences. Neuroplasticity enables us to intentionally shift our point of view. We do so through awareness, observation, and repetitive, conscious choosing. This builds trust in our ability to seize the moment and move ourselves out of negative, fear-based patterns into beliefs and behaviors that reflect a deep and abiding trust in our own ability to meet life's challenges.

my truth, your truth, the truth

What about "The Truth"—unequivocal, absolute truth, the way it is, period? I think the best way to address this point is through an ancient parable about three blind men and an elephant. They enter into a heated disagreement about the nature of an elephant. Each, encountering a different part of the elephant—his side, trunk, and leg—is convinced that he is right and that the others are wrong about what exactly an elephant "is." In "truth," all of them are partly right and all of them are wrong. The elephant is more than they can imagine.

Let's imagine for a minute that this elephant is death, and the blind men are devout practitioners of three different religions or worldviews. One believes there is heaven or hell after death. Another insists there is nothing. The third is certain that this life that is ending is simply part of a cyclical process of reincarnation. Is death (or the elephant) any one of these things to the exclusion of the others? Or do all have elements of truth in them but not the entire truth? Can we who are living really know death? Or are we merely speculating about it? Does death exist? Yes. Are we capable of unequivocal certainty about the nature of death? No. We can inherit a point of view about death, possibly explore our own beliefs about it, but never "know" the truth about death while living. There is mystery in this world. There are those things that exceed the capacity of our limited human ability to comprehend. I remember smiling deeply in college when I finished reading Ludwig Wittgenstein's *Tractatus Logico-Philosphicus*, in which he advised, "Whereof one cannot speak, thereof one must be silent." Some say he put his pen down and became a gardener after that.

I have three personal conclusions on the matter of what constitutes the truth. First, I think our scientific method of proof has led us far afield from being able to stand in awe at that which is beyond our ability to comprehend or to measure scientifically. We try to concretize, name, and frame things with a total lack of humility for our own limitations. I prefer a god I can stand in awe of to one that I can explain. Secondly, I value the fact that we all have the same perceptual equipment yet are capable of seeing and experiencing things so differently. As one of those blind people around the elephant, I want to expand my point of view by listening to and understanding what others see that is so different from what I see. I prefer curiosity and expansion to myopic vision. Unfortunately, we are so programmed by the right/wrong mode of thinking that we are far more inclined to singularly elevate our own point of view and, in so doing, to put down and dismiss any view that does not agree with ours. My third conclusion is that our perceptions of what is true may be based on faith as in "I believe this to be true" or they may be based on experience as in "I know through experience that this is true."

I'd like to share an experience I had in 1997 that moved my consciousness in an instant from a lifelong conceptual belief in God to experiencing and knowing God's presence. In other words, it moved me from conceptual truth to experiential truth. Here's what happened: I was driving at about 60 mph on the Taconic Parkway in New York State on my way to work early one morning. Suddenly, I hit a patch of black ice. The car, beyond my control, crisscrossed the road four times. As I headed toward a ravine on the right, I heard a voice call out from deep within my gut, saying, "I'm not ready to go yet—so please take good care of me!" In that instant, my car did what I have since been told is mechanically impossible—the car thrust into reverse, making a full circle and driving me backwards down the ravine into a swampy area. The car rear-ended against a tree that severed the trunk in half. My seat broke, my eyeglasses and earrings flew off my head onto the floor, and I lay face up just inches from the tree which had smashed the rear window to smithereens. I was surprised to notice that I was alive. I did not get a single cut or piece of glass in my hair or clothing. My only injury was shock and a concussion that made it difficult for me to think for seven months. However, just after the accident, I found myself in a state of euphoria realizing that I no longer *believed* in God. I *knew* God. Through that accident, I received irrefutable, yet nontransferable, personal proof of God's presence in my life.

By the way, two weeks before her death, my mother had her own personal epiphany that moved her also from a lifelong conceptual belief in God to knowing God's presence beyond the shadow of a doubt. One of life's great ironies is that experiences such as ours are nontransferrable from one person to another. They are purely personal.

unitive consciousness

Rather than living in an either/or state of mind, there is a kind of liberation, elevation, and transformation available to those who cultivate a "both/and," or unitive, consciousness. This is a consciousness that allows for multiple points of view to peacefully coexist and acknowledges that there exists a level of reality that is not apparent to our intelligence or senses. Elements of this kind of consciousness are referenced frequently in various religious and spiritual traditions. For example, in the framework of Christian spirituality, Jim Marion, author of *Putting on the Mind of Christ,* notes the frequency with which Jesus referred to "the kingdom of heaven." He suggests it was intended to refer to a state of consciousness—a place you come from rather than go to, a way of seeing God, ourselves, and each other as a continuum, a oneness infused with profound meaning that is invisible to the dualistic mind. This is a completely different way of thinking and processing information and experiences. With regard to life and death, let's experiment with this in the following exercise.

Exercise 7: Exploring My Unitive View of Death

Answer the following questions:

1. What do I need to do differently to live more consciously in my living and dying?
2. What can I do to open my heart to death as well as to life?
3. Do I believe that death serves some kind of higher purpose? If so, what do I think that is? If not, why not?

4. Do I talk to anyone about my thoughts and feelings regarding death and dying? If not, why not? If so, what has motivated me to do so and with what results?

———————

We are called upon to embrace the reality of our mortality—to face our fears, to embrace the unknown nature of death, and to explore our beliefs about what death is and is not. In so doing, we develop skills and tolerance for the full range of the human experience; we find ways to support ourselves, each other, and our society in developing a healthier relationship with death. And we can learn to talk about it rather than treat it as something unspeakable.

There is higher ground to stand upon than our preferences, but we have to sacrifice them to go there. We have to be willing to experience all of life in order to enter into its mysteries and the deeper gifts that await us. To go beyond right/wrong thinking about death means expanding our perceptual field beyond a myopic focus on pain, suffering, and loss. Death and dying, more than any other life experiences, call us to think through the filter of our heart and soul and to become aware of a very different level of reality. The poet Rashani Réa captures the spiritual dimension of death's presence in her poem "The Unbroken":

There is a brokenness
out of which comes the unbroken,
a shatteredness
out of which blooms the unshatterable.
There is a sorrow
beyond all grief which leads to joy
and a fragility
out of whose depth emerges strength.
There is a hollow space
too vast for words

through which we pass with each loss,
out of whose darkness
we are sanctioned into being.

There is a cry deeper than all sound
whose serrated edges cut the heart
as we break open to the place inside
which is unbreakable and whole,
while learning to sing.

In the words of Jalāl ad-Dīn Rumi: "The wound is the place where the light enters you."

four practices to strengthen unitive consciousness

Essentially, the work at hand is twofold. First, we acquire intellectual understanding. But we reap the real harvest of change by activating our new understanding in changes of behavior. The state of our consciousness forms the bedrock upon which our lives unfold. How we think and how we perceive and process information and experiences determine the contours of our lives.

When we live in fear, we contract into fight, flight, or freeze mode and tend to live on the surface of life. Alternatively, when we are open to participating in our life as it unfolds in all its mystery and surprises, we are able to keep our awareness present and act with conscious intention. We have greater tolerance for pain and suffering, and we sincerely trust ourselves and the cycle of life and death. The journey from right/wrong thinking and living in fear to living consciously in a trusting relationship with ourselves and God is a process of awakening. These four intertwined practices allow us to open our unitive level of consciousness.

1. Conscious presence. Our perceptions of ourselves, others, and the world are on autopilot when they are based on little or no conscious awareness or the intention to create greater health and well-being. When we are on autopilot, our lives are defined by the automatic recycling of our existing attitudes, judgments, illusions, delusions, memories, memory patterns, thoughts, feelings, fears, hopes, and dreams. We exist in a veiled state, unable to see what is right in front of us. Within the privacy of our own consciousness— in the theater of our mind—we create our own sense of reality, which we inhabit as our role in the great drama of life. Our habitual way of being is a complex foundational structure, like a skeletal system for our consciousness.

To step into the process of creating our lives through conscious presence simply means encountering each moment anew—freely and authentically with a sense of personal accountability, curiosity, and responsibility for our own creations. We are able to encounter and integrate our new experiences, remaining open to change and pain as appropriate. A fluidity and aliveness to our experiences emerges rather than a rote repetition of the past or following the status quo. We begin to focus more upon the deeper questions of our life's purpose and become more aware of the wisdom being presented through our experiences.

This practice begins with observing when something distressing happens. See if you can keep open to the present moment rather than extrapolating your current experience into fear patterns of what might happen in the future. Remember, when our focus leaves on the fast train of fear, our intelligence is not available to deal with the situation at hand—we've already left the station. In *Grist for the Mill*, Ram Dass describes how to be consciously present this way:

> Being conscious is cutting through your own melodrama and being right here. Exist in no mind, be empty, here now, and trust that as a situation arises, out of you will come what is necessary to deal with that situation including the use of your intellect when appropriate.

Your intellect need not be constantly held onto to keep reassuring you that you know where you're at, out of fear of loss of control. Ultimately, when you stop identifying so much with your physical body and with your psychological entity, that anxiety starts to disintegrate. And you start to define yourself as in flow with the universe; and whatever comes along—death, life, joy, sadness—is grist for the mill of awakening. Not this versus that but whatever.

2. Reframing pain and suffering. For those under the influence of the Death Taboo, death is perceived as the ultimate source of pain and suffering. Interestingly enough, most people are more afraid of the emotional and physical pain and suffering of dying than of the reality of being dead.

———

Exercise 8: My Beliefs About Pain and Suffering

Record your responses to these questions. Be sure to consider the different manifestations of pain and suffering—physical, mental, emotional, spiritual, or existential.

1. What are my beliefs and assumptions about pain and suffering?
2. What specific thoughts and behaviors do I have that are my ways of avoiding pain and suffering?
3. What forms of pain and suffering do I resist the most?
4. What, if any, benefits have I ever experienced through pain and suffering?

———

Here is a personal example of how the avoidance of pain and suffering functions in our lives and how it can be reframed. A number of years ago, I discovered that I was a master at avoiding pain and suffering. I realized that I had an unconscious mental construct, whereby I automatically reacted with disapproval and judgment when I experienced any kind of discomfort. Frustration would rapidly escalate to anger whenever something happened that I didn't like—even little things like a minor traffic delay or needing help and getting an inefficient, undecipherable, or incompetent technical support person on the phone. I held an underlying belief that I shouldn't have to experience these things and reacted against what I perceived to be the source of any discomfort.

Once I became conscious of this pattern, I began probing into it more deeply. I discovered that somewhere under the surface of this reaction was a fundamental belief that my suffering was obvious evidence that God was incompetent, and therefore I had better take charge. I got into defensive mode—I fired God, under the illusion that I could take charge and do a better job of controlling events and circumstances in order to restore my illusion of peace and safety. I discovered this in my fifties and realized that I had been functioning this way for most of my life. I suspect I was not alone in that.

The ironic thing about avoiding pain and suffering is that the evasion itself heightens the experience of pain and suffering by acting like a magnet attracting to us what we focus upon. In a 2014 interview, Tara Brach, Western teacher of Buddhist meditation, addressed the question of how nonacceptance of a painful experience prolongs suffering, saying:

> When we're non-accepting, we're tightening against, and the very tightening itself separates us from our own wholeness and the wholeness of the universe. So, it's a contraction that actually fuels the suffering. . . We are conditioned to tighten against what's unpleasant and so it's part of what our nervous system does. . . It's helpful

to be able to tolerate what's there even though every-thing in us is saying . . . pull away, push it away, get away.

I think of this as learning to breathe into the experience rather than running away from it. It's an acquired art, one that it behooves us to practice. In terms of bypassing the conditioning, the demands, and the expectations that are running our lives, in *Passage into Spirit* John-Roger advises that we do so not by forcing ourselves or pre-tending. It is a process of awareness, acceptance, and action.

It is fairly normal to minimize our distress, but my own avoid-ance of pain and suffering was an all-encompassing intolerance. I remember explaining my experience to someone by holding my arms straight out in front of me with my hands turned upward at a ninety-degree angle. I had a big "aha" moment seeing the connec-tion to why I had carpal tunnel syndrome in my wrists and bone spurs in my shoulders, and why my thumb and wrist had been fro-zen and unable to bend for several months. In that moment, I made the connection of how my mental and emotional avoidance of pain and suffering were manifesting in physical dysfunctions. As I prac-ticed working with these dysfunctions rather than fighting against them, I was able to reduce and eventually heal these problems.

Since pain and suffering come with the territory of being human, a wiser and healthier approach is to learn how to move through these life passages without losing our sense of well-being while har-vesting whatever lessons they bring our way. Thus, we learn to rise above personal desires into acceptance and cooperation with what is present in our lives and to build tolerance and skill in experienc-ing the fullness of life.

Psycho-spiritual healer and author of *Knowing Your Shadow* Robert Augustus Masters makes an important distinction between pain and suffering. He notes that pain is a normal part of the human experience. It is simply unpleasant sensation. Suffering, on the other hand, is the story we tell ourselves about our pain. Our tendency is to get so caught up in the story of our suffering that it focuses our attention on feeling the pain. Masters advises that we end our suffering by entering into our pain and moving through it. Imagine the difference between the experience of a birthing woman who is actively working with her breath to move through the pain of her labor versus the one who resists and fights against her pain by screaming about how much it hurts. The path through our pain is to accept its presence rather than to resist it or try to get away from it. We create the habit of suffering by the very act of resisting pain. Through resistance, we draw pain to ourselves. Through suffering, we attach ourselves to our pain.

3. Building trust. Unitive consciousness involves grounding our perceptions and responses deeper within ourselves than surface, automatic reactions. It involves building a core place of reliance on our own integrity, ability, and character that, no matter how unpleasant an incoming experience might be, recognizes that we are capable of moving through it and that there is something about it that is there to serve a higher good. While going about the business of handling the physical, mental, and emotional challenges being presented in any situation, we also seek to connect to and perhaps surrender to this deeper sense that there is nothing wrong. There is something for us in this experience.

In *The Power of Now,* Eckhart Tolle says:

> Do you truly know what is positive and what is negative? Do you have the total picture? There have been many people for whom limitation, failure, loss, illness, or pain in whatever form turned out to be their greatest teacher. It taught them to let go of false self-images and superficial ego-dictated goals and desires. It gave them depth, humility, and compassion. It made them more real.
>
> Whenever anything negative happens to you, there is a deep lesson concealed within it, although you may not see it at the time. Even a brief illness or an accident

can show you what is real and unreal in your life, what ultimately matters and what doesn't.

Seen from a higher perspective, conditions are always positive. To be more precise: they are neither positive nor negative. They are as they are. And when you live in complete acceptance of what is—which is the only sane way to live—there is no "good" or "bad" in your life anymore. There is only a higher good—which includes the "bad."

For me, the key to shifting my relationship with pain and suffering involved learning to trust in myself and in God's goodness. Trust is a kind of reliable ground I stand upon. I realized that I'm not the only blind person around this elephant, and I do not need to take issue with others seeing the world differently.

As I leaned into trusting myself and God, I found I was less attached to the ups and downs of my life. Instead, I maintained my balance with a steadier inner focus and trusted my ability to encounter all kinds of experiences. I used the metaphor of light going into the darkness to dispel my illusions, recognizing that the light can go into the darkness, but the darkness cannot go into the light.

And as I learned to cultivate and accept the existence of pain by consciously practicing moving through pain and suffering when it showed up, I built a kind of confidence that I was okay regardless of whether or not the situation at hand was to my liking. By enduring the presence of pain rather than emotionalizing it, which would merely escalate the degree of my suffering, I entertained the belief that everything that happens in my life is for my highest good. Little by little, I replaced my defensive posture with an inner calm of trust. I began to see that life is not so much about being comfortable as it is an opportunity to learn life lessons and gain wisdom.

I learned to allow for the mysteries of life that are beyond my perceptual capabilities. I realized that there was nothing wrong that I had to fix. I had to let go of my preconceived notions about pain and suffering and the desire to know what was going on or to be in the illusion of being in control. I discovered trust is about letting go of "shoulds," "have tos," demands, expectations, fears, illusions, and delusions. Opening to and creating space inside of me to receive and cooperate with God's perfect wisdom and timing in my living and dying is not a passive action. Rather, it is a different way of participating in my life and a different vantage point from which to make decisions. The bottom line is that when I trust myself and God, then I have no need to avoid pain and suffering and am free to be my authentic self in a trusting partnership of cocreation with God.

We earn this kind of profound trust by elevating our consciousness day by day—getting some altitude. I have never heard a more piercing description of this trust than this poem by an unknown author that was left by the body of a dead child in one of the Nazi concentration camps. It calls us to a far greater, deeper wisdom about human pain and suffering:

Oh Lord, remember not only the men and women of
good will,
but also those of ill will.
But do not remember all the suffering they inflicted on
us,
Remember the fruits we have brought thanks to this
suffering.
Our comradeship, our loyalty, our humility,
our courage, our generosity,
the greatness of heart that has grown out of all this.
And when they come to judgment
Let all the fruits, which we have born, be their
forgiveness.

4. Turning our thinking inside out rather than outside in.
Essentially, this shift in consciousness involves turning our focus inside out—living from a place of inner trust rather than outer

defensiveness and reactivity. In the avoidance model, our mental, emotional, and physical selves focus outward, acting as sentinels of self-defense spinning a web of illusions and fears and then reacting as if they were true. Alternatively, when experiencing life from a place of inner trust, the mind, emotions, and body can simply be useful tools for perceiving and cooperating with whatever happens in our lives. We breathe into each life experience, trusting that we are capable of moving through it.

Exercise 9: Seeing Death Through New Eyes

Imagine that you have just been given a terminal diagnosis with the prognosis of dying within one year. Describe in writing what it would look like for you to respond to this information from a right/wrong point of view. What would it feel like? What would you be doing?

Now, describe what it would look like for you to respond to this information from a unitive point of view. What would it feel like to be without negative judgements? What would you be doing?

Finally, describe how the quality of your inner and outer experience would be different in these two scenarios.

---

changing our minds about death

Let's explore the blessings and life lessons to be found in death if we are open to receive them. For the dying, for example, death may bring an end to suffering and, depending on one's spiritual beliefs, may represent a return home to the heart of God, a reunion with deceased loved ones, or finally finding out what really happens after death. At the end, my mother was impatient for her death, wanting to know what was going to happen next. She would ask me, "When is it going to happen?" My response was, "Have you asked God?" to which she would sheepishly say, "Yes, He says, 'Patience, darling.'"

For loved ones who will be left behind, death may bring a period of grief that also involves finding a new way of living one's life, perhaps with greater independence, time, and renewed motivation to pursue an unfulfilled dream. It may also teach them to be brave, courageous, and loving in the presence of their fears, to value the gift of life more dearly, and to become more generous and bolder in expressing love.

For me, rising to the occasion of caring for my mother at the end of her life allowed me to know her more intimately. It gave us the opportunity to take our love to far greater depths and showed me levels of courage and love within myself that I didn't know I was capable of before that. Did we walk through the Valley of the Shadow of Death? You bet we did! And I would do it again without hesitation for the gifts it brought to me in terms of greater self-knowledge, wisdom, confidence, and loving. Had I recoiled in fear, I would have been deprived of all these gifts.

The following exercise invites you to imagine how your own life and the lives of your family and society would be changed if the fear of death were removed. It guides you to explore action steps you are willing to take to move in that direction.

Exercise 10: Gaining Altitude on Death

Imagine living in a world in which death is seen to be as normal as birth and life itself. Make lists of at least five differences, each that you suppose you would experience in yourself, in your family, and in society at large if you lived in such a world. Alternatively, if you and/or your family already perceive death this way, you might look at what it is like for you to live in this society with its strong Death Taboo.

For each difference, identify at least one small thing you could do to contribute to disempowering the Death Taboo and decide if you want to take that step, and if so, give yourself a "deadline" for doing so—pun intended!

The key to cultivating a higher perspective on death is the willingness to participate fully in your own experience and to consciously experience your participation. As spiritual teacher John Morton says: "When we are not aware of God's constant love and blessing, it simply means that we are 'off' in how we are viewing life. What may be required is something referred to as 'altitude.' That means we must lift our consciousness to see situations from a more elevated perspective."

chapter 7

key #2:
investigating your deepest beliefs
and fears

*"*You never know how much you really believe anything until its truth or falsehood becomes a matter of life and death to you.*"*

—*C.S. Lewis*

O UR DEEPEST BELIEFS AND FEARS about living, dying, and death are part of the bedrock upon which we experience the ups and downs of our life. Unfortunately, many of us take them for granted as simply part of how we are, and we never challenge or explore them. In Chapter 7, we investigate our beliefs as well as the process of inheriting conceptual beliefs from our parents and society. We look at how we either embrace our inherited beliefs or find another point of view that resonates more deeply for us. We see how our beliefs function as filters for our thoughts, feelings, and behaviors. Pain and suffering are reframed as the little deaths of daily life, opportunities for us to override our autopilot fight-or-flight instinct. They also strengthen our ability to handle all of life, not just the parts we like. We look at our core fears about death and dying and articulate our specific wishes regarding our own dying process.

core beliefs

What we believe to be true is the ground we stand upon. What we believe determines the posture with which we meet the world as well as how we leave it. Unless we are exposed to other points of view or otherwise intentionally challenge our beliefs, we are likely to assume that they are the truth. Sooner or later, if we are lucky, we are motivated to know ourselves more intimately by investigating our deepest beliefs and fears. This introspection breathes life and wisdom into us. Alternatively, if we never take this journey, we are not as likely to really know ourselves, nor will anyone else know our deeper self.

When was the last time you contemplated your fundamental beliefs in terms of such existential questions as:

- Does God exist?
- Who am I?
- What is the purpose of human life?
- What is death? Is it the end of our existence or just the end of our body and current identity?

Knowing what we believe about such things places our everyday lives in the context of a more expansive worldview. If you haven't investigated these thoughts during your life, you most likely will find them critically important to you in your dying. Knowing who you are and what you believe can be an enormous comfort and benefit when facing your death or that of a loved one.

It is easy to become so consumed by our busy lives that we seldom go below the surface of our daily routines. Taking the time to explore our core beliefs, if considered at all, usually appears to be a luxury at best. Yet it is perhaps the most essential thing we can do to live deeply and purposefully. It takes effort and intention to poke below the surface of our lives to explore the foundation upon which we are living.

Some of us spout our beliefs with great conviction. Yet that does not necessarily mean we are significantly familiar with what we are talking about. For some, strong beliefs are little more than intellectual concepts inherited from parents, friends, or society. For others, beliefs are profound convictions that resonate as truth deep within the self.

Where do our beliefs come from? Clearly, society and family beliefs play a major role in molding our point of view as individuals. Here's an example. I remember going to catechism classes as a young Catholic girl, where I was taught to memorize and recite questions and answers from *The Baltimore Catechism* about the purpose of human existence. To this day, I remember some of them by heart:

- *Who made us?* God made us.
- *Who is God?* God is the Supreme Being, infinitely perfect, who made all things and keeps them in existence.
- *Why did God make us?* God made us to show forth His goodness and to share with us His everlasting happiness in heaven.
- *What must we do to gain the happiness of heaven?* To gain the happiness of heaven we must know, love, and serve God in this world.

The recitations continued from there to explain the role of Jesus and the Catholic Church in supporting humanity in achieving its purpose. I had no idea what these questions and answers meant. Success was not measured through understanding but by one's ability to memorize and recite these words. I was not encouraged to be curious about what these statements meant, nor did anyone attempt to help me to understand them—just recite them.

Children do in fact inherit belief systems from their parents, culture, and society. Regardless of the merit of the beliefs being programmed, they are reinforced through repetition forming the go-to neural pathways of the child's brain. While experience and exploration play a role as well, unless and until challenged, these implanted concepts run on autopilot.

Through personal exploration below the surface of our inherited concepts, or by rebelling against them, we activate our own inner knowing. It is a kind of inner resonance or recognition of deep truth that occurs when we encounter ideas and beliefs that we simply know as our own.

For me, this process of awakening happened most noticeably when I was twelve and my mother gifted me with a book about the world's great religions that Christmas. I began to experience resonance with ideas and beliefs of certain non-Christian ideologies. My awakening and curiosity were again stimulated in college when I studied Buddhism, Taoism, and other Eastern perspectives on the purpose of human existence. I began to welcome that resonance of inner truth each time I experienced it being activated when encountering elements of truth and wisdom in these other ways of viewing life as well as the tradition in which I had been raised.

Similarly, our newly emerging culture of death, as discussed in Chapter 4, presents an exciting opportunity for us as individuals and as a society to reconsider our perspective on death and dying. By challenging the good/bad view of life and death, we can evolve our thinking, which in turn will change our beliefs and experiences of death and dying.

We each have the opportunity to be powerful creators of our own consciousness or to be passive heirs to the autopilot programming of our own history and external authorities. Whether we choose to embrace the beliefs we have inherited or not, there is an opportunity to breathe life into what resonates as true within us and to live more consciously in the context of our own beliefs.

Exercise 11: My Deepest Beliefs

Document your responses to these questions. You can come back to them later, but for now, begin to record and date your present perspective:

1.   What really matters to me deep in the core of my being?
2.   What are the five most fervent beliefs that inform how I live my life?
3.   Am I pleased with myself as a human being? How do I think I am doing being me?
4.   What is the most profound purpose of my life?
5.   Do I think life is precious? Why or why not and how is that apparent in how I live my life?

Regardless of our beliefs, whether God exists or not, whether our dreams ultimately come true or not, whether we feel loved or not, successful or not, each moment of each day we have the opportunity to do our best—or not. My friends are amused by my favorite expression: "I'm doing the best I can, and THIS is what that looks like!" When we engage more profoundly in our lives, we participate with greater conscious intention and discernment. We choose to participate in our experience and to consciously experience our participation. In my book, *The Wedding Ceremony Planner*, I note that "We are all tested by the routines of daily life, by chance and circumstance, and by the full cycle of the seasons of life. We must encounter life's sorrow no less than its sweetness, its frustration along with its grace and ease, its disappointments along with its fulfillment." We meet our lives anew each moment, whether on the autopilot setting of the walking dead or the turbocharged, Technicolor of passion, loving, caring, hope, and kindness.

I am convinced that, no matter what one believes, the only path that allows us to transcend the option of sleepwalking through our lives involves an introspective awakening to a deeper sense of who we are and of our life as pilgrimage—a journey to a sacred place within ourselves or in search of an exalted purpose. As John Brierley, author of *A Pilgrim's Guide to the Camino de Santiago*, puts it: "Life itself is a sacred journey carrying with it the responsibility to act accordingly."

In numerous books and studies, I have read that caregivers of the dying often report hearing that the biggest regret of their dying patients has to do with having lived according to the expectations of others rather than living true to themselves. What a great motivation to get to know ourselves more intimately.

Exercise 12: How Intimately Do I Know Myself and Others?

Have you shared your answers to Exercise 11 with anyone else yet? If not, pick somebody you would like to know better and ask them if they would be willing to answer the questions for themselves and then get together and share responses with each other. Practice meeting any differences in your points of view with a spaciousness of mind, curiosity, inquisitiveness, and an absence of judgment. If you have already shared your beliefs with someone, pick someone else and do it again. Practice making it more normal to talk about these things with your partner, parents, children, and friends.

Those who choose to know themselves more intimately step into the driver's seat of their own lives. American memoirist and teacher Mark Matousek says: "It's uncanny what happens when people wake up. Their wattage increases. Their hearts amplify. You see the juju in their eyes."

Life becomes more precious when we realize how fleeting it all is—a string of moments offered to us one after the other until we have spent our allotment. Not knowing how short or long our life will be is a powerful incentive to go for the gusto moment by moment. In "Ecstatic Poem #5," Kabir, mystic poet and saint of India, amplifies this point:

> My inside, listen to me,
> The greatest spirit, the Teacher, is near,
> Wake up, wake up!
> Run to his feet –
> He is standing close to your head right now.
> You have slept for millions and millions of years.
> Why not wake up this morning?

Soren Kierkegaard adds: "If I were a physician, and if I were allowed to prescribe just one remedy for all of the ills of the modern world, I would prescribe silence. For even if the Word of God were proclaimed in the modern world, how could one hear it with so much noise? Therefore, create silence."

How do we awaken ourselves, extracting our awareness from the mundane routines of daily life or alternatively finding wisdom and fulfillment in them? It simply takes effort, time, and practice to live with greater conscious intention and to awaken ourselves to a more profound understanding of life and death.

beliefs as filters of our thoughts, feelings, and behaviors

I have been studying consciousness for most of my life and have come to recognize that our thoughts, feelings, and behaviors are a fait accompli of our beliefs. It is our beliefs that act as the primary filter through which we experience our lives. For example, if you believe in God, then the way you live your life will likely be structured around your relationship to God as either a divine presence within you or a being or force outside of you. You may have a concept of a life purpose that relates to God and move through your daily life with a conscious or unconscious set of rules about what is acceptable behavior and what is not and hold yourself accountable to behave accordingly. In addition, you may have a belief in some kind of afterlife, the quality of which will be determined by how you live your life.

Alternatively, if God is not a part of your worldview, you might source your sense of purpose from a more social and ethical belief in being a good person and see life as a discreet biological event with a beginning and end and no afterlife. In yet another possibility, some religious traditions such as Buddhism have no concept of God rather, a foundational belief in reincarnation and karma that motivates a sense of personal accountability in one's life and the impact of this life upon the next life. Sometimes we don't realize how powerful our core beliefs are in determining our everyday life choices.

how we live our lives

If we really understood how our beliefs serve as the foundation upon which we live our lives, we might become eager to get to know everything about ourselves. If we don't know what we believe and how our beliefs are directing our lives as well as how we will approach our deaths, then we are likely to be living adrift, bumping into life experiences and having knee-jerk reactions to them.

Each of us has the option of living our life from the inside out. This involves awakening to who we are and what we believe and living brilliantly from that deeper place rather than simply existing on the surface of our lives. Why is this important? First of all, it means we get to really live our lives with gusto instead of merely existing. We get to take advantage of the opportunity to master the art of being. Second, it allows us to befriend ourselves and get into the driver's seat, consciously doing our best with who we are and what matters to us. Third, it enables us to have more intimate connections with others. And finally, it gives us the ability to meet the end of our life with existential maturity, sated and at peace. As American journalist and author Hunter S. Thompson said: "Life should not be a journey to the grave with the intention of arriving safely in a pretty and well-preserved body, but rather to skid in broadside in a cloud of smoke, thoroughly used up, totally worn out, and loudly proclaiming, 'Wow! What a Ride!'"

beliefs about death

Our beliefs about death have a lot to do with how we live our lives as well as how we will meet our death or react to the deaths of others. Birth, life, and death are a continuum through which each of us must journey. Death itself is not merely a medical event of the body. In whatever manner our death comes, each of us, or those who are making decisions for us in the event we are unable to do so for ourselves, will need to decide when and how to recognize and surrender to our time to die.

This next exercise explores your fundamental beliefs regarding life and death so you can communicate them to those close to you as they serve as the basis upon which critically important decisions will be made.

Exercise 13: My Existential Perspective About Life and Death

This exercise explores your fundamental beliefs regarding life and death so you can communicate them to those close to you. This deeper truth within you serves as the basis upon which critically important decisions will be made.

Record your innermost responses to the following questions:

1. What do I really think about the consistent reports of near-death experiences that suggest something beautiful happening when we die?
2. What dies at death?
3. Does anything survive at death? If I believe that something survives at death, then why do I think we pay more attention to the dying part than to the part that lives on?
4. What do I think will happen to me when I die?
5. Does anything scare me about death? If so, what?
6. What, if any, religious or spiritual beliefs do I have that inform my view of death and dying?
7. How is my acceptance or fear about death apparent in the way I live my life?
8. Who has taught me the most about death and dying? How were these lessons transmitted?

Sometimes it helps to take our thinking to extremes to challenge it and to see where it leads us. For example, those who view death as something that shouldn't have to happen might benefit from exploring that thought further. Indeed, what would it be like to never die? To have endless time, no "bucket list"—just one to-do list after another moving through eternity? What would motivate you? What age would you be? Would everyone be the same age? Would there be any growing up or aging, or would life be more of a static monotone? What if flowers and fish and insects never died either? What if Buddha, Jesus, Hitler, and the billions of others who have gone before us were all still here too? Would that be better than having everyone die? Where would we put everyone? How would we share our resources? What political systems would emerge to handle it all? Alternatively, can you see any cosmic wisdom in the design of human life that includes death with an unknown expiration date? All we know is *this is our time*. What are you doing with yours?

Perhaps there is some holistic wisdom to the nonnegotiable reality of death. Thinking more deeply about death can challenge and dissolve patterns of resistance, denial, and fear. If we were not so afraid of death, we might be less inclined to fight against terminal disease as though death were the enemy to be fought to the bitter end. Instead, we might more calmly consider the hard decisions we face regarding the potential future quality and quantity of our remaining life, and we might seek awareness of the wisdom of what is happening to us. There are no perfect choices in this territory, only ones that are more or less coherent with our personal beliefs and circumstances. Imagine the freedom that some people experience through a true acceptance of their mortality. Have you ever been around someone who knew they were dying and had made peace with that?

No doubt, death plays a vital role in determining how we live our lives. Be aware of the fact that, in the absence of any exploration of your personal beliefs and fears regarding death, your brain is being bathed in our cultural Death Taboo that instills deep fear in your psyche.

the little deaths of daily life

We all encounter little deaths or mini losses every single day. How we respond to them has everything to do with how we will face our life's end. Do you judge or reject unpleasant experiences? Do you feel victimized by them? Or, do you use them as steppingstones? Minister and motivational speaker Temple Hayes said: "The subtle deaths of daily life . . . [are such things as] not ever speaking your mind and your heart with people around you. . . or the person who is miserable in their work or career . . . all the ways that we do not listen to ourselves . . . They take away our energy and we are not able to live a vibrant life."

I think of the little deaths of daily life as encompassing the ways we encounter pain and suffering—physically, mentally, emotionally, financially, existentially, and spiritually. Each one is a potential moment of transformation, unless we push against them or away from them. Perhaps the biggest price we pay by trying to sanitize our lives of pain and suffering is losing sight of the fact that these experiences are often the very ones that help us to clarify what really matters to us. They often bring with them the courage to pursue our dreams. In this context, it is interesting to consider a school of thought called hedonics that explores the human experience of pursuing happiness. Researchers agree that our sense of well-being is impacted more powerfully by how we choose to look at things than by any other factor.

In *Buddha's Daughters,* Pema Chodron has this to say on the subject of encountering the little deaths of daily life:

> When things fall apart and we're on the verge of we know not what, the test for each of us is to stay on that brink and not concretize. The spiritual journey is not about heaven and finally getting to a place that's really swell. In fact, that way of looking at things is what keeps

us miserable. Thinking that we can find some lasting pleasure and avoid pain is what in Buddhism is called samsara, a hopeless cycle that goes round and round endlessly and causes us to suffer greatly.

The very first noble truth of the Buddha points out that suffering is inevitable for human beings as long as we believe that things last—that they don't disintegrate, that they can be counted on to satisfy our hunger for security. From this point of view, the only time we ever know what's really going on is when the rug has been pulled out and we can't find anywhere to land. We use these situations either to wake ourselves up or to put ourselves to sleep.

the God question

There is no question that those who have an abiding belief in God have access to a kind of comfort that those without such a belief or experience are not able to draw upon. In this regard, I consider myself fortunate for the shift in my consciousness that occurred during my 1997 car accident. Embedded in this—one of the most terrifying experiences of my life—was what I can only call an existential awakening that was a kind of spiritual initiation that tore the blinders off my eyes. In an instant, I was transformed from being a person who conceptually believed in God to one who had a visceral experience and knowing of God's presence. I suddenly knew what the sixteenth-century Dutch theologian and humanist Desiderius Erasmus meant when he said, "Bidden or not bidden, God is present"—or, as my eight-year-old friend Sarah, heard this phrase—"Bidden or not bidden, God is president."

There is a powerful image that has held special meaning for me since my accident. Originally portrayed by the English

Pre-Raphaelite artist William Holman Hunt (1827-1910) and called *The Light of the World*, this allegorical painting illustrates Revelation 3:20:

> Behold, I stand at the door and knock; if any man hear My voice, and open the door, I will come in to him, and will sup with him, and he with Me. (KJV)

In the image, Jesus is about to knock on a long-unopened door that has no handle on his side because it must be opened from within. In my spiritual tradition, we refer to this as the fact that spirit or the divine or whatever term you prefer does not violate the human consciousness—we must open ourselves to receive.

As I wrote in my second doctoral dissertation titled *Life as a Trust Walk*: "I learned that the sacred dimension of life, the presence of the Beloved, does not exist because we say so. Rather, God is there, awaiting our invitation, our awakening into awareness that we are indeed spiritual beings—souls sharing a profound divine oneness." This proved particularly important for me in breaking free of the ways I had learned to avoid pain and suffering in my life. It led me to the conclusion that, if I trusted myself and God, then I had no need to avoid pain and suffering and was free to be my authentic self, to live in a trusting partnership of cocreation with God. I came to see pain, suffering, and death as trust strengtheners rather than as wrong, bad, or something to be resisted. By breathing into all our life experiences and trusting ourselves no matter the outcome, we open the door to becoming wiser, more skillful, and compassionate human beings. In so doing, we are developing our potential to thrive rather than shutting down in primitive fight-or-flight response to the challenges that life presents.

core fears

There are two mnemonics for the word "fear" that are helpful in understanding what fear really is and how it works. They are:

Fantasy Expectations Appearing Real
and
False Evidence Appearing Real

All fears function in the same way, though their magnitude varies. In the theater of our minds, fear catapults our consciousness out of the present into some imagined future that, in turn, causes us to put the brakes on ourselves in our present reality.

According to Bruce H. Lipton and Steve Bhaerman in their audio recording, *Spontaneous Evolution*, fear literally contracts our energy and paralyzes us from thoughtfully and compassionately responding to the object of our fear.

> When we are in a happy state, we are in a state of growth, and when we get afraid, we get in a state of protection. And when we get in a state of protection, it completely changes the blood flow to the body because when you are in a state of growth, you are nourishing the viscera, which is really the organs that take care of maintaining our health, etc. But when we start to get afraid, we want to send the blood to the arms and legs because the arms and legs are what we are going to use for fight-or-flight to escape the issue or deal with the problem, so the hormones and stress cause the blood vessels in the gut to squeeze shut, which forces the extra blood to go to the periphery where we are going to nourish that fight or flight behavior. Well, interesting enough, the same hormones affect blood vessels in the brain because when we are in a state of happiness and growth, we are using

our conscious reasoning and our thinking and our logical thought. But in a state of reaction to a threat, conscious reasoning is not very helpful because it is a very slow process. So, basically what happens is in the presence of stress hormones, blood vessels in the forebrain, which is the center of conscious reasoning and logic, are squeezed shut just like the blood vessels in the gut, and this forces the blood to go to the hindbrain. Well, the hindbrain is reflex and reactive behavior so basically it says from the moment you get under stress you actually shut down the thinking processes of the conscious mind and open up the reactive, reactionary processes of the hindbrain. . . Simply, when we are under stress, we become less intelligent.

This is enormously important for us in considering the levels of stress we create for ourselves through our fears.

When what we fear is death, quite a conundrum is created because no one can avoid death. Unless we learn to transform the energy of fearing death, we live in fear and die afraid. And as Lipton notes, we do so without much access to our intelligence. Thich Nhat Hanh, Vietnamese Buddhist monk, teacher, author, poet, and peace activist, says: "Without fear, we are able to see more clearly our connections to others. Without fear, we have more room for understanding and compassion. Without fear, we are truly free."

Contracting in response to our fears or things we have a hard time accepting literally fuels our suffering. We have been trained to pull away from and tighten against what we do not like. But if we can expand our tolerance for the normalcy of pain and suffering in our lives—even death itself—we are able to quite significantly reduce our stress. This in turn heightens the intelligence of our response and the enjoyment of our life. How? The answer lies in being more mindful and consciously choosing to endure what we fear.

A simple yet powerful technique is to begin by breathing into some of the less threatening experiences we have automatically resisted and, over time, do the same with more challenging issues and experiences. Here's an example. Let's say you are going to the doctor to get your flu shot, and you hate getting shots. This time, in anticipation of the experience, you remind yourself that you have survived and benefitted from many shots in the past. You intentionally take some deep breaths as a technique to relax yourself. When you are about to get your shot, you breathe and expand into the experience with the conscious intention of remaining relaxed, particularly at the site of the shot. You relax your muscles and skin and exhale deeply as the shot enters your body. In doing so, you are focusing on your breathing and relaxing rather than on getting the shot.

Similar practices of mindfulness and intention can be used to build tolerance to increasingly difficult experiences. Little by little, we gain acceptance and skill in meeting life just as it is—the unpleasant along with the pleasant. When we reframe the roles that pain and suffering play in our lives, we work from a base experience of acceptance rather than rejection and resistance. As a result, we discover that the degree of our physical, mental, emotional, and spiritual suffering is lessened because we are not holding so tightly to our fear of and resistance to the less pleasant experiences of life. In other words, we are dealing directly with what has presented itself rather than avoiding it. It is interesting to note that American surgeon Atul Gawande reports that many of his dying patients say the last days of their lives, when surrounded by friends and family, are the best days of their lives.

Those who have yet to learn a healthy way of being in relationship to their fears typically experience a general uneasiness—a kind of ubiquitous anxiety and groundless uncertainty in the face of fear. They armor themselves against whatever it is they think is going to hurt them. A radical but liberating alternative is to get to know fear by turning toward it rather than away from it. This is what Pema

Chodron and her teacher Chogyam Trungpa Rinpoche refer to as smiling at our fears. This requires that we stay present rather than shutting down and pushing away what makes us uneasy.

Exercise 14: Smiling at My Fears

Record your answers to the following questions:

1. What do I do when I am afraid? How do I feel? How do I behave?
2. What are at least five things about death and dying that I fear and/or experience distress when I think about them?
3. For each one, describe your typical physical, mental, and emotional reactions.
4. Choose to smile at your fears. Literally, engage in an inner dialogue with each of your fears with a smile on your face and in your heart as you relate to them fearlessly. Record your dialogues.

Fear displaces our consciousness from awareness in the present moment into our imagination, and then we respond to our envisioned future as though it were a certainty that we don't see ourselves being able to handle. Fear has a paralyzing effect. It can render us unable to function by freezing us in a state of panic, surprise, and confusion. Sometimes, fear is so overwhelming that we push it into our subconscious mind and some part of us expends an enormous amount of energy keeping it out of our awareness. This is much like trying to hold a beach ball under the water. When we smile at our fear, we trust our ability to handle whatever life brings our way.

your specific wishes regarding your own dying process

As mentioned earlier, according to the US Center for Disease Control, 28 percent of the 2.8 million Americans who die each year are under the age of sixty-five. The idea that only old people die is a Death Taboo myth that discourages us from taking control over the end of our life by planning in advance of need.

Everyone over the age of eighteen should be educating themselves about end-of-life issues and options and documenting their own end-of-life preferences. The alternative is to leave loved ones to make these decisions on our behalf without our input and to be subject to the laws of the state regarding who will decide on our behalf. Regardless of our age, we all live with the possibility of dying. While the probability of our death varies according to our age and other factors, the possibility is always present.

The preparation and documentation of end-of-life wishes is an evolving process in our society. What has been woefully missing is sufficient education about the issues and options available. Three kinds of anticipatory decision-making issues need to be considered for each and every one of us. They include:

- Advance healthcare planning that delineates our wishes regarding medical treatment and care at the end of our life
- Estate planning that specifies how we want our personal property and money distributed after our death
- Expressing preferences regarding religious or spiritual rituals to be performed after our death and the disposition of our body

At this point, education in these areas is quite hit-or-miss and typically not done until we are old or when a life-or-death crisis occurs. Healthcare proxies and advance healthcare directives, if considered at all, are either part of the paperwork included in creating a will or estate plan or part of the hospital admitting process. In neither case is there typically sufficient time or attention given to educating the individual making these critically important decisions about all the nuances and finer points to be considered. It's too often a case of too little, too late.

We need to take it upon ourselves to make time to think deeply about what we anticipate being our needs, preferences, and priorities when we come face-to-face with our own dying:

- How will you choose to make the most of the time you have left when the end is in sight?
- How will you measure the quality of that time?

These considerations need to be an ongoing process of educating ourselves, thinking deeply about our preferences, and then documenting and communicating our wishes to our healthcare providers and loved ones. Equally important, we need to secure agreement from doctors and loved ones to honor our wishes when called upon to do so. Since options and technologies are always changing, as are our thoughts, it's a good idea to review documentation of your three areas of end-of-life planning at least annually or whenever a major life change occurs. Decisions about medical treatment options involve not only a weighing of probable costs-versus-benefits of a particular treatment, but also the consideration of what one foregoes by seeking further treatment at all.

A basic overview of the three areas of end-of-life planning is presented in Chapter 14. This information needs to be put into action. Consider opening the conversation of end-of-life preferences with one or more family members or loved ones. Take the opportunity to explore your respective beliefs and wishes regarding your own death and dying within the context of your beliefs about living and dying. The more specific you can be about your wishes, the easier it is for others to honor them and for you to relax in the knowledge that you have done your best to communicate what is important to you. Expressing your thoughts in the next exercise in no way serves as a substitute for filing legal documents that record your wishes. However, this is a good opportunity to calmly and thoughtfully take a fresh look or a first look at the kinds of specific decisions you will be making at your life's end. This exercise will help you clarify, affirm, or update your point of view. It is intended to present you with levels of detail not always typically explored in filing end-of-life legal documents.

Exercise 15: What Matters to Me About My Own Death and Dying

Consider the following questions and statements. If a statement is not true for you, edit or rewrite it to reflect your wishes. If your answers depend on any factors such as your age or condition at the time of your dying, note your thoughts about that. If you are unsure of what you think, note that and follow up later. Be sure to indicate the date that you record these answers, so you can revisit these questions and update your responses if and when they change (again recording the date). If these are difficult questions for you to answer, consider asking someone you trust and feel safe with to help you talk through your concerns, and perhaps you can help them to do so as well.

1. What preferences, if any, do you have about who you would like to have taking care of you when you are dying? Is there anyone you wish not to have serving you in that capacity? If so, who?

2. What specific concerns do you have regarding being cared for at the end of your life? For example, do you worry about being a burden or not having sufficient financial resources, or being in a nursing home?

3. If you are no longer able to live independently and are diagnosed as being in the final six months of your life, where would you prefer to live? Number the following possibilities in the order of your personal preference (1 = first choice, 6 = last choice):
    * Your own home
    * The home of a family member or friend (please specify)
    * A hospice or palliative care facility for the dying
    * The Intensive Care Unit of a hospital
    * A hospital
    * A nursing home

4. Which of the following statements resonate as true for you—even those that may seem to contradict each other.
    * There is a natural course of life and death that should be honored.
    * There is a point at which aggressive medical interventions to prolong life could interfere with the will of God.
    * I am concerned about the tradeoff between extending the duration of my life and its impact on the quality of my life.
    * I am more concerned about the quality of the end of my life than the duration of my life.
    * I am more concerned about the duration of my life than the quality of the end of my life.
    * I want absolutely everything medically possible done to extend my life regardless of the side effects of treatment or the probability of success.
    * Other. Please specify.

5. Preferences vary depending upon our specific circumstances. Consider these four end-of-life situations you might find yourself in.
    * In the event of a medical emergency if my doctors believe that a particular intervention is indicated or required on a temporary basis to save my life.

- If my doctors believe this intervention would have no impact on improving the quality of my life but would merely postpone my death.
- If I have permanent and severe brain damage and am not expected to recover.
- If I am in a coma and am not expected to wake up or recover.

For each of these possible situations, which of the following life-sustaining treatments would you like to receive under the stated circumstances. Note if and when your answers are contingent upon such factors as your age and/or specific conditions:

- Medical devices to help me breathe
- Artificial hydration and nutrition (tube feeding)
- Cardiopulmonary resuscitation (CPR)
- Major surgery
- Blood transfusions
- Antibiotics
- Dialysis
- Other. Please specify.

What is your current attitude toward the idea of having hospice care at the end of your life? If you are open to having hospice care, at what point do you imagine bringing them aboard? If you do not want hospice care, explain why not.

6. What activities are most important to you to engage in for as long as possible? For example, walking, reading books or being read to, visiting with loved ones, eating your favorite foods, etc.? Be as specific as possible.

7. What are your thoughts, concerns, and preferences regarding pain management at the end of your life?

8. Describe what would be most important to you about the environment in which you spend your dying time. Think in terms of all your senses—are there any particular kinds of music, fragrances, quality of light, views, privacy, photographs, or other things that would be meaningful to you?

9. Again, if it is determined that you are dying or likely to die within a period of six months or less, please specify which of the following would be important to you in terms of social interaction:
    - I want a peaceful, cheerful, and uplifting environment and do not want to be exposed to any discord among my friends, family, and caregivers.
    - I don't want a lot of visitors or phone calls.
    - I want lots of visitors and phone calls.
    - I want to be treated with kindness and compassion, not sadness and drama.
    - I want people to demonstrate to me how upset they are that I am dying.
    - I want my loved ones and caregivers to honor and respect my wishes even if they don't agree with them.
    - I want my spiritual or religious community notified and kept abreast of my condition and would like them to visit me if possible. (Specify contact information.)
    - I would like to have pictures of the following people and pets visible from my bed.
    - I would like (specify person) to provide my loved ones with updates on my condition on a website such as CaringBridge.com.
10. If it is determined that you are dying or likely to die within a period of six months or less, who would you like to be in communication with and/or have visit you? Who would you specifically not like to be in contact with or see?
11. Which of the following forms of media would you like access to:
    - Television
    - Computer
    - Cell phone
    - Music
    - Other (please specify)

12. What, if any, religious/spiritual readings, poetry, books, etc. would you like read aloud to you when you are near death? (Be specific.)

13. What, if any, religious, spiritual, ethnic, or family customs, traditions, or rituals would you like performed on your behalf during the end of your life? Indicate any specific guidance regarding how that can be done and by whom. If there are any customs, traditions, or rituals you specifically do not want, indicate that as well.

14. Do you want access to spiritual/religious counsel? If so, is there anyone in particular you would want to be available to you?

15. What are your thoughts regarding how your body is disposed of after death? Please indicate such things as whether or not you specifically want or do not want to be cremated, buried, or to make body or organ donations?

16. Please indicate anything else that comes to mind here.

Death and dying and our particular end-of-life preferences are difficult topics because we have been taught to be afraid of them. No one has taught us how to broach these subjects in an open-minded way. This is a social handicap that each of us needs to overcome if we want to have what some call "a good death"—one that is approached according to our own particular beliefs, values, and wishes. If we face death without ever having explored our beliefs and preferences, we abdicate responsibility and the power to have a thoughtful say in what happens to us. As Thomas Moore said:

> People say that human beings don't have the privilege of knowing what happens at and after death. But the truth is we don't really know anything fully. We gather

facts and draw our conclusions, but we know very little. In this situation, we need other responses besides knowledge. We need faith in life, hope that the whole thing makes sense, and love of the world rather than merely an understanding of it. Compared to our usual trust in research and knowledge, these are alternative ways to be, and they operate under the power of love. The whole secret to dying is to love life and trust it.

Ultimately, it is a profound act of love for ourselves and our family and friends to push through our resistance by exploring and documenting our end-of-life wishes.

key #3:
giving of your tender and vulnerable heart

*"*I'm asking that you go to the place that responds when you hold a child, the place that awakens when you help someone just for the pleasure of doing it. Connect with the sacred energy that comes alive when you express loving.*"*

—*John-Roger*

WHEN WE ARE AFRAID, WE contract. When we are afraid of death and dying, we avoid being around the dying, who need us more than ever. Love is the great unifier that makes us stronger as we face our living and dying together. Our interconnectivity gives us tremendous influence over the quality of each other's lives. Chapter 8 is about learning how to lead with our hearts rather than falling into dysfunction because our fears, judgments, and hurt feelings are getting in the way of our loving. It takes willingness to express our tender and vulnerable hearts, especially when we are used to racing around, consumed by the routines of daily life. Suddenly we find ourselves pulled out of what is normal for us to respond to what we most fear. It is our heart that opens the door to the treasures available at the bedside of the dying.

Making the effort to show up for each other, offering forgiveness, and expressing gratitude all lead to a greater intimacy. In this chapter, you will learn nine ways to demonstrate your love for a dying person as well as seven ways for the elderly and dying to let love in. The roles of hospice and primary caregiving are also explored, as is the importance of tending to the religious and spiritual needs of the dying.

and the greatest of these is love

---

*"*Loving is the most important quality you can nurture in yourself.*"*

—John-Roger

No matter what riches, fame, or other treasures we accumulate during our lives, none will ever be as precious to us as the love we have been blessed to experience, that sense of underlying oneness that transcends all other experiences. Those of us who are most fortunate figure this out sooner rather than later and give our love generously. Patrick Clary, a physician involved in hospice since 1988, says it this way: "Now I see: living is a kind of slow burning, and love is what we salvage from the fire."

We are all connected in the web of humanity, and no matter what our life circumstances, at life's end we all have the same needs—to be loved and cared for. In the US, the vast majority of us will eventually and inevitably face weeks, months, or even years of decline, accompanied by an increasing need for support from others. Some of us will experience a chronic progressive illness or simply the normal decline of the aging process. Others will face a terminal diagnosis that may offer carrots of hope through a labyrinth of possible treatment plans, each having its own attendant probabilities and side effects. People used to die of major organ failure or disease without the possibility of a cure or halting of decline. Today we might live reasonably well for many years with something that used to be a death sentence. As prolonged illnesses have become more prevalent, so has our need for caregiving, compassion, and understanding.

loved ones and other people

We hold places in one another's lives. We belong to each other no matter what the quality of our relationships. This belonging gives us a certain power over the quality of each other's lives, and we are wise to hold ourselves responsible and accountable for our impact and contributions. When all is said and done, what we all want is to have others bear witness to us and to love us. "Late Fragment" by American short-story writer and poet Raymond Carver captures this truth:

> And did you get what
> you wanted from this life, even so?
> I did.
> And what did you want?
> To call myself beloved, to feel myself
> beloved on the earth.

The way we color each other's lives is particularly important when we are around the dying. The quality of a gesture has the potential to define the character of an entire experience. A nurse who makes a point of making eye contact with a patient communicates a level of respect, comfort, and connection that is lacking from the one who breezes in and out of the room, treating the body but not the person in the body. It doesn't take more time to be kind. It does, however, take awareness, heart, and the willingness and choice to nourish the dignity of one another.

The more we overcome the influence of the Death Taboo within ourselves, the greater opportunity we have to be sensitive and caring to each other. Sadly, in our current medical model it is perhaps expeditious and a matter of emotional self-preservation for so many doctors and other hospital and nursing home personnel to interface with patients in a strictly clinical manner. Many say they simply have to function this way because they have too many patients and too little time to engage more personally without becoming overwhelmed and exhausted. We must remember that they too are under the spell of the Death Taboo.

A patient in an institutional environment needs the comfort and warmth of friends and family. Often referred to as "loved ones," some deserve this title while others do not. Even in the best of times, the loving that exists between us ebbs and flows, gets blocked and unblocked. There is no perfect loving. We are constantly faced with choices about how we will behave with each other. We are wise to choose to be loving every chance we get.

Highly dysfunctional or toxic families and friends can burden the dying person with enormous mental and emotional stress. Petty jealousies, power struggles, unresolved conflicts, and inheritance greed can all rear their ugly heads, creating anything but a peaceful environment for the dying.

Each individual may feel justified to behave as they do, but do they pay attention to the larger picture as well? We need to look at the impact of our behavior on the family dynamic and the emotional environment being created for the dying family member. Chances are if two or more family members have a contentious relationship, it is infecting the entire family as well. If you find yourself in a situation like this, consider being the one who takes the first step to clear the air. Name the elephant in the room and encourage others to join you in taking advantage of the opportunity to heal the situation. The option is always there to untether ourselves from past wounds and injustices.

Choosing to heal and free ourselves of these past dynamics

allows us all to lighten up and focus on what is important—giving the dying a loving sendoff. You might be quite surprised at how a few sincere words can crack through layers and years of bad feelings or an aloof manner to reveal an awaiting tenderness and invitation to love and care for one another again. At the very least, keep your own emotional pain from being an added burden on the dying. Take responsibility for checking your anger, blame, guilt, regrets, and grieving at the door before you enter. The following exercise gives you the opportunity to consider how you have dealt with death in the past and how you might now behave differently.

Exercise 16: 20/20 Hindsight

Think about any past experiences you have had with dying, death, and bereavement when you had difficulty being tender and vulnerable because your fears, judgments, and feelings got in the way of your loving.

For each specific situation or general sense of your way of dealing with death, describe the situation in writing from your point of view at the time, being sure to address why you behaved as you did.

For each situation, list at least three things you now see that you could have done differently if you were leading with your tender and vulnerable heart rather than your fears, judgments, and hurt feelings.

---

the willingness to open your heart

There are three enormous motivations for intentionally opening your heart and becoming more tender, loving, and kind in your everyday life, especially around the dying:

- It enriches the quality of your life.
- These behaviors are contagious and therefore serve the greater good by helping to create a more tender, loving, and kind world.
- Ten percent of us will die suddenly and there will be no time to tend to unfinished business or to say goodbye.

John-Roger often said: "The willingness to do creates the ability to do." When it comes to being truly tender, vulnerable, and authentic with each other, too many of us have learned to prefer a dentist's drill. Some, by virtue of the imprint of our particular upbringing, culture, or gender, are less capable of speaking from our heart to our loved ones. Others of us have armored our hearts in response to the ways in which we have been hurt, disappointed, or betrayed over the course of our lives. Many of us have evolved ways of being that feel safe, living on the surface of life, consumed by jobs, responsibilities, hobbies, and to-do lists of significant but not urgent priorities without paying mind to the price we pay for living this way. We replace intimacy with proximity and tokens of affection gifted on special occasions. As Marianne Williamson says: "We are not held back by the love we didn't receive in the past, but by the love we're not extending in the present."

I think of our ability to love as being similar to the aperture of a camera—an adjustable opening, the diameter of which limits or expands the amount of light that can pass through. Metaphorically, our hearts act in the same way in terms of our ability to be tender, vulnerable, and authentic with each other. We choose how open we will be, and that choice affects the quality of our relationships.

As someone who has spent much of her life yearning for more profound connections to others, I find our social norm of surface busyness to be very sad. It pains me that so many people choose to transport their awareness away from where they are and who they are with to connect through mobile devices to someone somewhere else who is texting to simply say, "I'm bored" or "What's up?"

When I think of the depth of caring my mother and I achieved in our relationship at the end of her life, I am hungry to create more meaningful connections with my loved ones and to inspire others to do the same thing. Why wait till someone is dying to open your tender and vulnerable heart to them? Do your loved ones really know who you are and how you feel about them and about your life? How open and honest are you with your loved ones?

This next exercise provides you with a personal laboratory for experimenting with and creating deeper connections in your life. Hopefully, you will not wait until you or someone you love is dying to let them know what is in your heart.

Exercise 17: Expressing Greater Tenderness and Vulnerability

Make a list of at least five to ten people you care about who are actively a part of your life now and/or have been in the past. For now, select one of these people and focus on your relationship with this person. Later, come back to the list until you have completed the process with everyone listed. Over time, you may find yourself adding names to the list and, hopefully, this exercise will become a new normal way for you to express your caring for people who touch your life in a meaningful way. For each person on your list, answer the following questions:

1.   How do I feel about this person and why? Hint: Be careful

of saying you care about a person because of the role they hold in your life, such as "because she is my wife." See if you can go deeper than that to what it is about this person that matters to you.

2. If there are hurt feelings, judgments, resentments, etc. that diminish(ed) your closeness, identify them as well as the consequences they have had in your relationship. If asking for or extending forgiveness might close the divide between you, consider doing Exercise 18 about this person.

3. Specifically, how do you demonstrate how your feel about this person?

4. Does this person know how and what you feel about them? How can you tell they know?

5. If your relationship might benefit from your becoming more expressive, tender, and/or vulnerable, what might you do differently to make that happen?

6. If you are willing to do so—go for it. If not, ask yourself what you are making more important than connecting more meaningfully with this person and see if you can move past that.

---

forgiveness and other kinds of unfinished emotional business

Many of us avoid communicating our beliefs, attitudes, and feelings. As a result, we are not very good at it. There is no time when we pay a higher price for this than when death is at hand and we don't speak our truth. Dr. Albert Mehrabian, author of *Silent Messages*, reminds us that our spoken words are only 7 percent of the message when communicating about our feelings and attitudes, while 38 percent comes from the way we speak, and the remaining 55 percent is carried in our facial expression. Instead of stopping yourself because you can't find the right words, consider letting your love and caring and forgiveness show through your eyes. Then you can find whatever words you need to add to your communication.

There are three primary forms of unfinished emotional business at life's end. They are what Ira Byock, palliative care physician and author of *The Four Things That Matter Most,* calls "mending, tending, and celebrating our relationships."

- Mending involves forgiveness and apologies.
- Tending is about being a good friend now by keeping the loving alive through kind acts and keeping in touch.
- Celebrating can be taking a stroll down memory lane together and sharing gratitude for how you have enriched each other's lives. Why wait to have a celebration of a loved one's life as a memorial service after they are gone? Make expressing your gratitude for the gift of having someone you hold dear in your life a normal part of living, not a special occasion.

Your gratitude can be expressed through words, kindness, and thoughtful actions every day. Communicate your heart's appreciation through a simple touch, or by making it a point to acknowledge the things you most appreciate about this other person. Why keep your gratitude a secret when it could otherwise make someone's day?

If we make it a habit to express our gratitude for each other, to speak up when something hurts us, and to give voice to our love for one another, then we reap the benefits of more open, honest, and loving relationships in which we truly feel supported by each other. Living without unfinished business allows us to die with no regrets, whether we go suddenly or after an extended illness.

For the 10 percent of us who die suddenly as the result of a car accident, fatal heart attack or stroke, gun violence, a terrorist attack, or some other unforeseen final curtain, there will be no time to tend to our unfinished business and say our goodbyes in a thoughtful way. We will simply be gone, and our loved ones will be left in shock. Many will suffer the regrets of things unsaid or left undone. This is why I advocate living with no regrets by embracing life's impermanence and the uncertainty of the timing and nature of our deaths. Married couples have long been advised to never go to bed angry; rather to kiss and make up, so to speak. We would all be well advised to heed this counsel in all the relationships in our lives. Don't let ill will fester. Be heart brave. Be an emotional ecologist—always keeping the air between you and others clean. Don't let anything be more important than loving one another. At the very least, hold this intention and challenge yourself to find your way to forgiveness and loving kindness no matter how others respond.

Whether you are the person who is dying or someone who cares about someone who is dying, it can be a great gift to each other to extend any overdue forgiveness or clean up other unfinished business between you. When you choose to forgive someone or to ask for their forgiveness, you are choosing to reopen your heart to the possibility of a shared healing.

True forgiveness is really a gift you give yourself rather than something you do for the other person. In essence, it is a choice to lessen your own burdens—to travel more lightly though this world. Sometimes, it simply builds character to own up to having been stupid or stubborn or just plain wrong. Far better to clear the air with humility and perhaps a bit of embarrassment than to let one of you die with unsettled emotions between you. Sometimes, knowing time is running out can make us braver than we have been to clear the air and to connect in far more profound ways than ever before. It's a funny thing, but somehow having shared a breakdown in your friendship actually provides the opportunity to choose healing and a deeper intimacy than was available before. Choosing to heal a relationship strengthens and deepens our bonds. When we never learn to bring forgiveness into the equation, hurt feelings can fester into wounds, or we build high emotional walls between ourselves and others.

There are two primary ways to effect forgiveness. One is within your own heart and the other is in communication with the other person involved. I strive to do both because I find that, when I clear the issue within myself first, I can actually be in a more loving or neutral state of consciousness when I approach the other person.

Remember, most of our communication is non-verbal—our demeanor speaks volumes. Inner forgiveness is a choice to put down the burdens we carry that prevent us from feeling and expressing our love for each other.

Exercise 18: Inner Forgiveness

Bring to mind a judgment you carry or hurt feelings that cause you to withhold your loving from someone. If more than one situation comes to mind, do this exercise for each one separately.

Call to mind what it feels like in your heart, mind, emotions, and body when you are at your best, experiencing loving kindness toward yourself and others. It may help to remember a specific experience you had in the past.

Now, call to mind this person and the hurt feelings or judgments that stand between you. Feel the distress in your body, mind, and emotions. See if you are willing to release these feelings. If so, can you get a sense of setting these burdens down, leaving just the two of you facing each other? See if you can find and go to the place inside of you where you experienced love for this person before the upset occurred between you.

From this place of loving, silently say the following statement repeatedly until you feel complete with it: "I forgive myself for judging myself for judging _____ as _____ for having _____." Example: I forgive myself for judging myself for judging my brother as letting me down by failing to really be there for me and Cake in her final months. Notice that you are forgiving yourself for judging this person—this is not an act of condoning the behavior that hurt you. It is an act of letting go of your anger, hurt feelings, and judgment in reaction to what occurred.

Next time you see this person, do your best to approach him or her with your open and loving heart. If you are unable to do so directly, perhaps you could find some kind gesture you could do behind the scenes, or simply affirm your intention to yourself to let go of this burden. With my brother, for example, a hardness and distance had grown between us. It took me over a year to clear my upset with him. When I did, I went to him and told him how I had been feeling so let down by him, and how I had been standing in judgment of him. I shared that I had finally been able to forgive him. He was grateful and relieved and then able to share his own profound disappointment with himself, and how he was still struggling for inner forgiveness. This honesty brought us to an even better place than prior to our mother's death. When I am in one of these situations, sometimes the best I can do while still moving through my own healing process is to silently and repeatedly recite, "I love you. God bless you. Peace. Be still."

Sometimes in-person forgiveness is also needed to clear the air, whether apologizing, asking for forgiveness, or extending it to another. Whether you are the dying person or a loved one, do your best to bring forward forgiveness where needed. Here are several conversation starters you might use:

- I'd like us to clear the air about _____.
- You mean a lot to me, and I'm hoping you would be willing to talk about _____ so we can put that behind us.
- I know our friendship hasn't been the same since _____.

I want to ask your forgiveness for _____ and to let you know that I forgive us both for not clearing the air sooner.

For whatever reason, the other person may not be willing to move past the discord. That is always their right. I had that experience with my sister when our mother was dying. I remember how, days before death, our mother told me that it was really important to her that my sister and I make one more effort to heal our broken relationship. Cake knew that I had repeatedly and unsuccessfully sought resolution with my sister over the years. In her dying, it was a piece of unfinished business for my mother to try one last time to get her daughters to make peace. She had always asked us to promise to look after one another after she was gone. Unfortunately, my sister was unresponsive to my plea or our mother's request, and to this day we remain estranged. I am comforted, however, by knowing I did my best to honor my mother's deathbed wish and that she was grateful for my effort. It also helped me to make peace within myself. While the estrangement continued, I knew I had done everything possible to reconcile with my sister. I did go to her in good faith, with an open heart and willingness to heal through mutual forgiveness. In so doing, I completed my side of the relationship. It takes two to tango, and I honor my sister's right to make different choices than I did. For me, it was a death of another kind that I had to mourn. No matter what the other person's response, it is always worth the effort to seek healing. Sometimes it leads to profound new levels of connection and revitalization. Seeking healing and wholeness are always options but are not always easy to achieve.

Please don't assume that your loved ones know you love them. Show them and tell them again and again. It's not so much about saying "I love you" as it is consistently demonstrating your love through your attitude and behavior. As death approaches, it behooves us to say and do what is needed before time runs out. Ira Byock says that in essence the dying want to say, "I love you," "Thank you," "Please forgive me," and "I forgive you." And to their

children and grandchildren, "I'm proud of you." These simple statements allow us to clear away hurt feelings and to connect in deeper
ways with our loved ones. How I wish we were all better able to use
these phrases in the normal course of our lives rather than holding
grudges, judgments, and hurt feelings toward one another. Before
it is too late, when death is coming, don't let yourself be at a loss for
words. Think of these phrases as the only gifts that really matter at
life's end.

what the dying need and what they care about

Since none of us have died yet, it is helpful to gain wisdom from
the dying about their needs and concerns. The importance of initiating more intimate conversations with the dying is heightened
when they feel frightened, confused, or unable to express what
they're feeling or what they need. Sue Brayne and Peter Fenwick
of the Neuroscience Division of the University of Southampton,
England, are authors of *Nearing the End of Life: A Guide for Relatives
and Friends of the Dying*. It offers insight into the kinds of things
that typically concern the dying. For example:

- Many people fear being in pain and need to be reassured
  by their medical staff that they will receive appropriate
  pain control. They need to discuss with their medical team
  how best to stay ahead of their pain.
- We all have "soul needs," such as feeling heard, cared-for,
  connected, and emotionally safe.
- They may be afraid to die and need to explore their fear
  with clergy, counselors, their family, and friends.
- Some want to know how much time they have left and
  what to expect in terms of the process of decline leading
  to their death.
- They may be concerned about being a burden to loved

ones. I needed to repeatedly reassure my mother that, while caregiving was often consuming and overwhelming for me, I wouldn't have wanted to be anywhere else than right there with her. I made sure to let her know I was honored and grateful to have the opportunity to serve her and give back to her in this way.

- The dying may have anger about being cheated out of more life, or they may feel let down by God.
- Some want to ensure the best quality of life for their remaining time and may have a "bucket list" they would like to fulfill.
- They may feel emotionally isolated and desperate for someone to ask them how they really feel and not just "How are you doing today?" in a tone that invites only a perfunctory response.
- Some are hanging on to hope for a miracle cure and are in denial of the real possibility or probability of dying.
- Some feel as though they have wasted their life or are grieving, having never gotten around to doing what really matters to them.
- Many are concerned about those who will be left behind and how they will cope.
- Some want to review their lives and consider the legacy they are leaving.

Those who are dying may also be preoccupied with the need to reconnect or reconcile with others, such as ex-partners or estranged family or friends, and to say goodbye. If you believe there is reconciliation needed in your relationship with the dying person, do them the favor of initiating that. Paying attention and gently probing to discover which of the above concerns are present for your loved one can provide guidance in how to support them in making peace with their lives and their journey to the end of their life.

This next exercise gives you the opportunity to take the time to articulate what you imagine will be most important to you when you are dying. This is a more free-form approach to gathering this information than in some previous exercises and might stimulate some ideas that were overlooked before. It would be wise to review and update your responses annually when reviewing your other end-of-life plans and documents.

Exercise 19: What I Imagine Will Be Important to Me When I Am Dying

This exercise gives you the opportunity to take the time to articulate what you imagine will be most important to you when you are dying. Make a list of at least twenty-five things you would appreciate others do to support you in your dying process. Here are a few examples:

1. I would like my ministerial community alerted to my condition, updated regularly, and asked to provide a Circle of Light for me when I am actively dying.
2. I would like to listen to inspirational music and talks by the following people: _____.
3. I want people to be honest with me.

Next, make a list of anything that you want to avoid or minimize. For example, "I don't want to die in a hospital or other institution."

Review these lists with your loved ones and encourage them to make their own lists and review them with you as well.

---

the nine most important ways to demonstrate your love for a dying person

1. Show up. Ira Byock, MD, has this to say about the challenges many of us face in showing up for our dying loved ones:

> People are often put off by the trappings of illness: the tubes, pill bottles, bedside commodes, bedpans, and the unpleasant odors and visible physical decline. In modern times, the tendency has been to avoid all that by turning care over to hospitals and the people in white who work within them. By trying to sanitize illness and dying we inadvertently separate and isolate the people we love—we isolate ourselves. Isolation is the opposite of loving connection.

We give ourselves all kinds of excuses—"I hate hospitals," "I don't want to see her/him like this," "I don't know what to say," or "I don't have time." Quite bluntly, when someone you love is dying, it's time to push yourself out the door and just show up! Open up your heart by putting their best interest above your own fears and discomforts, and you'll likely be surprised by all the ways you can draw benefit from moving past your resistance. Know that simply walking in the door communicates volumes about your caring for this person. Show up in your authenticity, sadness, love, gratitude, and caring.

2. Be yourself. Don't let your own fears of saying or doing the wrong thing stand in the way of communicating your love. Remember, you are still the same two people—keep the energy and nature of your friendship alive and true. Practice just being yourself in a new situation, fully present, moment by moment, trusting your ability to rise to the occasion. Sometimes it takes courage to practice what Byock calls "love as a deliberate strategy for dealing with the pain of unacceptable loss."

Next time someone you love has a chronic, progressive illness or receives a terminal diagnosis, be there for and with them. Lend them your ear by listening, make your shoulder available to cry on, offer a gentle touch, words of support, and most of all your willingness to be there, no matter the inconvenience. Remember if you have been a comfort and a good friend to someone in their living, they are likely to be grateful and comforted by your being there for them in their dying.

Bear in mind that how you behave around the dying will either be a comfort or a constriction. When we are brave and truthful with the frail or dying, we give them permission to do so with us as well. Sometimes it takes a health tragedy or the knowledge that time is running out for you or one you love dearly to stop wasting precious moments on surface banalities. Don't hide your truth with a brave smile under the delusion that you are protecting your loved one from a truth you deem too dark to share. Thrust out your heart and connect in the truth as you know it. Be yourself. Remove your social masks and let your heart shine through so you can be a warmth and comfort.

3. Follow the dying person's lead. Always take your lead from the energy level, apparent needs, preferences, and interests of the dying person, and just roll up your sleeves to help make the best of the situation. When in doubt about what to do, ask them such simple questions as: "Is there anything in particular that you would like to talk about?" "Is there anything I can do for you?" Support the dying person in dying their own way. If they don't know what that is, help them to figure it out. Share your point of view if they are open to it, but never shove your opinion down their throat. Being right is of little value if it forces someone you claim to love to go against their own will in an effort to please you. Just remember that it is more important that they die according to their beliefs and values rather than yours.

If a choice must be made whether to proceed with a high risk "last hope" medical treatment or to forego the treatment, surrender your preference to that of the patient. Remember that each one of us has the right to self-determination as long as we are deemed to be mentally competent. Sometimes letting go is the most loving thing we can do. No amount of last hope treatments is going to ultimately change the fact that death and dying will come. It is wise to consider the quality as well as the duration of the dying process.

No matter how much we love someone, we may find their beliefs, preferences, and ways of going about things to be sometimes maddeningly different than our own. Generational, cultural, and educational differences can be significant. Regardless of how smart we think we are or how much better we think our way is than that of the dying person, we must never forget to honor their autonomy and ultimate right to live and die according to what is true for them. Always follow their lead and support them in their journey. Atul Gawande cautions, "The battle of being mortal is the battle to maintain the integrity of one's life—to avoid becoming so diminished or dissipated or subjugated that who you are becomes disconnected from who you were or who you want to be."

The needs of someone who is dying change and evolve as they progress through their dying process. As long-time hospice nurse Judith Redwing Keyssar explains in *Last Acts of Kindness*:

> Toward the end of life, a drawing inward is common. Surroundings and things matter less and less. Attachments to the material plane loosen. Even attachments to people can change. As one goes inside, the outer world gets smaller and less important. The external environment loses meaning as the internal process of dying takes over.

Pay attention to the signs and clues of the dying person. When it is time, support them in their pull inward. Become quieter along with them.

4. Don't burden the dying person with your own distress.
While it is important to be real and natural around the dying, it is even more important not to burden them with your own fear, denial, anger, judgment, unwanted opinions, dysfunctional family/community dynamics, or your resistance to the situation at hand. Never bring these into the environment of the dying. Consider it sacred space where only loving kindness, peace, and tender caring are welcome. Check your emotional baggage at the door, and work on clearing up your own emotional environment on your own time—preferably before showing up. While we may feel helpless and powerless to change the course of the dying process, we are powerful cocreators of its quality. Channel your efforts there.

5. Be of loving service. In a recent interview with Oprah Winfrey, Elizabeth Lesser, co-founder of Omega Institute, said it best: "Look for a way to lift someone up." It is wise to learn to make this your way of being throughout your life, not just around the dying. Chapter 12 will discuss in detail numerous specific ways to nurture, support, and serve the dying. As a general rule of thumb, keep your eyes and ears open for opportunities and remember that helping the primary caregiver or doing something thoughtful for the nurses also helps the patient. Boxes of really good quality chocolates for the nurses were some of the best investments I made in the quality of Cake's care.

There are many ways to express our loving—a simple touch, doing the laundry, or cooking a meal for the primary family caregiver. The key to opening our hearts to the situation is to expand beyond our personal concerns and ask ourselves: "What is the most loving thing I can do for this person and their family?"

6. Accept that the person is actually dying. Accepting that death is coming is not the same thing as giving up on the dying person's life. Giving up is acting as though death has already occurred. Acceptance is an active process of facing the present reality and participating in it rather than holding on to false and unfounded hopes. It enables us to support the dying person in what they are actually going through rather than looking for false evidence and engaging in magical thinking to avoid the truth.

7. Grieve along the way. Grief is the territory of both the dying and their loved ones, which will be discussed in greater detail in Chapter 11. The dying person is losing a future—time to do, be, and have what has yet to manifest in their life. Time itself is running out, and the person dying must grieve the loss of more opportunities and experiences. For those whose dying is extended over months and years, there is a loss of one capability after another. For Cake, it was her hearing, her ability to walk without pain, her eyesight, and on and on. It's important to be brave, but it is normal and wise to acknowledge and grieve these losses as they occur as well. Death does not come upon most of us in just an instant but over time. For the dying, grieving is about accepting and making peace with each loss rather than fighting against them or pretending nothing has changed.

The loved ones of the dying bear witness to a process of deterioration, simultaneously aware that this will someday be their fate as well and feeling the heartache of losing this treasured person in their life. It is important that we entertain these thoughts and feelings and, with a bittersweet heart, make the most of the time we have left together. Fighting against the dying process and denial of the signs of decline are part of the grieving process. However, it is important to move beyond denial in order to make ourselves available to treasure the precious time that remains. Denying death postpones grieving and allows one's grief to become a mountain of sorrow rather than a flowing river of shed tears.

8. Be open to the mystery and awe of death. As Judith Redwing Keyssar describes:

Dying is intense labor. Imagine how hard a woman must push to separate her baby from her womb. In dying, we do the opposite—we must push hard to separate the spirit from the body. Just as in birth, many believe that in death the spirit is sent out through a long, dark tunnel or passageway of some kind into a bright and brilliant light. Those remaining at the bedside are awestruck.

I remember my hand being on my stepfather's chest as he took his last breath. It was suddenly motionless and peaceful. No more breaths. No more struggles for him. We live on such a precarious razor's edge—one breath away from death at all times. We watch our loved ones do this thing called dying that we have been programmed to fear so much. We think that they are brave in their dying, and then they are peaceful in death. What are we so afraid of?

9. Let go and say goodbye. The love that binds us does not die at death. The individual is simply no longer available to hug or to answer our phone call. By grieving as we go along during the process of letting go of the dying, we communicate to them without words that we are dealing with the reality of the situation. Numerous stories are told about the dying lingering for the benefit of others. When we emotionally let them go, they get it and are free to go in their own timing. Yes, we will miss them, but clinging doesn't help them. It is important to consciously make the choice to accept your loved one's death and release them. This is an intentional act of love, so that we do not hold them back from letting go of this life. Say goodbye.

For some of us, saying goodbye is the hardest thing of all to do. I'm one of those people who has anxiety saying goodbye to my cats when I leave for just a few days! Knowing this about myself alerted me to how difficult it would likely be for me to say goodbye to my mother and other loved ones who have died. I have since then always made it a point to say goodbye to a dying loved one making eye contact if possible and speaking from my heart. The words never seem to matter as much as my heartfelt intention to bless them and wish them well on their journey to the other side of life and death. I also let them know that I will always carry fond memories of them in my heart. I'm careful to specify that it is the memories and not the person that I will carry forward in my heart so that my love does not hold them back in any way. I remember becoming aware of the importance of this with my mother. I knew she was worried about me being able to carry on without her. I made it a point to tell her that I would miss her, but I also knew that I would be okay and didn't want her to worry about me. I wanted her to trust that I would take good care of myself. During those last nine days of her being unconscious, I also found myself whispering in her ear, "You are free to go now, Cake. Happy trails to you until we meet again."

When someone has Alzheimer's disease or other forms of dementia, loved ones often face two goodbyes—first the mind and personality and later the body. I remember my friend Max's mother's eightieth birthday. She was so sad as she looked into my eyes and told me that not one of her four sons had remembered her birthday. Her sons were all standing around her at the time, and in her lap was a picture of them she had just unwrapped. These families are called upon to practice and express enormous patience and kindness while grieving the loss of their loved one who still walks among them.

Just as hearing is the first of our senses to arrive in utero, it is the last to go before we die. Therefore, it is always best to assume that your loved one can hear and understand everything you say, whether suffering from dementia or seemingly sleeping or in a coma. There have been many reports to confirm this. Be extremely careful not to discuss the individual who is dying in the third person as if he or she is not there or to have heated discussions in their presence. Maintain a sense of peace and sacredness around the dying. Also remember to speak kind words with tenderness and authenticity and to let your heart override any mental or emotional negativity you are experiencing when in their presence.

I treasure the memory of the last words spoken between my mother and me. Just before she closed her eyes and became unresponsive for her final nine days, she looked deeply into my eyes and said, "I love you," and my heart leapt out to her with the same three words and that was it. I am so grateful to have had that magnificent moment of completion with her.

the seven most important ways for the elderly and the dying to let love in

1. If you haven't already done so, put your affairs in order. It is negligent and unkind to put your loved ones in the position of having to second-guess your wishes because you haven't bothered to legally document them or effectively communicate them. Taking care of your personal business is an act of supreme love for your loved ones. Specifically, everyone over age eighteen needs to identify their preferences regarding such practical matters as advance healthcare directives, body disposition protocols, and a will or estate plan. Making appropriate funeral or memorial service arrangements is also a great help. If you do not have these plans in order, ask someone you trust to help you get it done carefully but expeditiously. Chapter 14 reviews these topics in detail.

There are endless tragic stories about what happens to people in terms of their healthcare at life's end and the disposition of their body and belongings as a result of not putting their affairs in order in advance of need. Don't let your story be added to this sad litany of negligence.

2. Be honest about your needs. Often, we are really trying to protect ourselves, not the other person, for fear of falling apart emotionally or to avoid having to bear witness to their reaction. The withholding of difficult information under the guise of protecting one another is a form of dishonesty and mutual deception. We need each other more than ever at these times. Keeping secrets and withholding truth isolate us from one another. As Maggie Callanan says in *Final Journeys:* "Silence severs the possibility for human connection, the essential support we all need during this difficult time."

This was an issue between me and my mom in lots of ways. Sometimes she withheld things because she was mad at me or embarrassed, didn't want to bother or concern me, or didn't want to face whatever truth was becoming apparent to her. Each time there were consequences, sometimes life threatening, that taught us the importance of being more honest and vulnerable with each other. For example, about four months before she died, Cake attempted to move herself from her bed to the commode instead of calling me for assistance. She fell and scraped her shin to the bone, which remained a weeping wound requiring constant care until her death. Let your loved ones and caregivers in.

Know that what you don't tell them may well be suspected, and their imaginations may create fears far worse than the reality you are trying to hide. Let them feel useful—tell them what you need and allow them to serve you. Practice receiving. Keep them posted on what is really going on for you so they can adjust, adapt, and respond to your changing needs.

3. Keep your sense of humor if you can. The dying process, in all its seriousness and sadness, can deliver some truly light-hearted moments. Here's a bit of levity for you. Despite my mother's natural elegance, she was subject, as are the rest of us, to the gaseous occurrences of the human body. I remember her telling me that when her mother reached a certain point in her aging, she could no longer control her farts and they would come in rapid succession. Whenever the mood was just right, my mom would imitate how her mother used to counter-productively call attention to her streams of uncontrollable farts that she was trying to hide. First would be a startled, helpless, and horrified look on her face, and then she would begin to exclaim, "Oh! Oh! Oh! Oh, I'm so sorry! Oh! Oh, I'm so sorry! Oh! Oh!" punctuating each emission as she backed herself out of the room with her hands on her behind. After each of my mother's performances, she and I would convulse in laughter. It didn't take much to amuse us.

When Cake's turn came to face this same humiliation, she did it with great pride. Periodically, she would go through bouts of tremendous, gastric distress. In those final months, she spent a lot of time rubbing her stomach and taking antacids, and finally relief would come in a stream of belches that were totally inconceivable to be emanating from her small body. They would be worthy of a large truck driver's pride. They went on and on and on as though coming from the soles of her feet and working their way up through all the pipes, picking up sound effects as they passed her vocal cords. They were mighty belches indeed and a cause for great relief, celebration, and hilarity. I used to howl with tears running down my face as Cake smiled with pride when she was done. The reality that someone is dying doesn't mean everyone has to be sad and serious all the time. There is always plenty of room for humor. Sometimes a good laugh lightens and refreshes the atmosphere like a breath of fresh air.

4. Be willing to receive help. A duet that is not always very graceful typically ensues between the aging or dying person and his or her loved ones and caregivers. Giving up little pieces of one's autonomy, dignity, and sense of control can be an untenable price for the dying to pay to meet the safety concerns of others and an increasing dependency upon them. The path of greatest wisdom for the one who is dying is to recognize this predicament and to practice graciously accepting and appreciating the help of others. This allows the quality of the relationship to be nurtured as our relative roles shift and change through time. If financially affordable, hiring trained professionals to assist with the hands-on care can relieve the family caregiver to focus on being a loving family member or friend while protecting the privacy and dignity of the patient.

People have all kinds of reasons for resisting help. Some stubbornly fight for their independence, while others are concerned about being a bother to family and friends. But how will others feel if they find out you needed them and didn't ask? Will they feel guilty if you die alone and in pain? Not asking for help when you need it inevitably causes more, not less, suffering for your loved ones. The most loving thing we can do under the circumstances is to be open to the help we need.

Sometimes we simply must humble ourselves to what reality brings our way and cooperate with the situation rather than fight against it. Perhaps you can also remind yourself of a time when you were enriched by helping someone and see your need now as an opportunity to extend that experience to others. We all need each other, and we need opportunities that allow us to rise to the occasion of demonstrating our love. Open the door and let those around you in. Let the circle of love go around and around. As Mother Teresa said, "There is more hunger for love and appreciation in this world than for bread."

I remember how my mother and I struggled with each other every time we made the precarious journey of twenty-seven steps from her bed to the toilet during her last weeks of mobility. At the time, she was on oxygen and using a walker. I would ask her to give me a moment to gather the thirty feet of oxygen tubing so they wouldn't get under her feet, but she would ignore me and forge ahead pushing the walker in front of her and walking forward to meet it. No matter how many times I begged her to walk within the walker as trained rather than pushing it ahead, which increased the likelihood of her falling, she stubbornly did it her way. I always felt like she was giving me the finger when she did that.

5. Be specific about what help you need. Guide your loved ones by being as specific as possible about what kinds of help you need.

Otherwise, they will try to help according to their ideas of what you need, which may or may not bear any resemblance to your reality. Be ready with some specific ideas when someone asks, "What can I do to help?" Be ready to give those willing to help the opportunity to be of service to you.

6. Express gratitude for the help you receive. Just because you are dying doesn't mean you get to forget your manners. Saying "thank you" motivates others to do more. Give them an "A" for effort, even if they don't do it exactly as you would have done for yourself. You can always give them gentle, remedial guidance and hope they hit the target better next time.

7. Say goodbye. Remember that saying goodbye is a two-way street. Your loved ones need to know that you know you are dying and that you are ready to go. Let them know that you are okay. Do your best to complete unfinished emotional and practical business before you go. If time permits, speak individually to your loved ones, expressing your appreciation for them in your life. Let them know how they have enriched you, wish them well, and say goodbye.

the hospice decision

One of the unfortunate side effects of living in a culture that resists death is our difficulty and reluctance to appreciate the significance of hospice care for people with terminal illnesses and those for whom dying is inevitable and irreversible. As long-time hospice nurse Maggie Callanan describes it: "The first focus of hospice care is making sure the patient is as pain-free and as functional as possible, because if people are hampered by physical suffering, they are not mentally, emotionally, or spiritually free to deal with anything but their suffering." Surely, we want that for our dying loved one, yet we resist letting go of what we perceive as hope. Too many of us equate choosing hospice with giving up hope. Our hopefulness is too often a form of denial that ultimately subjects many patients to yet one more painful medical procedure that delivers little benefit. The comfort of hospice is only available to those who open the door. Unfortunately, most wait until the last minute—foregoing possibly months or weeks of mental, emotional, spiritual, and physical support customized for the dying, their family, and caregivers. Choosing hospice is not giving up—it is a loving choice of opening to receive the sensitive care of a team of people dedicated to optimizing the quality of your remaining life.

being a compassionate caregiver

Usually the role of being the primary caregiver falls on the spouse or an adult daughter. Others typically come and go as they please, as their schedule permits. In reality, the primary caregiver ends up sacrificing more and more of their previous life activities while becoming a constant companion, chauffer, nurse, hands-on caregiver, and time manager for medications, appointments, visitors, and helpers. The primary caregiver is the one who updates everyone else and the one who escorts and suffers along with the dying loved one every step of the way through the trials and triumphs to come. It can be an absolutely awful job on some levels, but in my experience, the blessings far outweighed the hard parts.

The final six months of my mother's life presented one crisis after another. I sought desperately to be in control of the situation—to anticipate her needs, to rally her doctors and caregivers to exceed their capabilities on my mother's behalf. I drove myself to drink and overeat until one day one of my mother's doctors, seeing how stressed I was, commanded me to take a break and leave her room and go outside to take a walk. I obeyed and found myself sobbing as I walked along. I was finally beginning to feel my helplessness in the face of the forces of nature that were leading my mother to the end of her life. I began to soften as I realized that my job was not to prevent my mother's suffering and decline, but to hold her hand as she went through it. I learned to let go of my efforts to fix the situation and to simply bring my heart to her bedside, so I could be a comfort to her.

I discovered in myself a capacity to walk into the Valley of the Shadow of Death, fueled by profound love for my mother and the shared knowledge that we were journeying side by side through the end of her life. Neither of us ran away from the challenges nor were we unrealistic about her prognosis. We learned to do our best in foreign and scary territory and let life be messy. We discovered it was also a magnificent time in unexpected ways. I didn't realize how many treasures were to be found in that dark and chaotic time. My love for Cake awakened a kind of courage in me I had never experienced before, and we burst through previous boundaries of our defined roles and relationship. I never loved or treasured anyone so deeply and tenderly in my life. It was a magnificent surprise to find how rich our relationship became during those last few months. The primary caregiver colors the experience of the dying like a cocreator, and journeys alongside the dying till the final fork in the road when they must part ways and the caregiver returns to his or her life a profoundly changed person. I have great compassion for any caregiver who is also trying to maintain some semblance of a normal work or home life while caregiving someone who is dying. For me, it was a full-time job, and I had to set the rest of my life aside for the final six months.

Perhaps the hardest task of all for the primary caregiver is to avoid making themselves such a low priority that their own basic needs go unmet. In other words, the caregiver must not withhold their self-nurturance in an effort to rise to the occasion of the bottomless pit of needs of the dying person. Just as a mother traveling on a crashing plane is instructed to put her oxygen and life vest on before those of her child, as a caregiver you must always take care of yourself first, so you can care for the dying without doing so at your own expense. Easier said than done! The immediacy and urgency of the needs of the dying can make your own needs appear less important. They are not. Your own need to receive tender loving care will increase, not decrease. When you don't take care of yourself, not only do you run yourself ragged, but you are likely to become irritable and less effective in your caring. It's important to take breaks and to hold other loved ones accountable for helping you, as well as helping the dying loved one. Don't deprive others of taking a turn because they are under the false impression that you don't need or want their help.

If you are someone else in the circle of family and friends, please honor the primary caregiver's role as the one who knows the most about what is going on even if, and especially if, they are frazzled. If you think they are making terrible mistakes, discuss your concerns with them in private and work together to make changes, not behind their back. Give your input but honor their right to the final say in the matter. Offer help, not criticism. Don't assume they have everything under control and don't need any support. They are probably doing everything because no one else is offering to help. Ask them what you can do that would support them best. Ask if there is a particular task that they could delegate to you, such as grocery shopping or making phone calls to keep others in the loop.

religious and spiritual matters

Typically, a dying person's spiritual or religious beliefs take on an intensified importance. I was so grateful to my mother's hospice team and caregivers for making sure that important religious rituals were performed for her, as well as giving her spiritual counsel and comfort.

Over the last six months of Cake's life, her favorite priest came regularly to serve her communion and on five separate occasions to administer the Catholic Sacrament of Anointing of the Sick, formerly known as Last Rites or Extreme Unction. He was so tender, sincere, and responsive in ministering to her that it was always apparent to me he naturally carried the presence of God with him wherever he went. I, too, felt privileged and blessed by his visits. I also was called upon to serve as his Greek chorus, doing the prayer responses each time he administered the Anointing of the Sick, finally reaching the point where I knew what I was doing. I was deeply moved by his piety and by my mother's visible transformation into a deeper peace as she surrendered her will and soul to God.

We lived in a circle of prayer that last six months, surrounded by the prayers of family and friends from near and far. In addition to my mother's support from the Catholic Church, my spiritual community also prayed for her through a worldwide network of ministers. We have a unique and dispassionate, yet fervent, way of praying whereby we send light for the highest good of all concerned or the highest good of the soul's progression. We use the term "light" as a mnemonic for Living In God's Holy Thoughts. Rather than focusing only on the physical, mental, and emotional levels of the individual in crisis and the often selfish and myopic personal preferences of loved ones, we pray from a consciousness of neutrality regarding results, surrendering to God's perfect wisdom and timing. We often do not know the people we are praying for, and in many ways this makes it easier to maintain our impartiality. According to several recent research studies, this form of prayer has been proven more effective than the kind of prayers that request a specific preference or outcome.

Sometimes my mother received cards from around the world from individual ministers and regional ministerial boards of my spiritual community, just letting her know she was in their prayers. Our favorite card, said, "Good morning, Grace, this is God. I will be handling all your problems today for your Highest Good. I will not need your help so have a great day." It was signed, "Just a little reminder from one of your Guardian Angels."

We were especially blessed to have Yvette join our caregiving team at the end, and I knew we had found another super-competent and loving angel. The second day Yvette worked with Cake at home, she asked her if she would like to watch the Catholic mass at noon on TV. I was surprised at Cake's eagerness, as she had never watched the new huge flat screen TV we had purchased and installed in her bedroom. Her macular degeneration had advanced to the point that she simply could not make out the images on the screen. However, this day she definitely saw something! She sat for eight hours trans-fixed with her earphones on and mouth agape! Routine interruptions like being served meals and going to the bathroom were not appreciated.

At 7:00 p.m., the Pope was performing the Mass of the Angels in Turkey, and Cake was totally there with him. When he raised the chalice during communion, I steadied her shaky hand as she took hold of her milk glass and raised it to her mouth. When he lifted the host, her eyes closed reverently as she opened her mouth to receive communion. Then she sadly opened her eyes, looked at me forlorn, and said, "I didn't get any." Without thinking, I took a piece of ginger cookie from her tray, placed it on her tongue, looked into her eyes and said, "The body of Christ." She closed her eyes to receive this makeshift host and then opened them abruptly, disturbed, declaring, "This is a ginger cookie!" When I explained that I had to improvise, she accepted that, knowing that I am a minister of God, and she was once again at peace, having received what turned out to be her last communion.

After mass, she wanted to know if the Pope had made the announcement yet that he had changed her name to "Joy." She looked at us and said, "If this is dying, it's great!" That day, her eyes became a little glassy, her words a little slurred, and she said she'd seen her mother out of the corner of her eye.

I believe the power of prayer that surrounded my mother and her heightened spiritual experiences enabled her to live much longer than she would have otherwise. They gave her the fortitude to stick around so she could complete her inner work. She did a lot of surrendering, forgiveness, cooperation, and balancing out of unfinished business during her final months. When she died, I believe she had finished her soul's work and was at peace, and I had been privileged to experience a whole new level of loving and being loved.

Time is particularly precious when someone is dying. The dying, loved ones, and caregivers may want to remind themselves to savor it by being more mindful of the simple power of kindness and gentleness. Time can be seemingly endless when the dying process is long, yet in hindsight it may seem to have passed too quickly. As Teilhard de Chardin said:

> Love alone is capable of uniting living beings in such a way as to complete and fulfill them, for it alone takes them and joins them by what is deepest in themselves.

chapter 9

key #4:
honoring your truth

*"*Each death I have felt as an abruption, a tearing away of part of myself. . . . When people die, they cannot be replaced. They leave holes that cannot be filled, for it is the fate—the genetic and neural fate—of every human being to be a unique individual, to find his own path, to live his own life, to die his own death. *"*

—*Oliver Sacks*

H ONORING OUR OWN TRUTH SOMETIMES takes great courage, especially in an environment of opposing and passionate points of view and when the stakes are a matter of life or death. In order to honor our truth, we must first know what it is, as explored in Chapter 7. Once we clarify our personal preferences, it is essential to communicate them clearly to family and loved ones, medical personnel, and caregivers and to enlist their support. This is easier said than done for those of us who have difficulty asking for help and are concerned about being a burden or being rejected or criticized for having a different belief. Far better to take this step well in advance of need than in the midst of a health crisis, but in either case, each of us is called upon to honor what resonates as true deep inside ourselves.

self-advocacy

The essence of what it means to honor your truth was captured by Hillel the Elder, the Leader of the Jewish Supreme Court in the Land of Israel in the early part of the First Century CE, who said: "If I am not for myself, who will be for me? If I am only for myself, what am I? And if not now, when?"

Self-advocacy is about holding yourself accountable and responsible for your life and how you are living it. When we are healthy and vibrant, self-advocacy is largely an internal affair whereby we navigate our way through our life experiences and interactions with others. When we are frail or dying, our willingness and ability to effectively communicate our wants and needs becomes critically important and perhaps even more challenging as we find ourselves increasingly dependent upon others.

For some of us, self-advocacy requires that we ask others to support us in honoring our truth when we know it conflicts with their beliefs or preferences. For example, if you are at the end of a terminal illness, you might want a Do Not Resuscitate Order (DNR) posted above your bed at home because you have made peace with your dying. However, if your loved ones or caregivers are with you and you enter into life-threatening distress, it might be unbearable for them to resist calling for help. Remember, it is your life and your death. Explain to your loved ones well in advance of any emergency why you are making the choice you are making and how important it is to you. This will help those around you to understand that calling 911 would be against your wishes, and you would prefer they simply hold your hand and comfort you through the situation. The alternative is to allow them to possibly subject you to additional pain and suffering that could have been avoided if your wishes were honored. Speak up for yourself! You matter, and you are the only expert on the planet who really knows what is right for you.

It is important to support yourself by legally appointing someone willing and able to speak on your behalf in the event that you are not able to speak for yourself. This person is called your Healthcare Proxy. When your loved ones or caregivers have significantly different beliefs than you do, it is especially important for you to appoint and empower a Healthcare Proxy who understands and agrees to honor your wishes. That person may not be an obvious choice, such as your spouse or grown child. Perhaps it is a friend that your family doesn't know very well but who is someone you know in your gut is capable of honoring your wishes and standing up for you when you cannot do so for yourself. Make sure to let your Healthcare Proxy know that you are counting on them to speak up for you to other family members and your doctors. This is especially important because, according to the findings of a 2007 research study in the *Critical Care Journal*, even when patients have documented their end-of-life healthcare wishes, physicians are often unaware of their patients' preferences. This large-scale study found that only 25 percent of doctors knew that their patients had advance directives on file. Make sure your doctor knows your wishes and let your Healthcare Proxy know this as well, so they can educate your doctor if need be. It is also a good idea to let close family members know whom you have chosen to be your Healthcare Proxy and that you want them to respect that person's authority.

Watch out for bullies. Just because someone raises their voice and is more passionately expressive about his or her point of view doesn't mean it should be imposed upon you. Always hold your own counsel and practice standing up for yourself. Remember that sacrificing your own truth in order to keep the peace with others is ultimately an act of self-abandonment.

Who but you can truly stand up for you and your truth? You are the only you who will ever exist. Do us all a favor and let us know who is living inside of you and what matters to you.

Exercise 20: Will the Real Me Please Stand Up?

Bring to mind someone you know who has a different point of view on death and/or someone with whom you imagine it would be very difficult for you to get them to honor your truth. Think specifically about what you see differently and why.

Imagine the worst-case conversation of you trying to share your point of view with them. Describe the encounter. What do you imagine would happen? How would this person react? How would you respond and why? How might you feel?

Next, step away from that scene and remind yourself of what your deepest truth is regarding your own death and that you have a right to your own point of view and to asking others to honor it.

Now, imagine encountering this person again while standing confidently in your truth regardless of his or her response. Describe this situation. What did you do differently inside yourself and in relationship to this other person? What did you notice was different about how they responded? How did you feel?

human frailty

Have you ever been laid low with an illness or post-surgery recovery period? If so, remember what it was like to feel weak, to be dependent upon others, and to lose your autonomy. Or maybe you were called upon to be a caregiver for someone else going through a period of frailty. Most of us take our health for granted and are ill-prepared and disquieted by being in a weakened state. We seek to restore health and well-being as quickly as possible. But for those who are dying, a restoration of one's previous state of health is not an option. We may have good days and bad days, but the overall trajectory is downhill. This unfamiliar territory calls upon the dying and their loved ones to take the time needed to come to terms with the increasing frailty of the dying person as well as his or her need for increasing support from others. This can be enormously stressful to deal with in the context of our busy lives. It's easy to become frustrated, resentful, and irritable, which only serves to exacerbate the problem.

A few years ago, I went through about a six-week-long mysterious illness that rendered me physically and emotionally fragile. For the most part, I slept long hours or sat in a chair under a blanket, too weakened to even read. I simply honored my limitations. However, it was extremely hard for me to ask for help and to deal with all the considerations that some people had about helping. My friends knew I was sick but seldom offered any help. I noticed how one person in particular offered help, but it always came as a mixed message. She didn't simply agree to help but rather presented me with all the reasons that she was really too busy to feel comfortable doing so—but of course would fit me into her busy schedule. My heart hurt from that, and I just didn't want to deal with feeling like a burden. In contrast, another friend with a very complicated life didn't skip a beat in coming to just sit with me and bring me food. Why is it so hard for so many of us to rise to the occasion of another's need without making them feel like a burden? None of us want to feel that way. Part of helping each other is being sensitive to the emotional dimension of the exchange. When my reluctant friend and I spoke after the fact, it was apparent that she wasn't even aware of communicating what an inconvenience it would be for her; she was simply trying to figure out her schedule out loud. Unfortunately, it was obvious that her goal was to minimize her own inconvenience, without any awareness of how that made me feel. In helping others, it is so important to be sensitive to the fact that the person may not be comfortable asking for help. How you help is often more important than the help itself. Remember to wrap the action up in a smile and kindness.

Knowing that we all matter and that our needs and preferences matter as well can be challenging when we are frail. It is important to remember that each of us is a unique being connected in the web of life to others—genetically, circumstantially—by bonds of love, disdain, dismissal, prejudice, or a myriad of other ways that we relate to one another. We all share in common that we were born, we are living, and one day each of us will die. Some of us seem to matter more based on our level of popularity than those who live fairly isolated and disconnected lives. But on a deeper level that is not so. Each one of us deserves to be treated with dignity and respect by ourselves and by others.

While I am encouraged by the ways in which our culture of death is evolving, I also recognize that many of us need help in learning how to be of loving service to one another with sensitivity and compassion. Our high-tech world has left us deficient in the high-touch skills of acting upon our declarations of loving and caring for one another. Our actions speak loudest to the heart of the recipient.

different approaches to death and dying

There is no such thing as a one-size-fits-all approach to death and dying. Again, this makes clarifying and communicating what is and is not meaningful to us in our lives and in relation to end-of-life issues so very important. Don't assume you know what another wants or that they want what you want. Always ask.

Dying is an intensely personal experience. Each one of us will die in our own way, influenced by our beliefs, experiences, circumstances, relationships, cultural and religious heritage, and personal history. All of these dimensions of our lives significantly color our point of view about end-of-life issues and how we will die. It is becoming increasingly important for medical and caregiving personnel to be sensitive to cultural and ethnic differences. H. Russell Searight, PhD, MPH, and Jennifer Gafford, PhD, researchers on cultural diversity, report:

> Ethnic minorities currently compose approximately one third of the population of the United States. The US model of health care, which values autonomy in medical decision making, is not easily applied to members of some racial or ethnic groups. Cultural factors strongly influence patients' reactions to serious illness and decisions about end-of-life care. Research has identified three basic dimensions in end-of-life treatment that vary culturally: communication of "bad news"; locus of decision making; and attitudes toward advance directives and end-of-life care.

When it comes to end-of-life decisions, loved ones, medical personnel, and caregivers are all called upon to educate themselves about the true wishes and preferences of the dying and to honor their point of view. No matter how strong your personal convictions are, you have no right to attempt to impose them on another. It's fine to ask the dying for permission to share your thoughts but not to do so with the intention of convincing them to change their point of view.

It is the responsibility of each and every one of us to clarify and communicate our end-of-life wishes. However, some of us become so concerned about what others will think that we forget to honor our responsibility to and for ourselves. I remember when my mother was finalizing her plans regarding burial versus cremation. Her personal preference was to be cremated, but she was choosing burial because she was concerned that my siblings would object to cremation. I suggested she talk to them to see if her assumptions were accurate. As it turned out, they had no objection to cremation and were able to honor her wishes.

For a variety of reasons, many people live their lives with greater concern for getting the approval of others than being true to themselves. In a very real sense, this results in abandoning one's own self. It's one thing to be respectful of cultural, religious, and family traditions, and quite another to neglect responsibility for your own life and death process. You are the one who lives inside of you—not the person out there in the world whose approval you want.

understanding the importance of telling each other the truth

Many of us hide ourselves from one another in the roles we assume in each other's lives out of fear of being judged or rejected for the ways in which we differ from them or their beliefs of how we "should" be. When the topic of conversation is about dying or death and our personal end-of-life preferences, the challenge is far greater. Living within a cultural narrative that edits out the topic of death intensifies the challenge and can seem insurmountable to the faint of heart or extremely private individuals. If your family and loved ones do not talk about death, consider it an opportunity to take the lead in broaching the subject. As a consequence of the Death Taboo, resistance is quite normal and culturally programmed into us all. However, sensitive persistence works and is a great service to all involved. Ultimately, our reluctance to speak frankly with each other about how we feel about each other's deaths and our own end-of-life preferences is a kind of sticker shock—we are not sure we want to pay the imagined price. But the stakes of not having these conversations are much higher.

Here's what you need to decide: Is it important enough for me to have my death my way or am I more concerned about rocking the boat on the way there if I speak up? Many of us have spent a lifetime dodging the disapproval of others and the potential consequences of telling our truth. Doing so can become so familiar that we think it is normal and preferable. The consequence of hiding who we really are is that nobody ever really knows us. We become so busy perfecting the illusion that we are how and what we imagine they want us to be that the real one who lives inside of us gets silenced and lost.

If ever there was a time to tell your truth, it is when you or a loved one is dying. It is disrespectful and unkind to lie to each other—it says, "I don't trust you with my truth" or "I don't think you can handle the truth." Yes, it can be difficult, especially in a cultural and medical environment where the mere word "death" is so taboo, and even the doctors are gun shy about broaching the subject. Each of us deserves to know our options, to make our own choices, and to count on our loved ones to see us through. Legally, we have that right, but it is up to us to exercise it.

Talking about the impending death of a loved one can be especially difficult for a family that has yet to break through the silencing of the Death Taboo. In reality, those who are dying usually know what is happening to them. I remember when my mother woke out of a deep sleep, sat up in her hospital bed, and announced to me in a startled voice, "I think I'm dying!" My instinct was to tell the nurses. Recognizing this as a red flag, they immediately moved her to the ICU where she was pronounced to have a 50/50 chance of making it through the night. She made it that time, but we both knew from that point on that time was ever more precious.

My mother and I were fortunate that we were able to talk openly about the fact that she was moving toward her death. We could both say how we felt about that and what we were each concerned about. Our bond grew tighter for the journey ahead. Many who are dying are not so fortunate and believe their loved ones can't handle the truth. In an effort to protect them, they don't talk about it and live in emotional isolation. This can prevent them from acknowledging their wants and needs and saying their goodbyes. The reverse is also true. Sometimes, the loved ones and doctors know the patient is terminal but fear the patient can't handle the truth and withhold it from them.

how to initiate honest and intimate communication

Sue Brayne and Peter Fenwick's booklet *Nearing the End of Life: A Guide for Relatives and Friends of the Dying* offers great advice about how to bridge the gap of these painful silences that isolate us from each other when we most need to be supporting one another. Here are some of the ideas presented:

- A gentle touch can often serve as a prelude to taking the conversation to a deeper level.
- Either the patient or the loved one might broach the conversation indirectly asking such philosophical or spiritual "tester questions" as: "What do you think happens after we die?" or "Do you think God really exists?"
- Another indirect approach might be to ask something like, "I wonder whether there's anything you want to talk to me about?" or "What can I do to help you at the moment?" Indirect questions have a way of empowering the patient by letting them know the door is open to such a conversation, and they have the choice to take it further or not. This kind of question communicates that you are safe to talk to, that you care, and you are willing to be of greater service.
- Some prefer a more direct approach by asking such things as "Are you frightened of dying?" or "Do you have any fears about dying?"
- When either the patient or loved one is told that the patient is terminal, do not withhold this information from each other. With my mom, I chose to be direct in telling her about my conversation with the ER doctor who suggested we might want to check out the services of hospice. Cake was quiet at first, and then she took my hand and said, "I know, dear. We knew this time would come." We comforted each other through adjusting to our new reality.
- Another approach is for the loved one to open up the

subject by saying something like, "I want to be prepared to help you if you get really sick. It would be a great help to me if we could talk about what you might want or need so I can take good care of you." This at least puts the possibility of the patient not recovering on the table for discussion. Just remember that no matter how much resistance you are met with, that doesn't negate the fact that you have done both of you a great favor by opening the door.

- Leading questions are another option. For example, to probe whether or not the individual has their legal ducks in order, you might ask, "If you become ill, would you like me to know where you keep your important papers?" or "Have you ever thought about what you want to do with your belongings?" or "Have you thought about what kind of service you would like at your funeral?"

- Statements that open the door to future conversation can also be helpful. For example, "If there ever comes a time when you want to talk about something or you feel frightened, please feel free to talk to me." This lets the patient know that you are available and willing to listen.

- It's okay to cry and to express your grief in a way that communicates how much the person means to you. Just be careful that you don't burden them with your grief. Making it safe to cry with each other makes it more comfortable for the patient to grieve openly for the life he or she is leaving behind as well.

- If either the patient or the loved one feels unable to have this kind of conversation, consider asking for support from a social worker, nurse, or hospice worker. Trust your own judgment about who you feel comfortable talking to about this and give them the opportunity to help.

- Sometimes, there are no words that need to be spoken. Just being there quietly at the bedside can be wonderfully peaceful for both individuals.

deeply listening to each other

Many of us need to be reminded that talking is only part of the conversation. The receptivity of the listener is equally important to truly honoring each other's truth. Here are some more suggestions offered by the *Nearing the End of Life* booklet about how to listen to what the other person has to say:

- Be respectful by not trying to force your point of view on the other person. Let the person who is dying do so his or her way. Loved ones are there to bear witness, not to stand in judgment or to take charge.
- Be honest. Tell your truth, but not in a way that makes the other person's truth wrong. Mutual honesty can be very liberating and soothing for the dying person.
- Engaged body language. Make direct eye contact, keep an open body posture, and pay attention to each other's tone of voice, facial expression, and willingness or reluctance to pursue the conversation.
- Reading between the lines. Trust any sense you get that the other person isn't really saying what they want to say. Ask if there is something they are avoiding saying and encourage them to share their truth with you.
- Give your undivided attention. When love and loss are involved it can be difficult to stay focused on listening deeply to what the other person is saying without being distracted by your own thoughts and feelings. Do your best to stay focused and to bear witness by listening deeply to the other's truth being expressed.
- Be emotionally brave. You might be embarrassed and unfamiliar with the level of emotional intimacy this kind of conversation requires. Notice that, but don't let it stop you. Or, you might be afraid that one of you will lose emotional control and cry or express vulnerability. Providing a

safe emotional space for each other is a great gift. Do your best and avoid shutting down the conversation. Breathing slowly and deeply can help you to center and calm yourself.

chapter 10

key #5:
taking time, making time

*"*To everything there is a season,
and a time to every purpose under heaven:
a time to be born, and a time to die;
a time to plant,
and a time to pluck up that which is planted.*"*

—*Ecclesiastes 3:1–2 KJV*

THIS CHAPTER IS ABOUT TAKING and making time for what is really important about our relationships with aging, dying, death, and grieving. We don't break free of the Death Taboo just because we recognize that it is a good idea to do so. We must choose to observe ourselves, each other, and the institutions and norms of our society to identify all the subtle and obvious ways that the Death Taboo directs us to have a fearful attitude toward death. Take the time to notice how it suppresses you and to consider alternative ways of thinking about and relating to death and dying. Practice greater acceptance of the normalcy of aging, dying, and death.

Our newly emerging culture of death calls upon us to be more conscious and communicative about our preferences, fears, wants, and needs when death comes knocking on our door or that of a loved one. Most of us have remedial work to do to overcome our Death Taboo programming so we can be more comfortable and skilled in encountering our journey through aging and dying. The quality of our living and our dying will be greatly enhanced by taking the time to make peace with death.

being responsible for our living and dying

Tick tock. Seconds and minutes and hours and days come and go in a seemingly abundant supply. Yet our time will run out as it does for everyone. What we have to show for our time is up to us. It is a vibrant currency of pure potential.

When asked by Oprah Winfrey what he thinks happens when we die, Jon Kabat-Zinn, PhD, a scientist, writer, and mindfulness teacher, responded that he did not know but thought a more important question is whether or not there is life before death. Indeed, each of us is offered the opportunity to either awaken to the inner vibrancy of our being or to exist in a kind of unconscious and disconnected state, bombarded and distracted by a plethora of external stimuli. The choice is ours. Our mortality is a great motivation for choosing wisely in what we create, promote, and allow our lives to be on the inside and from the inside out. Ultimately, this is about choosing to live and die consciously and responsibly within the context of some understanding of what we think this mortal journey is all about.

taking time to think about old age, dying, and death

Our youth-oriented society teaches us to view the aging process as something to avoid as though there were something wrong with it. We invest in supplements, creams, and plastic surgery to hang on for dear life to our fleeting youth. Many of us try to pretend we are younger than we are. We deny the signs of aging, saying things like, "You look really good for your age," or we complain about unmistakable evidence of our aging as though we are disgusted at drawing a short straw. Our culture doesn't have an aging problem, rather a cultural pathology around aging. This results from our obsession with youth at the expense of having a balanced perspective on the gifts and challenges of all phases of the human life cycle.

It helps to acquaint ourselves with reality, both in terms of dealing with our own normal process of aging and that of our loved ones. I remember how as a kid I used to roll my eyes when hearing my parents and their cohorts complaining about their aches, pains, and ailments. Now it is my generation's turn. Aging is a process of noticeable changes, and some catch us off guard or sadden us deeply. But why are we so surprised? Perhaps it is because our denial doesn't work when we're up against the hard facts of reality. Aging is normal. It is not a sign of weakness or failure. The United Health Foundation's 2019 report on the health of seniors found that the rate of depression among those over sixty-five increased 19 percent over the prior year.

In its 2015 report, which focused on specific diseases, the foundation reported that:

- Nearly 80 percent of those over sixty-five live with at least one chronic health condition.
- More than 70 percent have heart disease, and nearly 60 percent have arthritis, a leading cause of disability.
- 20 percent have been diagnosed with diabetes.

As a society, we are not gracious about the aging process. We do not have a longstanding tradition of honoring the wisdom of our elders and tenderly caring for them. Perhaps the demographic bulge of the Baby Boomers will force needed change in this area. As Pearl S. Buck, Mahatma Gandhi, and others have warned us: The true measure of the strength and character of a society can be found in the way that it cares for its helpless members.

In *Conscious Aging*, Ram Dass offers the following lists of physical and psychological changes that are common and quite normal in the aging process:

Physical Changes	*Psychological Changes*
Arthritis	Despair
Neuritis	Depression
Insomnia	Feeling abandoned
Constipation	Feeling worthless
Poor circulation	Frustrated
High blood pressure	Worrying
Nervous tension	Doubting
Atrophying muscles	Vulnerable
Bones breaking easily	Forgetfulness
Motor nerves signal slower	Losing self-confidence
Lungs inhale less oxygen	Irritable
Loss of mobility	Fear of the future
Can't hear as well	Obsessed with possessions
Can't see as well	Meaninglessness
Run out of steam sooner	Friendlessness
Days when you feel sick	Fear of being penniless
and nauseous	No one to touch
Issues with incontinence	Loss of psychological power
	Worship of doctors
	Fear of doctors
	Suspicion
	Paranoia

Aging is normal. It is not a sign of weakness or failure.

Exercise 21: How I Relate to Aging

1. Review the previous lists of the physical and psychological changes that normally accompany aging. If you are experiencing some of these changes associated with aging, write about how you feel about these things happening to you. If not, think about how you feel and react to others who are manifesting some or all of these behaviors as they age. What is your inner dialogue about this?

2. Describe whether you see yourself as adaptive and accommodating of these changes, or are you more likely to be resistant, in denial, and/or reactive? For example, if you are young, how does it feel to be driving behind an older person who is traveling more slowly than you would like? What kind of inner dialogue do you have when encountering this?

3. Notice how many of these physical and psychological signs of aging affect your life either as your own experiences or because someone you know is experiencing them. Note if you find any of them especially distressing and take time to explore why.

4. Would you describe your way of dealing with aging as healthy or unhealthy? Explain.

5. What could you do differently to have a more balanced, healthy, and compassionate response to the normal signs of aging? Be specific. Are you willing to do these things?

will you show up?

Aging, dying, and death are perfectly normal human activities. Everything that lives must die. It goes with the territory. Some of us feel inconvenienced by the increasing dependency and caregiving needs of the aging and dying. Some perceive the death of others as a shocking interruption in our daily lives. Our routines are thrown out of whack as if someone threw a bomb into our lives. The Death Taboo has trained us so well to ignore death that when it shows up, we are stunned. Most of us live such over-scheduled lives that trying to fit more and more into our days means either creating more stress for ourselves or having to give up what we already think is essential for us to do.

Exercise 22: Do I Show Up?

Imagine that a beloved family member who lives across the country has just been taken to the ER with a 50/50 chance of survival. Answer the following questions:

1. Do you drop everything to be by his/her side or do you try to connect and provide support by phone?

2. Do you make your decision based on love? On the desire to support him/her? On the degree of convenience or inconvenience this presents to you? Or based on some other measure?

3. What does your response reflect about you?

4. How do you think you will feel about yourself if you don't really show up mentally, emotionally, and/or physically for your dying loved one? How do you think you will feel if you do show up?

Here's an interesting perspective on service from a spiritual point of view from John-Roger:

> People often misunderstand the concept of service, not recognizing that it is an active form of moving the spiritual consciousness, which takes place primarily when you serve from the level of positive attitude. Although you could respond, "Oh, I have to help them again," it would serve you better—and who better to serve?—if you expressed the attitude, "Thank God I can be of service again."

I know a woman who suffered unimaginable abuse at the hands of both her parents from infancy through her mid-teens. Her father died a while ago. Then, several years ago, she entered into an ugly and expensive legal battle with her mother's opportunistic companion over guardianship of her mother. After winning guardianship, she spent the next few years commuting back and forth from her home to a distant city to visit and care for her mother and to tend to her medical and legal affairs. Even after having placed her mother in a posh facility and hiring additional round-the-clock caregivers, my friend still spent time every day overseeing her mother's care. When her mother was nonverbal and suffering from dementia, showing no appreciation for her daughter's attentiveness, she still went to be with her. Why? After being abused by this woman as a child, what motivated her to rearrange her life to care for her mother? Can you imagine being so devoted to your parent under such circumstances? This woman, who had every good reason to turn her back on her mother, was raised in a culture that believes in the responsibility to care for one's elders. As far as she was concerned it was the right thing to do and was neither negotiable nor optional. In her culture, it would be unthinkable to say, "I'm too busy" or "She doesn't deserve my help."

Cindy, a young woman who attended one of my retreats, spent

one full day each week just being with her best friend and helping take care of her. The friend was in a prolonged dying process. It's not that Cindy wasn't as busy as the rest of us. She was married, had several children, and was CEO of her company. What's interesting is that she didn't succumb to all the excuses that so many other people make about how they would love to help but are just too busy. In Cindy's mind, she loved her friend—where else would she be? The degree to which we demonstrate our caring for each other is not a matter of busyness, it's about what we give priority to in our lives.

Can you imagine what a gift Cindy's weekly all-day visits were to her friend? What a testament of loving to make time for her friend during her friend's time of great need. And what a beautiful example she set for her children and employees. Through the routine of once-a-week visits, Cindy provided the space for the normalcy of their friendship to carry on. They both looked forward to these visits—their "us time."

Showing up takes time, but more importantly it takes the kind of heart that chooses to make the necessary sacrifices to be of loving service to someone in need who matters to us. The irony about our Death Taboo is that it has taught us to run as fast as we can to get away from death and the trials and tribulations of life. Yet it is these hardships that have the greatest potential to strengthen us and to make us wiser and more compassionate beings.

As Rainer Maria Rilke said in *Letters to a Young Poet*:

> Why do you want to shut out of your life any uneasiness, any misery, any depression, since after all you don't know what work these conditions are doing inside you? Why do you want to persecute yourself with the question of where all this is coming from and where it is going? Since you know, after all, that you are in the midst of transitions and you wished for nothing so much as to change. If there is anything unhealthy in your reactions, just bear in mind that sickness is the

means by which an organism frees itself from what is alien; so one must simply help it to be sick, to have its whole sickness and to break out with it, since that is the way it gets better.

We are meant to experience the fullness of life—what a bore it would be to live in a monotone routine, sanitized of life's adversity! We would miss the sweetness of spring after a harsh winter or the joy of finding a true friend after being deeply hurt and disappointed in past relationships. Each of life's experiences has something to offer us—even death. Imagine living as though you absolutely believed that everything that happens to you is there to serve your highest good.

taking the time to care

For those of us who become caregivers to loved ones, it is often a gradual and subtle process that, in time, takes over our lives. It is much like an improvisational dance where the music keeps changing unexpectedly and the dancers must adapt and adapt and adapt to keep up. This was the way it was with my mother and me. Somewhere over the nine years that we lived together, she lost her independence, and I became her caregiver. It was a little something here and something else there. Gradually, I became her coconspirator in hiding her failings from others to protect her pride. As her need for my assistance grew, I increasingly withdrew from my own life endeavors.

Before there were websites and books for caregivers to consult, I made so many mistakes, including losing sight of the need to take care of myself. Little by little, I found myself making excuses for why I couldn't do things I used to do or go places I wanted to go. My wants and needs were increasingly sacrificed so I could be with my mom and care for her. We enjoyed each other's company so much that we acted like a couple who would just as soon stay home together, and when we did go out, it was together. On the rare occasion that I went out alone, I would run into people, and they would say, "Hi, how's your mother?" I would often be annoyed that they didn't first ask how I was doing. But perhaps this was a mere reflection of the fact that I lost track of myself in the process of caring for my mother.

Typically, the need to take time and make time for a loved one begins long before they are frail or diagnosed with a terminal disease. For me, it started when I tried not to be too obvious about hanging around home to keep an eye on Cake because she was too proud to acknowledge some of her inabilities as they seemed to flood over her. Emotionally, it was often awkward and challenging to find just the right way to respect her dignity and autonomy yet help as needed. More and more, it was an issue of my feelings of responsibility for her safety.

One of the insidious side effects of her increasing hearing loss was that she lost direct contact with a lot of people she loved who didn't have the patience to find their way through conversations with her. She stopped answering the phone, and I became her ears on the phone with doctors, at restaurants where the background noise was deafening for her, and with insensitive salesclerks and others who had no patience with her deafness. It was yet another example of how the elderly get marginalized.

Cake's hearing loss was quite frustrating for me too. I learned to pay attention to the fact that her ability to hear declined over the life cycle of each set of hearing aid batteries. Conversations could be going along just swimmingly when all of a sudden out of nowhere she would repeat some nonsensical thing she thought she heard me say in a questioning tone of voice. I would often become perturbed that she would think I would say such implausible things, until I finally made peace with the fact that she was living in a world of warped sound waves.

One day my mom and I were having a deep conversation about

self-judgment, compassion, and forgiveness when she declared that she had finally stopped judging herself for something that had plagued her for most of her life. I responded, "That's so totally cool!" to which she replied, "You said, 'God is French toast'?'" For the first time, I heard the pure innocence in Cake's voice as she struggled to stay afloat in our conversation, unable to take the time to apply the autopilot editing function from which the rest of us unconsciously benefit. I loved her even more, and it was easier for us after that. I stopped taking it personally and getting irritated. She was a great teacher. My experience resonated with something writer and broadcaster Andy Rooney once said about what he'd learned in this life—that the best classroom in the world is at the feet of an elderly person.

My mother turned over her checkbook to me when she couldn't see to sign a check anymore. When she was unable to see the dirt on the dishes she tried to wash, I would just redo them when she wasn't looking. When her hearing loss reached the point where she could no longer talk on the phone, she would say a quick hello and ask me to talk to the person and then fill her in afterwards.

I attempted to maintain my mentoring practice and to offer my services as an officiant for weddings and memorial services, and until her last three years, I was able to carry on fairly well. Our daily lives evolved into a new "normal": a rhythm of my doing the errands, cooking and cleaning, scheduling and escorting Cake to doctor's appointments, ordering her medications, and researching new drugs and treatments that just might help a little. My work with clients and weddings got squeezed in here and there. The last six months of Cake's life were so dramatic that I sometimes forget how challenging the previous years had been.

We both felt a tremendous loss of independence. She gave up her driver's license about two years before her death. We made light of it, but we both knew it was her first huge loss of autonomy. She could no longer just get in the car and go wherever and whenever she wanted. I'm sure she didn't ask, and I didn't notice the many times she would have wanted to go somewhere. She was very proud and never wanted to be a bother.

Cake was still walking fairly easily then but with a lot of joint pain. Some days were better than others as her mobility was being jeopardized by arthritis. We used to drive to a favorite country road, and I would drop her off whatever distance away from where I planned to park that she felt she could handle that day. Then I would go off on my brisk walk, while she slowly made her way to the car and sat—resting, knitting, and enjoying the country air, sights, and sounds of nature.

As her eyesight declined, our passionate crusade was to preserve whatever sight she had left. We drove two hours to New York City regularly to see a specialist at a major hospital but got no results. We must have purchased every innovative and high-powered magnifier on the market to maintain her contact with the printed page. However, her eyes kept deteriorating faster than we could find solutions. Her macular degeneration was robbing her of her great passion for reading. She lured me into reading to her and was so greedy for reading time that we turned it into a daily ritual. Each morning, I would serve her breakfast in bed, and we would read our book— usually a historical novel that took us to faraway places and times. We adventured through centuries, cultures, countries, and characters who captivated and intrigued us. Whenever I could find some spare time, we would read on through our latest exploration. It was a great way to take her attention off her pain and disabilities, while drawing us closer and closer together.

As her arthritis got worse and attacked her feet, she would try to walk to the road to get the mail and back, using her cane and resting every twenty steps or so. She tried to make it look like she had casually stopped to check out a flower or a bird, but I knew she was hurting or out of breath. She had a heart condition and was exquisitely sensitive to humidity. I learned to bite my tongue and to respect her journey through this time. She didn't seem to want to talk about it and rarely complained, except when it got the best of her. When she was unable to manage the pain with increasing doses of medications, she would ask for a footbath or for me to rub on a soothing ointment. She would allow herself to cry when she thought I wasn't looking. The barometric pressure was a killer for her. Her feet and back knew it was going to rain or snow long before the weather people and their Doppler Radar did.

It seemed that we were always researching remedies and treatment modalities for new ailments as they occurred. I would go online looking for elixirs or specialists and call upon my friends in search of new doctors and alternative practitioners to alleviate her pain. It was all very discouraging and time-consuming. For a year or two, she went to an acupuncturist for her arthritis and had some degree of success, despite her initial disbelief. Unfortunately, though, that required going down a flight of outdoor cement stairs, which proved to be too difficult for her and were often treacherous with leaves or ice.

A Florida trip in search of help for her eyes was particularly dispiriting for us both. She hated traveling in public in a wheelchair, as she found people surprisingly rude and unconscious of how to respect the space of those in wheelchairs. She found her lack of control over her personal space very scary and stressful. For me, it was a constant challenge. I had to prearrange the rental and return of a wheelchair, pick it up, go get her, and wheel her back and forth from the hotel to the doctor's office, to and from meals, and on any other jaunts we made. Managing a loved one in a wheelchair along with two pocketbooks and packages in an unfamiliar environment wasn't a lot of fun. Getting in and out of taxicabs to and from the airport with luggage to boot was awful. I gained new empathy for wheelchair occupants and their companions everywhere. As hard as all this was, I am grateful for the opportunity it gave me to awaken to what the aging process actually involves. It made me a much better person by teaching me how to be more aware of and compassionate, caring, and sensitive to the needs of the infirm and aging.

I always felt like I was living on the edge of calamity. For example, a few years before Cake died, she had a colonoscopy that resulted in a hemorrhage. We were at home at the time and there was blood pouring out of her rectum—it was everywhere. That was my first totally intimate cleanup job. Somehow, my love for her overcame my fear, repulsion, and resistance and empowered me to handle the situation. It seemed like the most natural thing to do, and I was relieved to discover that I was able to rise to such an occasion. We got her back to the hospital, where she received transfusions, and she was back home as good as new in a few days. That was our first of so many trips to the ER.

In the last year before her fall, we probably averaged about two appointments a week to see doctors or to have lab work or tests done. Our lives became consumed with filling out forms, waiting in doctor's offices, and managing her changing medications. We went to her cardiologist, general practitioner, specialists, and alternative practitioners and regularly drove down to New York City to see her world-renowned ophthalmologist. Nothing improved.

Sometimes things would plateau for a while, and we would settle into a new routine until something else took a dive and another emergency rearranged our lives. I admired her ability to keep track of her ever-changing medications. She worked hard at it every day. I ordered most of her drugs in three-month supplies from Canada for half the price we would have paid in the US. When her medications started to change more frequently, it became cost effective to pay higher prices locally for short-term supplies.

She eventually started to sleep in a recliner chair, unable to lie flat on her bed due to deterioration of a disc, arthritis, and sciatica. It was just awful to be so helpless to do anything to alleviate her pain and to learn to accept my role of helplessly witnessing her suffering.

We finally settled on trying another round of epidural shots. The three-round series had worked for her twelve years prior when she had her first attack of sciatica. This time, the doctor was a pompous prima donna with a hideous bedside manner. I was not allowed in the procedure room and was appalled when Cake emerged an hour and a half later from her first shot, shaking and in tears. She begged me to get her out of there. She kept saying, "I couldn't do it. I just couldn't do it." The doctor had insisted he could not administer the injection unless she laid flat on her back for twenty minutes. She was so desperate for relief that she endured unbearable pain just for the possibility of liberation. I bought her ice cream and tried to soothe her. It took a few days for her to get over that one. Unfortunately, the shot didn't work, nor did the second or third ones, administered with her on her side after having her GP intervene on her behalf. After a series of X-rays, CAT scans, and orthopedic evaluations, we were just about to do a second round of shots when time ran out.

While, clearly, this was a difficult time for both of us, it was also very sweet. Our friendship grew deeper, our patience was tested, the content of our daily lives became less predictable and beyond any illusion of our control. It was a great opportunity to stay in the moment and to handle whatever showed up, remembering to pray for God's mercy and assistance. All we could do was to try our best with whatever appeared and to love ourselves and each other as we sorted through our choices, big and small. It taught us to be so vulnerable and trusting with each other that we got to see what we were really made of and to be pleased with ourselves. We lived a very isolated life, but our togetherness was sweet and so very precious.

Not all of us are called upon to be the primary caregiver to a loved one. But there are so many big and little ways to lend a hand. Many of us find ourselves at a loss for how to respond when we hear that someone we care about has received a terminal diagnosis or lost one of their loved ones. The "right" answer is seldom accessed through the mind, but if you go to your heart and think of that person, you can always find just the right thing to say or do.

Exercise 23: Heart Time

Describe what taking and making time would look like for you in the following situations. What might you do and how would you do it?

1. You notice that your aging parents are reaching the point where they will need to leave their home and find a suitable next housing solution.
2. Your good friend lost her eighteen-year-old son in a car accident eight months ago and remains deeply depressed.
3. Your brother's wife has just been diagnosed with pancreatic cancer. You have never been very close to her but love your brother dearly.
4. It's your day off, and the husband of the couple who live next door was just rushed to the hospital with a massive heart attack.
5. Your family is severely afflicted by the Death Taboo, and no one speaks comfortably about dying, death, or preparations for the end of life.
6. You arrive at work and find everyone buzzing about the fact that the spouse of your boss or your colleague has just died unexpectedly.

Make time and take time for those who need you. It's a funny thing about life that when we are ready and willing to demonstrate our love and compassion for others, it is we who reap the greater gift of knowing our own goodness. As Ralph Waldo Emerson said: "The greatest gift is a portion of thyself."

dying can be hard work

Birthing and dying are transitions, and both take enormous effort. Dying, like birthing, can be hard work. Consider how hard a chicken works to break free of its egg, or a caterpillar after its fifth and final molt then creates the chrysalis from which it will emerge as a butterfly. While we think of human death as a moment, it is the dying part that takes time and exertion. The process of dying is effortful. Dying is not a matter of losing life but disconnecting one's physical, mental, emotional, and spiritual self from this world to transition to whatever, if anything, comes next. That's hard work at a very deep level! Our beliefs about God, death, and the afterlife have a significant impact on the quality of our experience of dying. Resisting and fearing death create unnecessary tension in our bodies and minds. Accepting, cooperating, and surrendering offer the opportunity for a more graceful exit. Those who believe that transitioning out of our bodies in this life will take them somewhere beautiful, struggle much less, and have an easier time letting go into their inevitable departure from this world.

letting go

There is a lot of physical, mental, emotional, spiritual, social, medical, legal, and financial work to be done at life's end. For many who are dying, knowing that their days are numbered, combined with a final to-do list and possibly diminished energy and clarity due to illness and medications, can be quite stressful. The following exercise gives you the opportunity to anticipate what might be important to you ahead of time. It also allows you to think about who your "go-to person" is and to practice talking about these important matters. Finally, it gives you a chance to see what is clear for you, what is not, and what you need to attend to so you can make peace with death and be well-prepared when the time comes. Plan on taking one to two hours for this next exercise.

Exercise 24: If I Were to Die Tomorrow

Find someone you would be comfortable with discussing your respective end-of-life priorities if you were to die tomorrow—perhaps your partner or best friend.

Take turns sharing your responses to the questions below. One of you will go first, answering the questions out loud while the other person might record your answers or simply bear witness to your answers. Remember, you can always decide to take longer and/or add to your answers at a later time. The person listening and/or recording responses should be silent during this part of the exercise. When the first partner is done, switch roles.

Answer the following questions:

1. In terms of religion and spirituality, what, if anything, is important to you before your death, at the time of your death, and after your death? Are there any specific individuals you want at your bedside who share your beliefs or are there particular rituals you want performed? How can your loved ones support you in this area?

2. Emotionally, how ready are you to die tomorrow? What, if any, specific considerations do you have? If afraid, discuss what you are afraid of and what your loved ones might do to help you.

3. Who do you most want to see and be with before you die tomorrow? Is there anyone you prefer not to have around? If you had a week, who would you add to your list?

4. What thoughts or concerns are going through your mind

other than your responses to questions 1 to 3. Is there anything left undone in your life or information you need to share? Is there anything that your loved ones will discover after you are gone that you are concerned about?

5. How at peace are you with yourself right now? Is there anything you haven't forgiven yourself for? Take a few minutes to complete the following sentence out loud: "I forgive myself for judging myself for _____." What are you most grateful to yourself for? Take a few minutes to complete the following sentence out loud "I am grateful for _____."

6. Is there anyone that you are not at peace with? What, if anything, do you want and need to communicate to them? If you also need to forgive yourself, do so now, silently saying, "I forgive myself for judging myself for _____." You may want to spend some time to continue your forgiveness process after this exercise.

7. Do you have any physical concerns about dying tomorrow? Explain.

8. Are your Healthcare Proxy and Advance Healthcare Directives in order? If you have not filled out these documents or if you do have them but haven't reviewed them in the past year, make it an urgent priority to do so after this exercise to be sure your preferences for how you are cared for are clearly stated.

9. Do you have a will or trust and a Power of Attorney? If not, or if you have not reviewed these documents in the past year, make it an urgent priority to do so. Don't let yourself die without these documents.

After you have both answered the questions, take some time to share with each other about your respective experiences with this exercise and on a scale of 1 (I am woefully unprepared to die) to 10 (I have all my ducks in a row) rate your readiness to die.

Take about five minutes to review your answers as recorded by your partner and create a to do list of what you need to do to be fully prepared to die.

We all need to take death out of the closet by breaking through the silence around this topic. By allowing and encouraging each other to talk about death, we liberate and teach ourselves and each other how to die with greater dignity and to support one another in the process.

---

chapter 11

key #6:
entertaining uncertainty, loss,
and sadness

ONE OF MY FAVORITE WAYS to understand the importance of
staying open to all of life is Coleman Barks' translation of Jalāl
ad-Dīn Rumi's poem, "The Guest House":

> This being human is a guest house.
> Every morning a new arrival.
>
> A joy, a depression, a meanness,
> some momentary awareness comes
> as an unexpected visitor.
>
> Welcome and entertain them all!
> Even if they're a crowd of sorrows,
> who violently sweep your house
> empty of its furniture,
> still treat each guest honorably.
> He may be clearing you out
> for some new delight.
>
> The dark thought, the shame, the malice,
> meet them at the door laughing,
> and invite them in.

Be grateful for whoever comes,
because each has been sent
as a guide from beyond.

acceptance

There is great freedom in accepting everything that comes your way. Real acceptance is not for wimps, nor is it a wishy-washy, passive way of making do with whatever is present. Rather, it is a conscious choice to drop all forms of resistance to whatever has shown up in the moment and making the most of it. Acceptance isn't about liking or approving of something. It is about letting life flow and unfold without getting in the way. It is about being receptive, rather than exerting resistance. Instead of focusing on the past or the future or wanting things to be different than they are, we open to what is actually happening in the moment. This absence of "againstness" allows us to more fully engage our reality in such a way that we can learn from it and strengthen our ability to function in this world. Whatever comes our way, our job is to accept it, decide how we choose to respond, and then to act accordingly.

Our first impulse may be to resist something we do not like that comes our way. Acceptance requires overriding this impulse by choosing to acknowledge the experience and doing our best with it, trusting that it has value and is for us and not against us. The truth of the matter is that resistance prolongs and intensifies the negativity of the experience, while acceptance allows for the possibility of changing our negative experience by altering our attitude toward it.

No matter how attached we are to preconceived notions or desires about how we want things to be in our lives, reality often presents us with something very different. If we try to resist our new reality by tightening our grip on our expectations and desires, that simply creates tension between what we want on the one hand and reality on the other. Consider Joe, who received a terminal diagnosis with the probability that he would be dead in six months. His initial reaction was to resist and fight against his prognosis—after all, there was a 10 percent chance that he could live longer than six months. He blinded himself to the probability of his imminent death and focused only on the small chance that he could live longer. Luckily, he had a very sensitive and astute doctor who suggested that Joe look at his entire situation and not just the part he hoped to be true. Little by little, Joe saw the wisdom in his doctor's advice. After two months of frantically pursuing every conceivable life-extending treatment option, Joe began to realize that no amount of wishful thinking about living longer than the odds predicted made it any more probable. He asked for hospice care and began working with his team to make peace with his reality so he could make the most of the precious time he had left. Joe was able to put his affairs in order, to say his goodbyes, and most importantly, to surrender into his own death.

living your own life

Each of us has but to live our own life—to do our best with it—nothing more and nothing less. To truly receive what comes our way in life requires that we be open to the fullness of life, trusting ourselves to rise to whatever occasion presents itself to us and allowing our consciousness to freely and continually flow on to each new experience. To entertain what we do not prefer requires building wisdom and trust that embraces the idea that everything that shows up in our lives is somehow for us and therefore to be received accordingly. Rumi advised: "Live life as though everything is rigged in your favor."

As described in Chapter 6, we have been culturally trained to avoid pain and suffering, which has left us like a deer in the headlights—unskilled in meeting life's challenges. In exploring my own response to pain and suffering, I discovered that I was so busy trying to protect myself from unpleasantness that I had no proficiency in dealing with the hard times when they did show up. I doubt that I am unique in this. We need to intentionally override our programming of resisting pain and suffering by practicing new behaviors. We need to recognize the uncertainties, losses, and sadness of life as natural, unexceptional, and the source of some of the greatest wisdom and intimacy of our lives. Not only is it important for us to intentionally experience these parts of our lives, but to support each other in doing so as well. We need to make room in our lives, hearts, minds, and relationships for painful experiences to reveal us more fully to ourselves. In *Practicing Peace in Times of War,* Pema Chodron shared this wisdom on relating to our preferences:

> All the wars, all the hatred, all the ignorance in the world come out of being so invested in our opinions. And at bottom, those opinions are merely our efforts to escape the underlying uneasiness of being human, the uneasiness of feeling like we can't get ground under our feet. So, we hold on to our fixed ideas of this is how it is and disparage any opposing views. But imagine what the world would be like if we could come to see our likes and dislikes as merely likes and dislikes, and what we take to be intrinsically true as just our personal viewpoint.

entertaining uncertainty

Life is a suspenseful thriller. Will I get the job I want? Will I find true and abiding love? Will my cancer go into remission, or is this it? How and when will I die? How much time do I have left? Who among us doesn't wish for some guarantees where none are available? Does God really exist? Some of us demand irrefutable, scientific proof; some take a leap of faith; some say they don't care; and some claim a visceral knowledge of God's presence in their lives. Could it be that we are all right from our respective points of view? If you stand on one side of a two-colored beach ball and I stand on the other, and your side is red and mine is blue, we could argue forever for our respective certainty about the color of the ball. However, sometimes there is more than one right answer, and our certainty is just a way to cope with uncertainty or a reflection of myopic thinking.

When we are uncertain, we typically respond with doubt and a lack of conviction. Depending on the nature of the uncertainty we face, we may be filled with suspicion as to the truth of that which is uncertain. We may seek to comfort ourselves by trying to force a verdict or decisive perspective on that which confounds us. We may hope and pray that the truth matches our preferences, but we must live with not knowing for sure until the truth reveals itself to us. And sometimes, it doesn't.

Everything is vibrant and moving and alive. Yet, we become attached to people, things, experiences, and memories. We want them to remain unchanged and to last forever so we can live happily ever after. We become deeply disappointed when they don't and sometimes feel betrayed because someone moved on or our preferential prayers appear not to have been answered. We want guarantees and assurances where none are available.

In reality, accepting the impermanence of all things enables us to be more realistic about the comings and goings in our lives. We learn to welcome, as well as to let go and say goodbye, when the time comes to do so. Practicing acceptance of impermanence and uncertainty saves us from the unnecessary suffering of holding on too tightly to our preferences, which in itself is very often the source of our suffering.

Part of the wisdom we gain when we accept the uncertainty of our lives has to do with developing a greater appreciation for the fertility and possibilities of each moment. When we give our awareness anew to each moment, we can perceive and choose more wisely. We learn to more deeply appreciate the sweetness of life and to build our capacity to weather its trials and tribulations. Of what value is immortality if we do not find this moment to be precious? As the British novelist Susan Ertz says in *Anger in the Sky*: "Millions long for immortality who don't know what to do with themselves on a rainy Sunday afternoon."

Even our breath is impermanent. Like waves in the ocean, each breath arrives and recedes, that particular breath never to return again. Such is the nature of living in time and space. We exist in a complex process of change, flux, and flow. Rather than trying to sanitize our lives of pain and suffering, let's embrace them by opening ourselves to the wisdom and learning they are there to bring forward to each of us and to those who love us. It is wise to trust the dance of life rather than trying to control and direct it.

Exercise 25: Trusting the Fullness of Life

Write your answers to each of the following questions/sentence completions:

1. The three things I resist most in my life are _____.
2. How I deal/dealt with each of these is _____.
3. The worst thing that ever happened to me in my life was _____.
4. How I deal/dealt with that is _____.

Now, go back through your answers and ask yourself, "How might I demonstrate/have demonstrated greater trust and acceptance of these realities in my life? What wisdom did they/might they offer me?

---

to hope or not to hope

Our life expectancy has been extended due to medical discoveries and improvements in sanitation. This presents us with a mixture of blessings. On the one hand, they have extended and increased the quality of our lives and given us options for hope where none existed before. On the other hand, they have brought with them new kinds of physical and emotional suffering associated with chasing after a medical miracle cure to beat the odds of a dismal prognosis. Unfortunately, many leading-edge treatment modalities subject patients to greater pain and suffering while fighting to the bitter end of their lives, hoping for a reprieve rather than surrendering into a potentially less painful dying process.

Sometimes hope blinds us to reality. This can be true both for patients, their loved ones, and doctors, who are perhaps too attached to the hoped-for possibility of extending life. At times, this can prevent them from objectively and reasonably considering the price the patient pays in additional suffering and the possible wisdom of doing less instead of more. Hence, the introduction of the concept of Slow Medicine in 2009 by Dennis McCullough, MD, who suggests that because a new medical technology is available or offers some promise does not mean it is necessarily a good idea to pursue. Rather, it must always be weighed against the option of doing less in terms of the relative risks, side effects, and quality-of-life alternatives.

In 1961, Eisenhower warned us about the economic, political, and even spiritual influence of the military industrial complex and how it had become an essential part of the very structure of our society and culture. Today, in addition to the military industrial complexity of our nation, we have added yet another powerful influence—the pharmaceutical, insurance, and medical industrial complex that is often the sole beneficiary of pushing the boundaries of extending life. Living within this context calls upon us to weigh our options carefully. This includes looking more deeply at the extreme ways that our fundamental avoidance of aging, dying, and death feed the growth of medical research and pharmaceuticals. I am not suggesting that these enterprises are without merit; however, we might benefit by tempering our enthusiasm for the latest elixir with a more normalized view of aging, dying, and death as essential parts of our journeys as mortal beings. Death is not an enemy to be fought against.

accepting loss

When we struggle with loss, it presents the opportunity to compare the nature of our relationship to that which we lost before it was gone. The possibility of loss is an ever-present reality. I might lose my job, my mind, my best friend, my partner, my belief in myself. I will lose my life one day. Loss comes with the territory of being human. As such, it is beneficial to develop our capacity to meet our losses in a way that integrates them naturally into our life's rhythm. Losses often make the most wonderful steppingstones into another stage of our life.

When I lost a job about thirty-five years ago, I was numb with shock and afraid of losing my home and security. Now I see that the loss was essential for me. It caused me to redirect myself into a new and much more rewarding kind of work. While that job provided me with a level of comfort and the illusion of security, it also prevented me from going after what I really wanted to do. The loss of that job freed me to dare to follow my greater passions. The same was true when my mother died. As much as I loved her and would miss her, I would no longer be consumed by caregiving, and I was able to begin writing this book.

Our lives, our relationships, our experiences all have beginnings, middles, and ends. Losses are always mixed blessings, calling us to loosen our grip on what has been and to open ourselves to what is arriving next. "Loss" is one of those words that has gotten a bad rap.

Yet loss is never all bad. The secret to dealing with loss is to always open our hearts and minds to the blessings inherent in the loss and to be grateful for having experienced who or what we now mourn.

moving through loss and sadness

Many of us hide a multitude of sorrows behind the mask of a smile. I know I learned to do this very young—to pretend that everything was fine when it was not, that I was fine when I was hurting. But there is a heavy price we pay for avoiding feeling our negative emotions. As Lisa Firestone, PhD, says in her article, "The Value of Sadness":

> Our tendency to avoid sadness is almost instinctive. From a very young age, we try to avoid sad feelings. As adults, we're quick to shush wailing babies or offhandedly say to sobbing children, "Don't be sad. Cheer up. You're fine. Stop crying." Though not intentional, we tend to pass on the message that sadness is bad and should be avoided. Yet, research has shown that sadness can be an adaptive emotion with real benefits. So, why is it that we are so afraid to feel sad?

In the movie, *Inside Out*, it is the lethargic, depressive character Sadness who is the hero—not Joy, in her eternal optimism, frenetically racing about, trying to control everything that happens. Through experience, Sadness is able to guide the main character, Riley, to stop pretending to be happy for her parents and to tell them the truth about how sad and miserable she feels. This opens the door for them each to share their respective sadness about moving and thereby to empathize with each other and reestablish their shattered connection.

As discussed in Chapter 6, our culture has normalized polarized thinking. This has naturally led us into a pattern of actively seeking positive experiences and avoiding negative ones. While it is perfectly natural to prefer enjoyment over pain and suffering, the reality is our lives will inescapably include both. Therefore, it is important that we learn to move through life's painful experiences in as healthy a way as possible as early in our lives as possible.

Consider the prevalence of addictions. The motivational impulse that leads many to drugs, alcohol, gambling, excessive shopping, and other addictive behaviors is the attempt to get high, feel better, or to dampen down or cut off unpleasant feelings. Unfortunately, escaping feelings doesn't make them go away and often results in maladaptive behaviors that further distress us and those around us. Unresolved feelings, when pushed below the surface of our consciousness, can silently accumulate and wreak havoc in our mental, emotional, and physical lives. The emotions we consider negative serve important functions in our lives, as in the above example of the character Sadness in the movie *Inside Out*. Negative emotions are perfectly legitimate and normal. In fact, when we limit our experiencing of them, we are pushing away from life itself and isolating and distancing ourselves from those who love us.

Another consideration here is that when we numb our pain, we numb our joy as well, thus narrowing our range of emotional experiences. When we simply feel our feelings, we allow them to move through us and to give ourselves the opportunity to respond appropriately. Our feelings are indeed essential tools that help guide us, connect us to each other, and correct our course of action when we get off track of how we want to be in our lives.

Let's look specifically at sadness. In the 1960s, psychologist Paul Ekman theorized that sadness is one of the six universal human emotions along with anger, disgust, fear, happiness, and surprise. In Western civilizations there continues to be ongoing debate about the universality of these emotions, yet fairly strong agreement about their consistency.

Sadness is a kind of heavy-heartedness whereby we are much

more likely to see our glass as half-empty than to perceive that it's also half full. Sadness is typically a response to specific experiences of pain or loss that is expressed in feelings of despair, helplessness, disappointment, and sorrow. When sad, we might be lethargic or antisocial. Unlike depression, which is a physical illness, sadness is a short-lived natural reaction to painful circumstances. It typically passes with time and a redirection of our focus.

When sadness occurs in response to a loss, it is important that we pay attention and not try to dismiss or override it. It's okay to be sad—and it's perfectly normal. One of the positive benefits of experiencing our sadness is that it reminds us what matters most to us in our lives and gives our lives deeper meaning. Sadness is a perfectly natural response to the loss of a loved one or the experience of rejection, hurt, or frustration in an important relationship. Allowing ourselves to experience our sadness also deepens our ability to connect with and be empathic toward others who suffer.

In the territory of death and dying it is particularly important that we give ourselves and each other the freedom to express our grief and sadness. Grieving is a process that takes time, energy, and effort. When you have lost a precious loved one, it is unreasonable to expect yourself to go about the business of your life as usual. Unacknowledged grief still exists below the surface and can be very powerful. It will assert itself in unexpected and often undesirable ways. Allowing ourselves to experience our grief and encouraging others to do so as well is an essential part of finding our way to new life after the loss. Be patient with yourself and pay attention to changes in mood, your ability to function both personally and professionally, insomnia, addictive behaviors, or other significant changes. Make sure you have at least one trusted confidant, whether a friend or a professional, with whom you can be completely honest about what you are going through.

It is also normal to feel sad and helpless in the face of another's obvious pain. We do not need to hide our sadness for fear they won't be able to handle it. Let your truth be known. It strengthens all of us! All we really need to do is to do our best. Everything else is beyond our control. The prospect of our own death or any major loss ultimately challenges us to actively engage in our lives, simply doing our best.

grieving our losses

Not only do each of us die in our own unique way, but we grieve differently as well. And sometimes we are surprised to find that we don't grieve any two deaths in quite the same way. Nor do all deaths end happy relationships—but that doesn't make them any less significant to us. For example, my dad and I had great difficulty with each other. I was quite taken by surprise to find myself sobbing for two weeks straight after his death. I remember walking through the airport on my way back from his home, where my siblings and I had gathered after his death. The kindness and caring of complete strangers who were sensitive to my weeping was like blinding sun in the eyes of someone coming out of a dark place. These strangers cared for and about me in a way my own father never did, and that startled me and intensified my tears. I had an epiphany when I realized that I wasn't upset about losing him; rather, I was experiencing a profound sense of liberation, a letting go of the tension that had always existed between us. I hadn't realized how stressful our relationship had been for me until then. It was as though some part of me had been stretched to its limits like a rubber band that was abruptly let go. I was relieved not to have to cope with that tension anymore.

In contrast, as much as my mother and I loved each other, we had both made peace with her dying and were impatient for the end to come. She wanted to know what would happen next, and I was ready to move on with my life. I shed no tears at first. I was happy for us both. As time went on, I periodically found myself weeping, sometimes uncontrollably sobbing. I accepted her death, but I missed her love and friendship and often cried in gratitude for all the ways that she had enriched my life. Grief had its way with me in unpredictable and unexpected ways. When it took hold of me, I always paid attention and made room for it. I instinctively knew it was far better to express it than to repress it. In experiencing and releasing my grief, I knew I was making space for something else to come into my life and heart.

I have known and worked with many people who were debilitated by their grief and unable to accept the death of a loved one. Usually this boils down to a kind of shock and unwillingness to surrender to the reality of death. These people tend to suffer in a hell of their own mental creation, unable to entertain living their life without this person—a spouse, a dear friend, a child. Powerless to accept the reality, they cannot integrate it into their lives and move forward. Some people stay stuck in this way for the rest of their lives. Unless and until they are able to accept their reality by entertaining a different way of perceiving the situation, they are stuck in resistance to the reality that has come their way.

It does not help to have others urging you to get on with your life or saying you shouldn't feel the way you do. Quite to the contrary, what we typically need is someone willing to bear witness to our pain who will encourage us to articulate it and who will not tell us we should be any different than the way we are. This is one of the wonderful benefits of grief counseling. Ultimately, moving on with one's life after the loss of a loved one becomes a matter of choice. It is about accepting the fact that our life is continuing and choosing to live it and to make the best of it. We must choose ourselves, rather than our grief.

the transformational nature of loss and grief

When we truly allow our grief to reverberate through our being, we usually find it to be an alchemical process of energy transformation. For the dying, grieving is a process of disconnecting from outer activities and relationships into an inner state of oneness as an individual being whose journey is ending. It is about letting go, saying goodbye, and accepting the loss of physical energy, caring, connecting, and being. For those left behind, the energy that flowed between the loved one and the deceased must be put to work in one's healing process. William Worden, a founding member of the Association of Death Education and Counseling (ADEC) describes the four fundamental tasks of the grieving process for the surviving loved one as follows:

- Accepting the reality of the loss
- Working through the pain and grief
- Adjusting to a new environment/life
- Finding an enduring connection with the deceased, while moving forward with your life

Typically, grief doesn't start when somebody dies; rather, it emerges when it first becomes apparent that death is probable. Grieving and letting go of those we love is hard work, yet it is an opportunity for profound inner growth. Whether we have treasured the dying person or had a difficult relationship with them, knowing that our time together and our opportunity to heal any hurt between us is running out implores us to give our best into the situation.

The moment the ER doctor told me there was nothing further to be done medically for my mother and suggested we consider hospice care propelled me into an entirely different relationship with my mother. Our way of being with each other was transformed in that moment. From chief cheerleader and advocate for her getting better, I became the one to intimately share the process of her letting go from this life. My new job was to lovingly yet helplessly bear witness to her withdrawal from this world.

There is no place for denial or putting on a fake, cheerful face in the dying process. It is so important to give each other the gift of our honesty, rather than hiding behind perky messages of hopefulness in the face of impending death. My mother's bravery taught me to be honest about my sadness, my love, my helplessness, and my prayerfulness for the well-being of her sweet soul. It also moved me to begin the process of leaning into my solitary life. Too often, in our efforts to protect each other from the truth we are actually attempting to avoid going into territory we fear will cause us to lose control emotionally. I don't really understand our impulse to stifle our tears in front of each other. I say, let them flow. In my experience, that serves two purposes. It allows us to be honest about how we feel, which increases intimacy with those who witness our tears. It also expresses, rather than represses, the energy of our sadness.

Our inner and outer lives can go through a great metamorphosis as the result of the death of a loved one. For example, a woman artist who never got the chance to pursue her own career because she was busy supporting her husband's thriving career was offered that opportunity when he died. A couple whose child died subsequently founded a research and support foundation to help others dealing with the disease that took their child. The parents of victims of the Sandy Hook school shootings of 2012 mounted efforts to stem gun violence.

Sometimes the survivors of a loved one's death find themselves at loose ends about who they are, what matters to them, and how to redirect their time that was so intimately intertwined with the life of the deceased. To embrace your own life and to discover who you are without the deceased is tender work for many. However, this new freedom offers the opportunity to explore new aspects of ourselves and our aspirations. For some, this feels overwhelming and isolating. Many believe that life has lost its meaning. At times like this or whenever you find yourself losing your sense of hope or direction, consider this next exercise.

Exercise 26: When You Can't Bear What You Are Feeling

Follow Pema Chodron's advice in the following quote:

> The next time you lose heart and you can't bear to experience what you're feeling, you might recall this instruction: change the way you see it and lean in. Instead of blaming our discomfort on outer circumstances or on our own weakness, we can choose to stay present and awake to our experience, not rejecting it, not grasping it, not buying the stories that we relentlessly tell ourselves. This is priceless advice that addresses the true cause of suffering—yours, mine, and that of all living beings.

It is easy to get caught up in resisting a new reality without even realizing it. It is far more fruitful to seek the strength and wisdom to make the most of what comes our way. It is important to harvest all of our life experiences—using them to grow, to gain wisdom, to learn what works for us and what does not serve us well, and accordingly to choose wisely. We are such powerful creators, purely by virtue of what we promote and allow in our lives. Choose to make a masterpiece of yourself and your life!

chapter 12

key #7:
nurturing, supporting, and serving

"What I must do inside myself is make sure that my relationship with you is up to date, present, and not based upon something that was happening last week or last month or last night or this morning, but is that which is present right now, here in my heart with you, so that I am here with you now."

—*John-Roger*

DEATH SENDS OUT TWO POWERFUL calls to be of service. First is to nurture, support, and serve the dying, and the second is to be there for yourself and others who are grieving.

While our culture of death is undergoing a much-needed transformation, we have a long way to go as individuals and in the process of transforming our institutions as well. Most of us are still ending up in hospitals and nursing homes at the end of our lives, despite the fact that the vast majority of us prefer to die at home, surrounded by loved ones.

Our healthcare system was designed to treat diseases, not people. As such, it is awkward and inadequate in meeting the multidimensional needs of the dying. Our favorite healthcare workers tend to be the ones who make it a point to connect with the human being they are treating. Others have to be trained to do so. Many doctors and other medical personnel have been trained to cope with the suffering, sadness, and grief of patients and their loved ones by disowning their own emotions on the job and staying clinically focused on the task at hand. New models of patient care are advocating treatment of the whole person—not just the physical body.

I hope that in time we all learn to treat the dying as people who need compassionate acknowledgment and support on their journey out of this world. For now, loved ones and compassionate caregivers need to fill the gaps. We only do our death once. Therefore, it is critically important that those on the front lines of transforming our culture of death be heard and supported in bringing forward more compassionate care for the dying.

For those of us who are aging and dying, there is often an inescapable accumulation of aches and pains—not just physical ones but heartache as well. We are all too often faced with the reluctance, resentment, and repugnance of those around us who feel irritated and inconvenienced by our need for them to speak a little louder or slowly, or to help us in big and little ways to alleviate our suffering. In a March 2015 TED Talk entitled *What Really Matters at the End of Life,* BJ Miller, author and hospice physician, notes that: "As Baby Boomers age, a record number of us are living with chronic and terminal illness, and into ever older age. And we are nowhere near ready or prepared for this silver tsunami." Miller urges that we educate ourselves and design an infrastructure that allows us to be responsive to the needs of the dying in the following ways:

- Shifting our perspective from one of being burdened by the needs of the dying to choosing to surround them with more love, compassionate care, and companionship
- Providing an aesthetic environment that calms the soul and pleases the senses, rather than surroundings that are sterile and inhospitable
- Responsively caring in a way that allows the dying to feel unburdened and not a burden to loved ones
- Creating a sense of normalcy with the dying process. Miller describes this as "making space—physical, psychic

room, to allow life to play itself all the way out—so that rather than just getting out of the way, aging and dying can become a process of crescendo through to the end"

- Allowing a sense of wonderment and spiritual awareness that is responsive to the beliefs of the dying
- Beneficence—being kind, charitable, or beneficial with the intention of making life more wonderful for the dying, rather than just less horrible. What scares us most about death is not being dead, but the process of suffering during the dying process

There is nothing more revealing about us, as individuals and as a society, than whether or not we are able to respond to the suffering of others with compassionate care and community. Not only are we prone to denying our own suffering, but that of others as well. As Miller points out, compassion is about suffering together—designing systems and learning how to open our hearts so we suffer together and share the burden. Never has this been more urgently needed than now as the Baby Boomers become Elder Boomers. A 2006 study by AXA Equitable Life Insurance Company about helping our aging parents delineates the challenge:

- Today's adults in their forties and fifties represent the first generation who will be likely to spend more years helping their parents than taking care of their children.
- In nearly one in four US households, there is someone caring for an elderly relative or friend. Generally, this involves helping the older person with a host of questions and choices, ranging from medical care to living arrangements, to finances, and to judgments about whether we may need to intervene in our parents' lives.
- The financial costs and the responsibility for physical care of a frail parent are not the only demands family members must face. Old issues of parent-child relationships may

be rekindled or dormant sibling rivalries may resurface. These emotional aspects of family relationships—and simply talking about the future—are often the most difficult hurdles to overcome.

- Most people feel ill-informed about the problems of aging, are unequipped to help, and are unaware of resources that are available to assist them. Our mobile society, with children often living far away from their parents, makes these issues even more complex and difficult.

creating the habit of being of service

We needn't wait until someone asks us for help. We can intensify our awareness of being connected in the web of humanity by making being of service to others a routine part of how we live our lives. Being exposed to the pain, suffering, and misfortune of others gives us an opportunity to familiarize ourselves with that territory in advance of our own need.

Some of us find it emotionally difficult to see a loved one who is frail and suffering. We try to avoid seeing them in an attempt to avoid our own painful emotions. It is wise in such a situation to see our resistance as a red flag that we need to do some inner work. Rather than avoiding those in need, we are called upon to take the time to get clear on exactly what is triggering us to run away. If this happens to you, here are some valuable questions to ask yourself:

- What am I trying to avoid?
- What specifically scares me?
- What am I afraid I won't be able to handle?

We need to keep asking deeper questions until we discover an "aha" moment that unlocks our fear. It helps to talk to the part of ourselves that is afraid to confide in a friend or therapist and ask for help to neutralize our distress. Consider this a golden opportunity to free yourself of your fear. Then go see your beloved friend or family member with an open and caring heart. Anyone who is entering the personal space of the dying should be reminded that something profound is happening in that place, and it should be treated as a sacred place where we bring the best of ourselves—like putting on our Sunday best before going to church. This doesn't mean to be fake or pretend to be cheerful. It means taking the time to connect to the heart of our caring for this person before entering their space. It means having reverence for the great mystery of death and dying that our loved one is going through. It helps to hold the clear intention of enhancing or supporting their experience. Handle your emotional needs before you enter their room. Otherwise, your apparent upset may burden them with trying to soothe you.

As discussed in Chapter 10, we need to take and make time to support the dying and their loved ones through loving kindness and practical help. We are all being called upon to minister to each other in our times of need. Rise, rise, and rise some more to meet the opportunity to be of loving service. Embrace, share, and give, and you will be blessed a thousand-fold!

service as a path to higher consciousness

My spiritual teacher John-Roger often reminded us that when service is done as a loving action that comes from the heart, it is the highest form of consciousness on the planet. When the impulse behind our action is love, we serve freely—not as someone who is burdened or self-sacrificing. True service is love in action. When we really get that there is nothing more important than loving each other, we put the expression of our caring in front of any other considerations we have with that person in terms of our role, relationship, or the task we are there to perform.

We receive a precious gift when we lovingly serve others. The more we give from our authentic self, the more we get to know ourselves as kind and caring individuals, and the more wisdom, grace, and balance we gain about the art of living and dying. Acts of heartfelt service actually nourish the giver more than the receiver. Service gives us the opportunity to exercise our goodness. The more we can do so, without tainting the act with an attitude of being put upon or begrudgingly going through the motions, the greater the payoff. Frank Ostaseski says it this way: "*When you fix,* you assume something is broken. When you *help,* you see the person as weak. But when you *serve,* you see the person as intrinsically whole. You create a relationship in which both parties gain." Notice when you are called upon to help. Is your response heartfelt? Or do you roll your eyes and wish you didn't *have to* interrupt your routine? Hold yourself accountable for your attitude.

taking care of yourself when you are frail or dying

Those who are weakened and fragile need to nurture themselves as well by taking the time to thoughtfully clarify, acknowledge, and communicate their changing needs. Many of us who serve as care-givers are clueless of what will be required and thus face baptism by fire. The more effectively a dying person is able to educate his/her caregivers about how to best care for them, the less stressful for all involved.

It's not easy to lose your autonomy and independence. If you are used to managing your own life or you are more familiar with the role of caregiver than being the one in need, it can be very challenging to ask for and receive help. Even the most well-adjusted person will have difficulty at times finding their balance and sense of well-being as independence declines and dependency increases. There is a lot of inner work to be done as we move through our aging and dying process. Here are some examples of what we need to be conscious of and some suggestions of how to work with them.

• **Not wanting to be a burden.** Often our concerns about being a burden on our loved ones and caregivers are expressions of our inability to make peace with and accept our declining condition. Perhaps we carry the false expectation that this should never happen to us. Yet, it does. Practicing an attitude of acceptance and neutrality helps. This means recognizing our decline as normal rather than as something wrong or optional. Be present with whatever experience you are having and work with it—not against it. There is a lot of grieving to be done as we experience the loss of our vitality and capabilities. We need to allow ourselves to express our sadness and loss. This is part of our grieving work.

We are meant to have burdens and responsibilities in our lives—things that we must bear that cause us worry and stress. They test our character and our ability to be of loving service. How capable are we of being of the mind and heart that says, "He's not heavy, he's my brother," and rising to the occasion? How ironic that those placed in the position to fear being a burden are actually doing a great service to those tending to their needs. The one who serves is given the opportunity to demonstrate who they are and what they are made of. I learned more about myself in caring for my mother than in any other experience in my life. I was deepened by it, immeasurably and infinitely enriched.

Sometimes, when it is obvious that a loved one or caregiver is treating us like a burden, we hesitate to speak up for ourselves for fear of exacerbating the issue. Just remember, if we don't stand up for ourselves, who will? We need to speak up by communicating negative feedback in a way that calls attention to the impact the other person's behavior is having on us. This includes a description of the action or behavior that the other person is doing that upsets us, a statement of how it makes us feel, and why it makes us feel that way. It helps to preface our negative feedback with an acknowledgement of appreciation for what the person is doing for us. Here's an example: "I want you to know that I really appreciate all that you are doing for me, and I know it is not easy. But I need you to know that when you look at me with disgust or get impatient with me, it makes me feel just awful inside. I feel trapped in my dependence on you, and I really am doing the best I can. Would you be willing to talk about this to see if we can figure out a better way to deal with it?" Rather than letting a situation fester, we need to take the time to figure out what we want to say. By speaking up we are giving the other person an opportunity to consider their behavior, hopefully to change it and to enter into a more honest, intimate, and respectful relationship with us.

• **Abuse or mistreatment by caregivers and loved ones.** Abuse should never be tolerated, no matter who the abuser is. Remember that emotional abuse can hurt even more than physical abuse. One client shared a story about her husband who was in rapid decline. Visiting his son's house, he had an episode of incontinence during a party. His son, disgusted, paused while escorting his father up the stairs to change his diaper and announced to his guests, "I'll be right back. My father just peed in his pants."

Speak up for yourself to any abuser, and if that doesn't change their behavior, get help immediately. If the abuser is a friend or loved one, tell someone else who loves you and ask them to take charge of removing the abuser. If you are under hospice care at the time, contact their supervisor. If you are a resident in a care facility and the person who is abusing or neglecting you is an employee of that facility, report it to your nurse or the administrator immediately. Every community or county has support services for the elderly. Call them and ask for help.

• **Effective pain management.** We are entitled to effective pain management but must do our part to communicate the nature, frequency, duration, and location of our pain and how it affects us. Palliative care has become integrated into the medical model and is not restricted to the dying. The purpose of palliative care is to provide relief from symptoms and stress related to pain and illness as a way to improve our quality of life. It is important to resist any temptation to take less of a pain medication than prescribed in an effort to minimize the possible side effects or the possibility of addiction. Many pain meds need to build up in our system to become effective. If we don't keep ahead of the pain by taking medications as prescribed, we simply reduce their effectiveness while increasing our own stress, which in turn heightens our pain even more. Doctors can explain the pros and cons of a particular medication and address any concerns we have.

• **Disappointment in loved ones.** We never really know someone until we see them handling a crisis or something that is challenging for them. As we become increasingly dependent upon others for our physical, mental, and emotional well-being, our eyes will undoubtedly be opened and our heart will be either touched and soothed or wounded by how others behave. We will likely be surprised to find that some of those we expected to be able to depend upon will disappoint us greatly while others will surprise us by stepping up to help. I remember when my friend Meyer was dying of AIDS, our mutual and very macho friend Jim, while perhaps the least likely to become Meyer's intimate caregiver, was the one who stepped forward to do so with a tenderness that surprised us all and changed Jim in such beautiful ways.

four keys for comforting the dying

1. Be sensitive and responsive to their pain and discomfort. To be helpful to others requires that we first notice their needs. Be attentive. Be sure that pain meds are being given in a timely fashion. If the dying person is wincing with pain, ask what you can do to help—perhaps shifting body position, calling the nurse, or simply a compassionate statement of willingness to help will be a comfort. If they are perspiring, a cool cloth on the forehead might be welcomed. If they want to talk—listen. Watch for the clues of how to help. Don't depend on the dying person to always tell you directly. Observe and respond. Gently anticipate and do what is called for in the moment.

2. Distract their attention away from their pain. Here are some interesting facts about pain. It attracts our attention like a magnet, and the very act of paying attention to our pain amplifies it. Research has shown that when we direct our attention away from our pain, not only do we feel less pain, but our heart rate and skin show less of a stimulus response. Thus, strategies to distract a patient's attention away from their pain can effectively reduce the intensity of their experience of pain. Shifting the focus of the dying person to some constructive activity can help them to coexist with their pain. For example, "Isn't it wonderful that Nancy is on duty today—she is such a thoughtful and caring nurse."

3. Serve, don't assume command. No matter how smart we may think we are or better-versed in the art of dying than the loved one whose bedside we are being called to, we need to remind ourselves that it is their death, not ours. We are there to serve and support, NOT to guide or make critical decisions on their behalf unless serving as their healthcare proxy. We are there to nurture and to be of service.

4. Don't lay your burdens on the dying. The dying person is often the recipient of endless excuses from loved ones who beg their understanding and forgiveness for being too busy to show up. Can you imagine how hard this would be to hear if you were the person whose days were numbered? Not only is the other person letting you know that you just don't matter enough for them to find the time to see you, but they want you to spend some of your precious, limited energy reassuring them that it is fine with you that you are not enough of a priority to them.

Next time you are called upon to help someone in need, check your attitude before communicating with them. If you are feeling put-upon or burdened, take time to look at that privately and try not to show it. Ask yourself these questions:

- Does this person ask too much of me?
- Do I have a hard time saying no?
- Am I looking at this opportunity to be of loving service as just one more thing I have to crowd into my busy schedule?

Try shifting your focus away from yourself and to the other person who needs your help. Do you feel compassion for them? Can you imagine reversing roles and how grateful you would be to them for helping you? Think about how it would feel to know the other person felt put upon. Now imagine how it would feel if they helped you with a cheerful heart and loving kindness. It's a whole different ballgame.

five keys for comforting the grieving

1. Say something. Not knowing what to say is a poor excuse for creating an awkward silence. There is no right thing to say, but the wrong thing is to say nothing. Acknowledge the loss and grief. It is a common mistake to tell ourselves that we should give the griever space unless they specifically ask us to do so. This is often a cop-out from facing the discomfort of bearing witness to their sorrow. Don't avoid the situation or treat it as an unspeakable subject. Express your sympathy for their loss and, if sincere, offer help. Depending upon the nature of your relationship, sometimes a gentle touch can communicate more than words to those who feel alone. But don't overdo it by trying to hold their hand or hug them unless they initiate that. They may be struggling to cope by containing their emotions. Give them space but let them know you care.

2. Avoid comparisons. No two people will grieve in quite the same way, nor will we grieve identically for different loved ones who die. Be careful not to assume that because you have grieved a parent, partner, sibling, or child, you therefore have any idea how someone else is feeling about a seemingly similar loss. Never say, "I know exactly how you feel." Instead, you might say, "I have a sense of what you are going through because my mother/sister/partner/child died, too." But be careful not to launch into telling the story about your loss, unless the one who is grieving specifically asks you to do so. It has a way of hurting rather than helping the one who is grieving. For them, it can seem to depersonalize their loss and shift the focus to you and away from them. Bear witness to their grief; don't focus on telling them about yours. Let them know that you are knowledgeable but be careful not to imply that you know what they "should" think or feel or do. Personalize what you say: "We've talked about how much our families mean to us. I'm so sorry about Ed's death." Shared feelings communicate more than well-intentioned advice.

3. Offer specific help. Many who are grieving are too tired or numb to decide what help they need or to find out what kinds of resources are available. Check in periodically by phone, text, or email and suggest two or three things you could do for them to help them through. For example, you might say, "I'd like to help make this time easier for you. Would it be helpful if I were to babysit your kids or cover your carpool days for a few weeks or bring over a meal once a week? Or maybe there is something else you might prefer." It can also be very helpful to offer to explore what resources are available that might be helpful to them. For example, Medicare, which pays for most hospice care, requires that free bereavement counseling be offered to surviving family members for at least thirteen months following a death. Many people don't know this is available.

4. Follow their lead. Pay attention to what the person who is grieving thinks they need, not to what you think they should need or do. There are many styles of grieving. Some grievers want your attention, and others want to be left alone. Regardless, letting them know you are there and that you care can be a comfort. Trust your own sense of the person. You might send a note at first rather than calling them. That respects their privacy while opening your door to them.

5. Create a safe place. There is a fine balance between being sensitive and hovering or being overbearing. The Death Taboo has made many of us quite awkward around the grieving. As we break down our resistance to the normalcy of death, we will learn to create a comfortable spaciousness without such awkwardness.

nine ways to help children understand death

"Why die?" four-year-old Ivan asked as I held his tender little hand in mine, walking together in silence and crunching the leaves beneath our feet. I was dumbfounded by his question and overcome with the responsibility of giving him a meaningful and worthy answer. His innocent eyes looked up into mine, awaiting my response, which was inadequate and forgettable, but I will never forget that moment.

One piece of fallout from our taboo is that we don't effectively prepare our children to deal with death. They are much more aware of death than we realize and need our support in developing a healthy understanding. Although age determines to some extent how a child will respond to the death of a loved one, each child has a unique journey of learning about death. Apply the guidelines listed below with sensitivity to the child's individual level of development, environment, ethnic, religious, and cultural background, as well as their exposure or lack thereof to the reality of death. Regardless of one's religious beliefs, death is about loss, and children need our help to accept loss and to grieve. Here are nine ways to help children to deal with death and grief.

1. Introduce the topic of death gradually. Don't wait for the death of a loved one to talk to a child about death. Take advantage of less emotionally charged opportunities such as seeing a dead bird or insect or driving past a graveyard to engage the child in seeing death as a normal part of the life cycle.

2. Be open and honest in sharing your own feelings about death to make it easier for them to do so as well. Don't try to protect children from death. What we think of as protection prevents them from accumulating life experience, learning how to express their feelings, and receiving needed support. The act of secluding them communicates that death is a scary and terrible thing.

3. Provide clear information that is appropriate to the child's age and level of development. Listen carefully, respond honestly and clearly, and make sure they understand what you have said. Children learn through repetition, so you may need to go over the same information several times. They tend to hear words literally, so euphemisms like "eternal rest" and "went away" should be avoided, as they can evoke a fear response. A child might be afraid to go to sleep and not wake up, or to have Mommy go to the store and not come back.

4. Be sympathetic and nonjudgmental in your responses to a child's questions and behavior. Children have many ways of dealing with death, ranging from silence to rage. It is important to see both extremes as calls for help. Tread lightly, comfort them, and don't force unwanted discussion.

5. Respect the fact that children feel loss just as intensely as adults do. They need patience and thoughtful support to develop an understanding of death.

6. Watch children carefully for signs of needed support. Don't force the child to participate in rituals or assume that you know what he or she is experiencing. Be alert to any misconceptions, fears, or worries. Encourage conversations about death, draw out their thoughts and feelings and let them feel your love. You might help guide their perspective on death by suggesting that because we all will die someday; it is important to be kind to each other while we are together.

7. Follow the child's lead about visiting a terminally ill loved one or attending a funeral/memorial. Children should be given the opportunity to visit the dying or attend funerals if they want. Both provide a sense of reality and closure and the opportunity to observe how adults behave in these situations. It is important to prepare the child for what he or she will see and hear.

8. Allow children to express themselves. Let them know that it is okay to be angry or mad or silent and that mourning a death is a process that takes time.

9. Consider these age-specific guidelines for helping children who have lost a loved one:

> **Infants and Toddlers (0-3):** These children do not yet comprehend death but are sensitive to the emotions of others and to changes in routine. Signs of distress might manifest as changes in mood, eating, or sleeping behavior. If possible, keep them in familiar

surroundings, maintain their routines, and give them lots of love and nurturance.

Ages 3-6: At this age of magical thinking children may not understand that death is permanent and instead believe that it can be magically reversed. Cartoons reinforce this idea. They may have nightmares, repeat the same questions, cling to adults, or behave in regressive ways. When talking to these children about death, physically touch them and look directly into their eyes. Be direct, clear, and sensitive. You might describe death as not eating or moving, talking, or breathing anymore. Be patient and repeat your simple answers as often as the child asks. They may express themselves through artwork or by reenacting a funeral. These are normal behaviors. Always let the child know when you are leaving his or her presence, where you are going, when you will be back, and how they can reach you. Reassure them that you and they are just fine.

Ages 6-9: Cause-and-effect thinking and feelings of guilt may be part of their reaction. For example, "I got mad at Grandma and said I never wanted to see her again, and now she is dead. It's all my fault." Emotional reactions include confusion, sadness, and fear of abandonment from other loved ones. Some personify death as a monster or a bad person that comes and gets you. They may fear that death is contagious. Others imagine they can escape death through magical thinking. Be a good listener, provide opportunities to talk about the death, and correct any misconceptions. Some will be inclined to work through their feelings through artwork or play activities.

Ages 9-12: Better able to comprehend the permanence of death, these children may think death is a form of punishment. Some appear emotionally unaffected on the surface, while others express anger toward self and others, including the deceased. It is helpful to provide opportunities to talk if the child would like to do so and to discourage the idea that people die if they are bad.

Teens: These young adults have a fairly mature understanding of death's finality. They may try to be strong and a comfort to others rather than dealing with their own emotions. They may be confused, angry, feel hopeless or lonely, or develop a philosophical perspective on death. Still others will take unnecessary risks with their life in an effort to overcome their fear of death or vulnerability to death by trying to exert control over their own mortality. Make yourself available to talk and be open about sharing your feelings. Avoid letting them assume adult responsibilities.

Above all else, always let children know that they are surrounded by your love, and that you are available to them to talk about their feelings and needs.

dealing with grief in the workplace

The American Hospice Foundation estimates that more than 8 million people are directly affected by a death each year in the US, while millions more will grieve other important losses, such as relationships, homes, and jobs. These losses take a toll in terms of stress and the resultant inability to function at our usual level of performance in both our personal and professional lives. Grief is experienced on many levels. We know that grief can be responsible for physical symptoms such as trouble sleeping, changes in appetite, fatigue, or actual illness. Grief affects the way our minds work—how we see the world and ourselves. During times of loss, it's a filter through which we receive information and make decisions.

The prevalence of grief in the workplace is extensive, inescapable, and costly. Grief impacts productivity through absenteeism, mistakes, and turnover. It also increases the use of health benefits. As reported in the *Wall Street Journal* in 2002 in the article "The Annual Cost of Despair," the impact of grief has been quantified and monetized as follows:

- Thirty workdays are lost per year by each employee experiencing grief with no support from coworkers or managers.
- 20 percent of grieving employees will continue losing workdays for over a year.
- The average annual cost in lost productivity due to grieving workers in an organization of four hundred employees is $125,000.

There is always grief somewhere in the room. As mentioned in Chapter 3, an average of one in four employees is grieving a major loss in their life at any given time. In light of the staggering cost to businesses in lost productivity and revenues, not to mention the emotional challenges, many companies are taking note of their responsibility to nurture, support, and be of service to their grieving employees. Many are developing networks of support for the grieving and their coworkers to normalize the experience of grief in our lives, rather than responding with the past familiar approach of avoidance—the proverbial elephant in the room.

An employee's grief does not stay at home when they come to work. They need to be supported by their employers and coworkers as well as their friends. The short-term response of an organization should be to offer compassion and understanding and to lighten the grieving employee's load. In 2002, the American Hospice

Foundation's *Grief at Work* study reported one business manager returning to his job two days after his daughter's funeral who said that throughout his workday, he thought about her. "I put in my full eight-hour day, but for six months I didn't do more than four hours of work each day."

Almost all of the 25,000 grieving people who were interviewed for the Grief Recovery Institute study said their job performance was affected. Cofounders of the institute, Russell Friedman and John W. James, discovered that a large percentage of workplace accidents are grief-related due to an inability to focus. While 92 percent of companies were found to offer paid bereavement leave, on average they offered only four days. Friedman and James advocate ten days.

Fortunately, more companies are recognizing the importance of offering grief counseling and educating their employees about company and community resources. Many are offering in-house programs that better equip management and employees to meet the needs of employees with at-home caregiving responsibilities and those who are grieving.

Businesses have the unique opportunity to help their employees overcome the Death Taboo both at home and at work by providing needed education and resources, and by funding community initiatives. In doing so, they also have a positive impact on the health of those communities in which they do business. Grief support in the workplace improves the culture of the organization by educating management and employees how to effectively balance compassion with business sense and by letting everyone know that their organization cares. Among the most effective organizational responses to grief are:

- Training sessions for managers, HR professionals, and employees that provide skills to proactively manage personal grief and to support each other
- In-house or community-based confidential stress and grief

counseling for employees involved in caregiving and those dealing with, or anticipating, the death of a loved one

- Paid bereavement and flexible working schedules for those with intensified caregiving responsibilities for a dying loved one or those grieving a death. (Some companies offer creative time-banking programs, where employees voluntarily donate working hours or unused vacation days to be used by fellow employees in need.)
- Employee education about the importance of advance healthcare planning and presentations by local resource organizations, such as hospice, to educate employees about area service options

Every organization should be well-versed in the hospice assistance and resources available to their employees as well as to those services designed for individuals dealing with caregiving responsibilities or grieving a death. For example, hospice supports caregivers by offering home visits by hospice nurses, nursing assistants, and volunteers who can take some of the pressure off family caregivers by helping with medical and personal care needs. They also offer short periods of respite care, placing the patient in a hospice in-patient facility to give the caregiver a break. Hospice also provides assistance to Human Resource departments or a company's Employee Assistance Program in how to support workers who are grieving the death of a loved one or colleague. At a minimum, companies should be sure to:

- Establish working relationships with local hospice providers.
- Include hospice coverage in employee healthcare benefits.
- Offer an employee assistance program and have a Human Resources department that ensures effective corporate policies for maintaining workplace morale and meeting the needs of caregivers and grieving employees.

Grievers need to become advocates for their own needs in the work-place as well. As the hospice study *Grief at Work* states, it is important not to expect too much of yourself. Rather, do things because you can—not because you should. There is no one right way to support someone who is grieving. The study advises: "For some, it hurts when others don't mention the loss—and sometimes it hurts when they do. Some individuals need some time alone to get their bearings, while others may wish to regain their identity by resuming their routine, even plunging into activities that keep them too busy to feel."

If you are grieving or involved in caregiving, and no one has reached out to you from your company, be proactive and contact either your boss or the Human Resources department. Discuss your preferences and needs and let them prepare others to support you accordingly. Be sure to let someone know what information you would like shared with whom and whether you want to talk about your experience or would prefer to concentrate on your work. Also, be sure to review your needs for time, privacy, and help with your workload. The hospice study notes: "There's no right way to grieve and no shortcut around it. But grieving is not a weakness, it's a necessity. It is how we heal from our loss and move on. . .the only way past grief is to move through it."

If an employee in your company or a coworker is coming back after a recent death, think ahead how you can best support them in returning to their job.

- Offer your condolences in person or in a note.
- Ask how you can help, unless instructed otherwise.
- Respect the griever's privacy and possible emotional sensitivity and vulnerability.

If you are in a management position and charged with responsibility to prepare coworkers for the return of a grieving employee, be sensitive to their needs as well. When tasks need to be redistributed, thank staff members for their extra effort. Acknowledge them for their cooperation in sharing both the emotional burden and the extra work. When an employee dies, make certain that affected employees know of funeral and memorial arrangements and that they have time to attend.

the ability to serve

One of my favorite and most challenging teachings from John-Roger is: "The willingness to do creates the ability to do." How often do we tell ourselves, "I'm trying" or "I want to, but . . ."? There is a world of difference between trying to do something and doing it. When it comes to being of service to someone in need, we are often challenged to cross this fine line. Some of us convince ourselves that we have a really good reason why we can't be responsive to this other person's need. But if the truth were known, it is we who pay the bigger price for our inability to rise to meet the needs of another. In justifying our lack of availability, we lose the opportunity to make our caring more important than anything else, and we isolate ourselves in our small world of personal convenience. There really is nothing more precious than living love and no better way to expand our hearts than choosing to step outside our comfort zone in service to another.

Exercise 27: My Willingness to Serve

Think about someone you love who is facing critical health challenges, becoming frail, or dying and answer the following questions:

1. What am I doing to nurture, support, and serve this person?
2. With what attitude do I serve?
3. What am I not doing to help them and why? How do I feel about that?
4. What, if anything, am I willing to do differently to help improve the quality of this person's experience of their suffering?

---

chapter 13

key #8:
unearthing your treasures

a precious human life

"Every day, think as you wake up…
Today
I am fortunate to have woken up.
I am alive,
I have a precious human life.
I am not going to waste it.

I am going to use
All my energies to develop myself,
To expand my heart out to others,
To achieve enlightenment for
The benefit of all beings.

I am going to have
Kind thoughts towards others.
I am not going to get angry,
Or think badly about others.

I am going to benefit others
As much as I can."

—*His Holiness the 14th Dalai Lama*

harvesting your life and wisdom

Over the course of a lifetime, each of us accumulates experiences, wisdom, memories, joys, sorrows, and relationships. There are treasures we hold dear—my mother's favorite hat that rides in my car with me, an audiotape of a famous friend reading spiritual poetry to me, love letters from my first love, my brother's friendship, and my writing as a vehicle of expression. Some of us have silly little signature gestures and expressions as well. My friends' son Dan always said, "Whaw, whaw" after telling a joke. During Dan's last week of life, while he was in a coma in the ICU, his father heard the life support machinery go "Whaw, whaw," and he knew that Dan was saying goodbye. Human hearts touch in the most unusual and extraordinary ways!

Whether you are reading this book because you are at your life's end, because you want to help your loved one whose life is ending, or because you work with the dying, this chapter applies to you personally as well as to those you love and serve. This material encourages you to celebrate, to speak up, and to document at least a sketch of who you know yourself to be. Whether you choose to share what you find with others in your lifetime or leave something behind for loved ones to find is up to you. I encourage you to share, because the very act of sharing validates your sense of self-worth and gives others gifts of yourself far more valuable than any material or financial bequest you might send their way.

This chapter is also about doing your part to contribute to a more authentic kind of genealogy in which you breathe life into your memory. Will your life-earned inner treasures die with you, or will you take the time to capture, record, and share them from your point of view? What value and purpose might they serve for those you will eventually leave behind? Your inner legacy becomes an immortal source of nurturance for future generations when gathered, recorded, and passed on in what I call a legacy journal—a gathering place for your stories, wisdom, life lessons, and ponderings. A legacy journal reflects a strong personal affirmation: "I am alive and my life matters!"

A client of mine in her eighties has suffered great loneliness in her life. With no spouse, children, or siblings at this point in her life, it is easy for her to assume no one really cares about her. I've encouraged her to write about her life. At first, she saw no point, thinking there was no one who would care. After I persistently prodded her on, she enrolled in an online memoir class where she wrote weekly responses to the instructor's prompts and discovered the cathartic relief of acknowledging her own truth. She was surprised, as was I, at how fluid and articulate she was about her inner and outer life. It wasn't that she had lived the most fascinating of lives, rather it was the way she captured the joys and sorrows of an ordinary life. This is the point of keeping a legacy journal. It is a way to know yourself more deeply and to gain appreciation for how you have moved through the challenges of your life. It captures a sense of what it is like for you to be you—it gives the insider's view. While seemingly written for others, a legacy journal enables you to bear witness to your own life, to come to terms with it, and to lay claim to yourself before you leave.

Do you want your memory to be interpreted through others, or do you want to tell the truth as you know it? Do you want others to speak for you through the filters of their own experiences of you based on the roles and relationships you had with each other? Or do you want to affirm your truth?

The most common objection to engaging in this process is "It's a nice idea, but I simply do not have the time." Consider the fact that we all have the same twenty-four hours each day. What we do with them is largely a matter of personal choice. Engaging in the process of keeping a legacy journal can fit into your life in small time segments here and there. It need not be burdensome or a big deal. Simply pace yourself and make it part of your daily or weekly routine.

When I was teaching a memoir-writing course at a local oncology support group, one participant, Mary, claimed to be there only to keep her friend company. She insisted there was nothing special about her, and she therefore could not write anything about herself. I coaxed her on with alternative perspectives on the matter. She seemed to respond to my question of what could be said about her that was true in response to future generations wanting to know more about what Grandma Mary was like. Each of us has our own way of being, our anecdotes of life, and stories about our favorite things. Mary surprised us all, but most of all, she surprised herself by how poignantly she wrote. In fact, as the weeks went on, we looked forward to hearing Mary read her assignments. Inside this person who thought she had nothing to say lay treasures that would never have been shared had she not happened upon a memoir-writing class.

Each of us walks through the journey of our life accumulating experiences and a point of view on our own selves, the world, and the others we meet along the way. We gain a sense of how hospitable or inhospitable we find this world to be. If we attempt to be anonymous, even to ourselves, several very sad things happen. First, we fail to appreciate this precious gift of life that is our opportunity to explore ourselves and the world about us. Second, we are likely to be alive but not to thrive—we forego the chance to really know ourselves, to give voice to our existence, to learn and grow and see and be all that we can. Finally, no one else gets to know us either or to benefit from the inner gifts we share. Instead, we silence ourselves and are interpreted by others who see us only through their own filters of understanding, which may or may not yield an accurate picture of who we really are.

It is important to take ownership of the full range of experiences in your life—not just the ones that are fun to share. When we try to paint a pretty picture of who we are and what our life journey has been like, we mislead ourselves and others about the greater realities of life. In fact, sharing about our life challenges and disappointments can give others permission to take theirs out of hiding as well. When we show ourselves, warts and all, we invite others to learn far more about us and through us. Into each life will come sadness, illness, death, betrayal, maybe a divorce or estrangement, and other personal and global tragedies. As you encounter memories of these parts of your life, writing about them can be a cathartic release of unshed tears. Giving expression to them is a way of letting them go or turning the light on them so they don't look so scary from the vantage point of the passage of time.

to share or not to share

A great way to align yourself with the idea of sharing about your life is to understand your motivation and intention for doing so. For example, it might be important to you to experience the catharsis of giving voice to your truth as a gift to yourself. There is something about bearing witness to your own truth that can be extremely liberating and healing. Or you may be focused on wanting to pass on your legacy to your family, friends, and future generations. Or perhaps you want to prepare something for presentation at a memorial service that will one day be held in your honor. Some people are motivated by a terminal diagnosis that imparts a sense of urgency to keep their story alive. So simply ask yourself, "What is my motivation or intention for recording my story from my point of view?"

Whether you are twenty-four or ninety-two, full of vitality or near your life's end, the best way to create momentum is simply to show up on a regular basis. For starters, make a commitment to yourself to focus on this work a minimum number of times each week for a minimum amount of time each session. For example, you might choose to commit to collecting and recording your thoughts and reflections at least three times each week for a minimum of a half hour each time. Set yourself up to win at this by choosing to commit to a schedule you are confident you can fulfill and book your time allotments in your calendar. My calendar is sprinkled with

"Sacred Judith Writing Time." Until you find yourself in the habit of doing this work, make your commitment nonnegotiable—you may have to reschedule certain sessions, but be sure you fulfill your specified weekly commitment. Once you get in the habit, it becomes quite easy and draws you forward.

You needn't limit yourself to words. You might want to create a multimedia legacy journal with memorabilia, photos, film clips, and other things that capture the story of your life.

If you are concerned about where to draw the line between your truth and what might be controversial or too revealing about someone else, be sure to qualify your statements as your personal recollections. Stay focused on those experiences that shaped your life and stay away from making judgments about others. For example, a divorce that occurred because you and your spouse grew apart over time should be referenced in terms of what happened inside of you that brought you to the decision. Write about how that was a turning point in your life.

It seems to me that too many of us don't authentically share of ourselves with each other. We tend to live lives too busy for deep connection and communication. Most of us rarely take the time to bear witness to each other's inner life journey—let alone our own. Our unfamiliarity with this territory makes it all the more challenging to invite intimate sharing of our most meaningful life experiences. This is why I think memoirs and legacy journals are so important, especially within families. They invite contemporaries and future generations to tell their stories as well—not so much about what happened, but about how it touched their lives and what it taught them. It models intimate communications for others and allows us to burst forth from our assigned roles as mother, sister, or daughter to report on the journey that this dynamic human being has taken thus far. It brings us to life as individuals for each other and gives us the opportunity to share our life lessons and wisdom in the hope that it is meaningful and helpful to others. A legacy journal provides links to the interior world of our ancestors. This kind of inner genealogy allows us to know more than just the names and lineage of our family. In fact, a legacy journal is perhaps the most important gift you'll ever give to your family and loved ones. It allows them to see behind your social mask or the role in which they have met you in their lives, to know you as you know yourself.

I encourage you to use this as an opportunity to break through the customary distances that many of us keep between ourselves and our loved ones. Be brave. Share. And be honest. Let your truth about what it is like being you be your most treasured legacy. In the event that you do not choose to share your legacy journal in your lifetime, be sure to let just the right person know where it can be found after you are gone.

family legacy journals

Why wait until you are in your eighties or at the end of your life to create a written legacy of your life? Some couples and families make it a shared project where everyone writes a weekly or monthly reflection. I advise several basic rules for doing so. Everyone promises to tell the truth as they know it and to capture what that truth feels like inside of them. Writing is mandatory, sharing is not. And everyone is encouraged to focus on recording their inner experience without blaming or judging themselves or others. When we allow ourselves to be more transparent with ourselves and each other, we foster an environment of honesty and truth-telling.

Research done in the 1990s by clinical psychologists Marshall P. Duke and Robyn Fivush revealed the impact of sharing family stories on the development and well-being of children in the family. They developed a measure called the "Do You Know?" scale that asked children to answer "yes" or "no" to twenty questions about their knowledge of family members and the family's origins. Correlating their results with a battery of psychological tests indicated that the more children knew about their family history:

- The stronger their sense of control over their lives
- The higher their self-esteem
- The more successfully they believed their family functioned

The key to this was not in the actual information the children knew about their families, rather the existence of a consistent process of passing down family stories which enhanced their sense of well-being and belonging to a larger family. This scale has turned out to be the single best predictor of children's emotional health and happiness. Nurturing intergenerational bonding through sharing both your own and your family's narrative is particularly important for children because their sense of identity tends to get locked-in during adolescence. Do your part for the children in your family. When you write about the harder parts of your life, be sure to include the positive outcomes of your struggles in terms of life lessons learned or your developing greater compassion for the struggles faced by others.

sharing as a service to others

As an author, I have learned many lessons on how sharing my life experience is a service to others. While we experience our lives quite personally, there is a universality to our joys and trials and tribulations that resonates with others. I am amazed and humbled by the tender and vulnerable emails I regularly receive from complete strangers who have read something I wrote that resonated deeply and helped them to know they are not alone in what they are experiencing in this world. A granddaughter reading the stories of her grandmother may recognize herself in an intergenerational pattern and gain a deeper understanding of herself and other family members. So, please—tell your story from the inside out. Let others know what it has been like for you to be you. You never know who will be blessed and helped by seeing themselves in the mirror of you.

how do I organize and package my thoughts?

Whether you ultimately choose to simply stick your toe in the water of reflecting on your life or to dive in headfirst and create a full-blown memoir or multimedia presentation, it all starts with choosing a receptacle for your ponderings—a computer file or folder, a journal, a box of mementos, or a combination of these. Start somewhere. I always keep a file for my notes on each new chapter, book, or project I embark upon. Here I keep random tidbits that show up along my journey and periodically review my entries for inspiration and inclusion in whatever form the project takes. It's important to always date your entries. Make that a habit. Otherwise, it's easy to lose track of the sequence of events in your life or the evolution of your perspective.

Begin with an outline or some sort of structure and set about organizing your thoughts and ponderings into that form. Or decide to give yourself the freedom to not care about organizing your thoughts until a structure or order reveals itself to you. Eventually, random bits and pieces will find their relationship to one another. Just start by opening yourself up to the idea of sharing your story, life lessons, and wisdom and invite your thoughts to emerge. If you find yourself resistant to the idea of sharing your story, write for your own eyes only. Alternatively, you might want to explore why you don't want to share your story by challenging yourself to move beyond your objections.

where to start

Start where your heart is. Ask yourself, "What is most important to me to share about myself and my life?" and follow your own lead. Alternatively, visit a few websites on memoir writing and explore some of the prompts they offer. Respond to whatever catches your attention.

Give yourself the freedom to write in an unedited stream of consciousness and write from your heart, not your head. As Nan Phifer, author of *Memoirs of the Soul*, said: "Record the voyage not of your ego, but of your soul. . . if you want to learn all you can about yourself, to really explore the depth of your soul, then write candidly and honestly." You will find your voice in time and can always come back to edit, but first you must unearth your treasures from within. Don't worry about punctuation, structure, or anything else. Simply gather what is yours and yours alone and have fun with the process. Yes, some memories will be hard and bring you to tears, but consider the fact that bearing witness to what you have gone through in your life can yield a wealth of appreciation and gratitude for your endurance and the life lessons you have harvested, as well as a deeper understanding of what you are made of and how your life's journey has evolved.

The exercises in this chapter are intended to help you gather your treasures from within. This first exercise simply focuses on your favorite things as a point of provoking your memories to flood forward.

Exercise 28: A Few of My Favorite Things

For at least ten of the items on the following list, identify your favorite(s) and share what made/makes them special to you. Include such things as how, when, where, why, and with whom you found this favorite person, expression, or experience and what kinds of feelings you had at the time.

Choose from these favorites:

- Memory from childhood
- Friend from childhood
- Person
- Holiday

- Food or meal
- Quotation or expression
- Book
- Time of year
- Place that is beautiful to me
- Place I have ever visited
- Age I have experienced
- Pet I have had
- Friend
- Movie
- Color
- Teacher
- Mentor
- Song or music
- Hobby
- Birthday so far
- Source of inspiration
- Job
- Smell
- Thing I have ever touched
- Item of clothing
- Piece of jewelry
- Person I loved, but they never knew it
- Surprise
- Celebrity crush
- Relative growing up
- Nonrelative growing up
- Famous person, living or dead
- Compliment someone has ever given me
- Photograph of me

You may want to come back later and record your answers to all the questions. You might also use this list to spark some sharing with your friends, family, and children. Expressing curiosity about each other can draw you closer and demonstrate openness and availability.

––––––––

The next two exercises introduce you to two powerful tools for excavating your memories of the richness of your life. They are an invitation to embrace the life you have lived so far, and to begin to string together the various dimensions of your life.

––––––––

Exercise 29: The Timeline of My Life

First, format your timeline: On a blank sheet of paper, draw a horizontal line across the middle of the page. Next, enter your birthdate on the left side of the line and today's date on the right side. Now, to the right of your birth date, count forward in ten-year segments marking each decade.

Next, record events on your timeline: Mark each event you add to your timeline by indicating the year on the bottom of the line and your age at the top of the line. Now randomly enter the dates of pivotal events and experiences of your life, such as major accomplishments, tragedies, marriages, births of children, beginnings and endings of essential relationships and jobs, moves, discoveries, deaths, changes in health, failures, achievements, and historical events, such as wars or natural disasters. You might want to color-code additional horizontal lines representing the duration of key time periods in your life such as the duration of a marriage or love affair or when you lived in a particular home. Remember to indicate the dates on the bottom of the line and your age and the item being recorded at the top.

Keep asking yourself, "What else?" until you run out of either space or ideas. You may also want to create mini timelines for each decade of your life so you will have more space to fill in more details about where you were and what happened at that time. Or you could do mini timelines for various themes of your life, such as your education, jobs, achievements, major relationships, or whatever inspires you.

Once you have completed this exercise, keep your timeline(s) handy so that you can add to it (them) as you recall missing elements. Also, use it (them) as a source of inspiration as you move forward or simply have it (them) as a visual reference point of your life to share.

———

This next exercise introduces the concept of mind mapping, which is a nonlinear way to access random thoughts, memories, and ideas from within you without having to worry about them presenting themselves in a tidy, sequential outline fashion. Mind mapping also helps to clarify the major themes you want to touch upon and how to organize and interrelate your themes. For example, you might want to capture information about the periods of time in your life, the roles you have played, or the kinds of lessons you have learned. Or you might want to mind map what you do and do not know about your family history to add to the family knowledge base.

———

Exercise 30: Mind Mapping

On a blank sheet of paper, draw a small circle in the center with your name in it followed by the phrase "my life so far" or pick a theme or dimension of your life such as family, career, passions, or whatever else comes to mind and write that next to your name. Draw branches coming off your circle to gather ideas about the theme you have chosen and label them. For example, if you have a branch labeled, "Things I am passionate about," ask yourself "What am I most passionate about?" Whatever responses come up for you, use them to label sub-branches off the "passions" branch. Then you create branches off each sub-branch to collect relevant details. Do this to whatever level of detail works for you to provoke ideas of how to organize your thoughts about your life. As with the timeline process, you may find a juicy branch and choose to do an entire mind map of that branch alone. For a visual representation of this technique, visit mindmapping.com.

Both your timelines and mind maps are wonderful reference tools where you can gather ideas. Use them when ready to write a new piece or when you want to tie together the themes of existing journal entries.

This next exercise invites you to focus on one idea or memory and to record and develop the specifics.

Exercise 31: The Moments/Events That Shaped My Life

Make a list of at least five moments or events that shaped your life and perhaps changed its course. For each one, write at least three sentences that capture the essence of why you chose that particular moment or event. Pick one and write 800 to 1,000 words about it, capturing what it was like for you to go through that experience, how it changed you and your life, and the life lessons that have come to you through that experience. Be as descriptive as possible of the people or situation being described to bring your story to life.

Making lists can be a useful technique to remember certain aspects of your life as well. When I start a list in my notes, I always consider them a running list. Sometimes, when I am uninspired during a writing session, I will revisit my notes, come upon a list, and either be triggered to write about something there or think of something to add to the list for later. In the event that you never get around to writing about the things on your lists, the lists themselves can serve as valuable and interesting insights into you for others to consider after you are gone.

Exercise 32: Using Lists and Sentence Starters

Sentence starters are yet another wonderful way to stimulate memories worth writing about. They focus your attention in a particular direction to be explored. Start several lists in your journal, using a blank page for each one. Lists might include some of the following, or you might think of others that are more productive and useful for you. Be sure to date all entries.

- Things I am afraid of
- Things that bring me joy
- The biggest decision(s) I ever made
- Things I worry about
- The times when I feel most free
- The times when I feel most restricted or confined
- People who have touched my life the most so far
- What I enjoy most about my life right now
- What I am learning the most from in my life right now
- What challenges me the most right now in my life
- The pets I have had
- Our family holiday traditions

Photographs and memorabilia have stories to tell as well, though unless we let others in on their significance, a pressed rose in mom's scrapbook is just a dead rose rather than the rose daddy gave her the day he first told her he loved her. Pictures tell important stories too—often revealing more about what isn't shown in the image than what is apparent.

Exercise 33: Pictures and Memorabilia

Go through old picture albums, scrapbooks, photographs, and other memorabilia to help jog your memory. Make a list of those pictures and items that are most meaningful to you. Gather them together or identify them in some way for reference to your writing. For each one, write at least two to three sentences to remind you of the memories you hold about them.

Be sure to gather and list at least ten of your favorite photographs of yourself. For each one, write about what is so special or pleasing to you about that picture and the backstory about who took the picture, where you were, and any other revealing details. You can use this list to inspire you in future writing sessions. For now, pick one picture or piece of memorabilia and capture the story and memory it holds for you. Be sure to include descriptions of people and events that engage the senses of your readers—tastes, smells, sights, what touched you inside and out, and what you heard. Provide vivid descriptions to engage your readers. For example, describe what you were aware of with your senses, such as pleasant or noxious odors, things you touched or the way your body felt, revolting or scrumptious tastes, and what sounds you heard—a mosquito buzzing by your ear or sirens coming closer. When you are describing a person, see if you can convey in words their stature, posture, their way of walking and moving, or any habitual gestures they had/have. Visualize their skin, teeth, hair, voice, or any other notable features.

Sometimes objects carry deep memories. Upon the occasion of his father's death and the need to empty the family home, a friend of mine began retrieving his personal treasures. He then took them one at a time and posted a photo and reflection of each one on Facebook. He has been remembering and learning all sorts of things about himself, and we are all getting to know him more intimately. Hopefully, these posts will eventually become a book.

When writing about your life, write in the first person—claim your experiences and feelings as your own. Use the guidelines of memoir rather than autobiography in your approach. In other words, rather than chronologically recording the facts of your life, gather anecdotal sketches by zooming in on defining moments, experiences, and people in your life. Seek to share the flavor of who you are and what it has been like for you to be you.

capturing the inner legacy of the elderly and dying

In addition to working on your own legacy journal, you may want to assist an elderly or dying person to unearth their treasures as well. I've done this using an audio recorder and many of the ideas offered in this chapter. In addition to helping to record the intergenerational genealogy of your family, just the act of showing interest can deeply touch the elderly and dying.

When we dig below the surface of each other, all sorts of surprises and wonders can be found. Doing this with someone who is terminally ill helps them to review their life, draws you closer together, and reminds them that they still matter.

This is about reflecting upon and celebrating the life each of us is living. At a recent memorial service for my friends' thirty-one-year-old son, I made it a point to emphasize that he was born one moment of one day and died one moment of another day, but he lived 11,074 days in between! It is important to celebrate the life lived as well as the passing of a person from this world. Please don't let the wisdom and other inner treasures you have gathered throughout your days disappear when you leave. Take the time to share who you know yourself to be and what has mattered most to you.

key #9:
putting your ducks in a row before you go

"Leave this world a little better than you found it."
—*Robert Baden Powell*

what does it mean to put your affairs in order?

As long as we are alive, of age, and deemed mentally competent, our life and how we live it is legally our business. However, if we become unconscious (even during surgery), become mentally incompetent, or die, we will not be available to make important decisions for ourselves unless we have filed legal documents that specify our wishes and appointed someone else to speak on our behalf. Otherwise, the laws of the state in which we reside determine who gets to make decisions on our behalf. The younger we are, the less relevant we tend to think end-of-life issues are. If you are of age and mentally competent, you have the legal right to have a voice in what happens to you in the event that you lose your mental competency or die. The catch is this: to activate our rights, we have the responsibility of documenting and communicating our wishes in advance of need in a manner that will be legally binding. Each of us must face the fact that unless we take the time to figure out what we want, others will decide on our behalf. They may or may not choose what we would have chosen for ourselves.

Putting your affairs in order is fundamentally about making thoughtful decisions in advance of need. There are three primary areas to consider:

1. Arranging for healthcare decisions to be made in the event that you are unable to speak for yourself. This involves documenting your healthcare choices and appointing someone as your Healthcare Proxy so they can be sure your wishes are honored.
2. Creating a legal will or trust that specifies what you want to happen to your money and belongings in the event of your death and who you want to take charge of honoring your wishes.
3. Determining whether you want any religious or civil ceremony or gathering to take place when you die and deciding what you want to happen to your body when you die.

Addressing these areas involves educating ourselves about our options and understanding the pros and cons of each choice so we can make informed decisions. It is important to understand that, in the absence of legally documenting and communicating our choices in each of these areas, decisions will be made based upon the laws of the state in which we live. Alternatively, legal documents prepared in advance of need allow our wishes to be fulfilled. Not putting our affairs in order represents our choice to have no say in these matters. It also subjects our loved ones to the awful task of trying to imagine what we would have wanted and possibly fighting over differing points of view, rather than being able to simply grieve their loss while honoring your wishes.

Many people think their affairs are in order because they have been to a lawyer and filled out the appropriate documents. If so, congratulations for taking this important step. However:

- Did you fill out your forms in haste?

- Did you have a sufficient understanding of the issues involved?
- Have you effectively communicated your wishes to a loved one or let someone know where your documents are located?

Many an executor of an estate must search high and low to find the deceased one's legal documents, important papers, and passwords for online accounts. In terms of preferences for end-of-life rituals, only a handful of us communicate with our loved ones about what would be meaningful to us.

why you should always be prepared

Being prepared becomes critically important when facing our own long-term illness or death, or that of another. Here are two sobering thoughts:

1. According to the US Census Bureau, 28 percent of us die before reaching the age of sixty-five.
2. About 58 percent of us die without a healthcare proxy and 50 percent without a last will and testament or a trust to direct the disposal of our personal belongings and assets.

We all need to understand the issues involved in end-of-life planning. A lack of understanding and preparation leads to unnecessary stress and ill-informed decision-making.

Whenever I go on a trip, even if only overnight, I always clean the house before I leave. Aside from wanting to return to an orderly home, somewhere in my consciousness I imagine that I may not return. In the event of my death, I want to give the impression that I lived an orderly life. There is wisdom in creating the habits that maintain order in our lives. Yet for me, as with most of us, just below the surface things can be quite chaotic. Keeping up with our lives, work, relationships, finances, hopes, and dreams is a lot to handle. Life gets very messy, and all of a sudden one day, usually when we are so overcommitted that there is not time for even one more minor errand on our to-do list, the phone rings and we are told that we have a terminal illness. Or our best friend's mother just died unexpectedly. Or someone we love who lives ten hours away and is about to die is asking to see us. Death comes with no regard for our plans. In spite of all the inconvenience, stress, drama, and trauma, we are called upon to rise to the occasion, to lovingly say goodbye, and in some cases, to carry out our loved one's wishes for bringing closure to his or her life. This work is meant to be done by each of us gradually and thoughtfully over time—not by our loved ones in a panic while grieving for us. No matter how young or old, rich or poor, nice or nasty, we all have one thing in common—there is a 100 percent probability that one day in the future we will die. The three big questions are: When? How? Will I have my affairs in order—mentally, emotionally, spiritually, socially, financially, legally, and medically?

With our increasing diversity of beliefs and family structures, we can no longer assume who will be there with us or how willing they will be to honor our wishes. Some family members may find it inconvenient to disrupt their own lives to comfort us or tend to our affairs, or they might be challenged to support our wishes if these conflict with their own beliefs. That's the hard reality for many of us. In far too many cases, loved ones are left to clean up a tangled mess that we had every intention of dealing with before dying but didn't know that time would run out first. If you want to prevent misunderstandings, second-guessing about your wishes, hurt feelings, family dramas, and potential lawsuits, you need to clearly express your preferences in legally binding documents. If you haven't yet put your affairs in order, there is another great payoff to consider. Just imagine that wonderful feeling you get each year when your taxes are done, multiplied by about 10,000 times! That's how wonderful you will feel and how proud you will be of yourself when you get this handled!

three motivational stories to move you to action

Hopefully, I have convinced you to get your affairs in order. If not, consider these three stories that illustrate the quagmire that can result from not legally documenting your wishes.

Story One: My Aunt Carol

Despite the fact that I was her closest living relative, my relationship with my Aunt Carol had evolved into holiday phone calls that lacked any intimacy. One day, I called her and was shocked to hear a recording that her number had been disconnected. I panicked but was determined to find out what had happened. I ended up doing a live-cam internet search of her street to find the name of her church down the block. I called the church to get a message to her friends, and I was able to make contact with a neighbor in her building, who turned out to be a Godsend in helping me understand and deal with Carol's situation. Carol had been in the hospital for over three months, and no one knew how to reach me.

Carol had rented a room in her apartment to a man who had been living there for several years. Apparently, this man had been psychologically abusive and threatening her, and Carol was desperately trying to get rid of him. The tenant, under threat of killing her dog, pressured Carol into appointing him as her Healthcare Proxy. He disconnected her phone, moved her from hospital to hospital so her friends couldn't find her, and blocked their visitations when they showed up. In the meantime, he lived rent-free in her apartment and did nothing to promote Carol's well-being. She was essentially lost in the system.

When I arrived on the scene, the hospital was delighted to find someone who actually cared about Carol. However, their hands were tied because this man had pressured Carol into appointing him as her Healthcare Proxy. Eventually, the hospital petitioned the court to appoint a legal guardian for Carol and recommended me for the position. The tenant was there seeking guardianship as well, but I was appointed. I went to the hospital immediately to take charge, signed all the necessary forms, and began a dialogue with her doctors to coordinate her care. Three days later, she died, and all my "authority" died with her.

The tenant blocked my access to Carol's apartment, preventing me from even getting her clothes for the funeral or from being able to search for the original copy of her will, which was needed for probate. The bottom line: her meager estate, which was intended to go to her church, was spent on legal fees. The tenant disappeared after stripping her apartment.

Story Two: My Friend Betsy

Several years ago, my friend Betsy, who lives in Connecticut, received an early morning phone call from the New York City Police Department. They were calling to inform her that a dead body had been found in her brother's apartment. The body had been there long enough to be decomposed beyond recognition, and the police needed dental records to determine the identity of the deceased. For two days Betsy was embroiled in a legal quagmire, along with experiencing the shock and emotional distress of knowing that it probably was her brother yet hoping that it wasn't. In the absence of knowing the name of her brother's dentist, the police could not verify the identity of the deceased, who turned out to be her brother. Consequently, they were also unable to verify that Betsy was indeed his sister. Legalities can be quite sticky matters.

There is an important, albeit unpleasant, lesson in this story. Some of us do die in unpleasant ways that require dental records to confirm our identity. Among your important papers, be sure to keep an up-to-date list of your key contacts, including your dentist.

Story Three: My Client Jeffrey

Jeffrey's mother, Ann, is in her sixties and recently retired from a job she loved. Within six months she became depressed and chronically ill. Dementia started to set in, and Jeffrey scrambled to put his mother's affairs in order before it was too late. In addition to her three children, Ann had a boyfriend twenty years her junior who had been living with her for the past ten years. Jeffrey suspected that his mother had been supporting her boyfriend.

Ann had repeatedly told her son that she wanted him to have her house but never expressed this or anything else in a legal will or trust. Ann is currently hospitalized with advanced dementia and a poor prognosis. Given the rate of her decline, it is too late for Jeffrey to move any of his mother's assets out of her name, due to possible conflicts with Medicaid rules. The three siblings are fighting with each other and posturing against the live-in boyfriend. No one has the legal authority to do anything. Jeffrey did manage to get his mother to appoint him as her Healthcare Proxy but not to file a legal will before her mental capacity was too impaired. Imagine how different this picture would be had Ann put her affairs in order.

You may not think that situations like these would ever happen in your family. The people in these stories didn't think so either. But situations like these can happen when advance planning is not done. Better to be safe than sorry.

my father's gift

One of the things I have come to admire about my father was the gift of ease and grace he gave us by thoroughly putting his affairs in order. For many years, prior to his death, he had an envelope on his refrigerator that said, "In the event of my death." Honestly, I criticized him unmercifully behind his back about that envelope. In fact, he had provided my brother, the Executor of his estate, with step-by-step directions and put him through what my brother called "the drill" every year to prepare him to take charge of our father's estate.

Dad's preparation was a gift of loving that really made it easy for us. For that I am enormously grateful.

My brother had our father's essential information entered in his computer and updated it annually after his January visit with Dad. Their annual drill consisted of updating the following information:

- Contact information for his accountant, broker, doctors, dentist, and banker
- Contact information on all friends and which ones to notify in the event of his death
- Keys to his home, mailbox, car, storage unit, and safety deposit box
- Brokerage statements plus his manual bookkeeping system for tracking all sources of income
- Checking accounts, both individual and joint, and monthly reconciliations
- Monthly bills and how to pay them
- All subscriptions and how to cancel them and get refunds
- A list of all online accounts, including usernames, passwords, and security questions and answers
- A list of items he specifically wanted to go to certain people
- Ownership documents for his home and car
- Insurance policies: life, health, auto
- Copies of his will/trust and Healthcare Proxy
- Contracts and instructions for his funeral, cremation, death certificate, and the disposal of his cremains
- The process of acting as Executor for distribution of death certificates and trust to establish legal standing, filing tax returns, disposal of apartment, car, and assets in apartment
- Sale and distribution of portfolio

My brother made it a point to get to know our dad's friends, attorney, accountant, and financial advisor. When Dad died, my brother knew what to do without a protracted and stressful discovery process.

In some ways, Dad's methodical and thorough preparation for death became a bit comical. He wrote down all prepaid newspaper and magazine subscriptions, so my brother not only had contact information for cancellation but could get the refunds. His Christmas card file had stars by the names of those who should be notified of his death. We were very blessed by our dad's attention to his own end-of-life affairs. It drew my brother and father closer and provided comfort to all in the family. Each of us is a repository of information and memories that dies with us if not recorded or shared. Helping a parent or other loved one to put his or her affairs in order can be a wonderful opportunity to establish a level of trust that draws you even closer than before.

acknowledging the elephant in the room

Hopefully, your journey through this book has helped you to create a healthier relationship with your mortality. Now that you have lightened up your consciousness where death is concerned, you are well-prepared to attend to your end-of-life planning with greater ease and grace. Even if you think you have done a great job of tending to your affairs, read on—you might pick up a vital tip you overlooked. For those who are beginning this process, this chapter highlights the key decisions you need to attend to. This is not something that should be done in a rush. Take your time, let it be a gradual and thoughtful process.

You might benefit from inviting your family members into this process as well. If you have a family that doesn't talk about death, you can do them a great service by taking the initiative to broach the subject of this giant elephant in the room. This is, after all, how we break through the Death Taboo—one person and one family at a time. If we don't do this work, we could go to our graves in emotional isolation from one another. Anyone over eighteen has the right to make their own end-of-life decisions. If they don't do so in advance of need, the state in which they live will make those decisions for them. When we educate ourselves and our families about these rights and responsibilities, we are all empowered.

If you would like to invite your family into a dialogue about an end-of-life planning process, start speaking to one person. Let them know that it is important to you to be sure they understand their legal rights regarding end-of-life planning. If they object to having the conversation, which many will do, be persistent and let them know it is important to you and explain why. Begin by asking basic questions like, "Do you have a healthcare proxy?" "A will?" If they don't, ask if they know the legal significance of these documents, why they are essential, and the importance of reviewing documents and keeping them up-to-date. As any salesperson knows, you have to ask for the sale—so ask them to commit to a time to start this work together.

In my experience, getting people beyond the first step of being educated about these matters to actually filling out the legal documents and communicating their wishes to their family, lawyers, and doctors can be filled with procrastination and other types of conscious and unconscious resistance. Persist. Keep your eye of the goal of supporting each other in doing this important work. Once you have one person's support, ask them to help you to engage the rest of your family in getting the legalities of their end-of-life wishes in order. This is a great service to your family, opening the door to far greater honesty and intimacy about other things you find hard to talk about.

The laws of each state are different, and medical, legal, and tax policies are always in a process of evolution. Therefore, it is critically important that we consult with medical, legal, and financial advisors to be sure that we are putting our affairs in order according to the current laws of the state where we live. Go to your state government's website to check for changes.

who needs to put their affairs in order?

Remember—end-of-life planning is not just for old people. The reality is you don't have to be old to die. Health tragedies and death happen every single day to healthy young people texting in cars, drinking and driving, on the football field, in domestic disputes, and in innumerable other ways. (For example, we have a new baby in our family who was just named after his mother's brother, who died at the age of seventeen in a bizarre car accident.) Anyone over the age of eighteen who is mentally competent and does not put his or her affairs in order is forfeiting the right to have a say in their health-care in the event of their loss of consciousness or decision-making capacity. They also forfeit the right to have a say in the disposition of their body and belongings in the event of their death.

the impact of mental capacity on end-of-life decision-making

Mental capacity means that you have the ability to speak on your own behalf. Specifically, you need to be able to do three things: understand relevant information, weigh the pros and cons of each, and communicate your choice.

For a variety of reasons, doctors, professional advisors, or loved ones may question our mental capacity. However, only a court of law can determine that we are either temporarily or permanently incapable of managing some or all personal affairs in our own best interest. Even if someone believes that we are incapable of making decisions, they must honor our expressed wishes unless a court declares us legally incapacitated. When someone is legally determined to be incapable of looking out for his or her own best interests, the court usually appoints a guardian or conservator to do so on their behalf.

An individual may be deemed clinically incapacitated by a doctor due to such temporary conditions as delirium, depression, coma, or intoxication. This can be a somewhat dicey area. Generally, a doctor's determination of incapacity is rarely litigated in court. However, situations may occur where a doctor's action on a patient's behalf is legally challenged by either the patient or a family member.

Mental capacity is a deal-breaker when it comes to having the authority to make our own decisions about our affairs. Once legally pronounced incapacitated, all rights to make our own decisions are lost. Thus, it is critically important to have preferences regarding end-of-life issues well documented to guide anyone making decisions on our behalf, whether as a guardian, proxy, one who holds a durable power of attorney for us, or the Executor of our estate after we have died.

the top excuses we use for not putting our affairs in order

While there are clearly excellent reasons for putting our affairs in order, there are also powerful reasons why we do not do so. Many individuals are paralyzed from taking action by deep irrational fears. Hopefully, reading this book will have dissipated your fears. Otherwise, your fears manifest as excuses that you use to convince yourself it's not that important for you to tend to these matters right now. You can just keep putting it off, and you don't have to take a look at the irrational fears that are running you. For example, some people tell themselves, "If I do the paperwork, then I will die soon. If I don't do it, I won't die because I won't be ready yet." Or "I'll do it later. I'm too busy." Or "I'm young, and therefore I have plenty of time." Others think planning will be overwhelming or creepy, too expensive, or they don't want anyone to know their business. This results in some frightening statistics. For example, in 2014, the *Forbes* magazine article "American's Ostrich Approach to Estate

Planning" reported the following survey results about why people don't have wills:

- 57 percent said they "just haven't gotten around to making one."
- 22 percent felt that making a will wasn't urgent.
- 17 percent didn't think they needed a will.
- 14 percent didn't have a will because they don't want to think about death.

It's unfortunate to think how many of us are causing unnecessary suffering for ourselves and our loved ones because of such poor excuses for not putting our affairs in order.

end-of-life healthcare planning made really easy

As discussed in Chapter 4, our culture of death is being overhauled. One of the key initiatives is to educate the public about Advance Healthcare Planning (AHP). The focus has been primarily on the forms we need to fill out and why they are so important. But there is so much more to it that is far more essential. Advance Healthcare Planning is about providing clear and convincing evidence of your wishes in the event of a life-or-death health crisis when you are unable to speak on your own behalf.

Here's how AHP works. The legal requirements, forms, and recommendations for expressing your wishes are regulated by each state and vary from state to state. Your state government's website will inform you of what is required in your state. Much of the information in this section is sourced from the National Hospice and Palliative Care Organization (nhpco.com). It provides extremely clear information about AHP and provides downloadable forms for each state.

If you spend a significant amount of time in more than one state or country, be sure to fill out forms for those multiple locations and carry them with you when you travel. This is important because not all states and countries have legal reciprocity with one another.

Generally speaking, there are two documents involved. The first is a Healthcare Proxy, which is a legal document in which you empower someone else to speak on your behalf regarding end-of-life healthcare. The second is a Living Will, which is considered a legal instrument in some states but not in others. A Living Will is intended for the purpose of giving specific information about what kinds of life-sustaining treatments you do and do not want. In some states, these documents are combined as one.

Unfortunately, most of us have been presented with these documents along with a package of forms that we are filling out with our attorney as part of our estate planning, or we are asked to fill them out when being admitted to the hospital. Both of these circumstances are typically stressful situations. As a result, we rarely understand the full implications and intricacies and fill them out in a rush.

Most of us who have filled out our Advance Healthcare Directives are woefully in the dark about some very important aspects of how this all works. Basically, filling out the forms simply isn't enough. That's only one of five critically important things you have to do to ensure that whomever you appoint as your Healthcare Proxy will be able to speak competently on your behalf. Here are five key things you need to do.

1. Educate yourself. Before filling out any forms, it is important to educate ourselves about all the terms and nuances involved. This includes understanding the purpose of each form as well as what it can and cannot do. Here are some fundamental points to be aware of:

- A Healthcare Proxy is a legal document that designates both a Proxy and Alternate Proxy to make healthcare decisions on your behalf. The alternate serves if the Proxy is unable to for some reason. This document has no expiration date but can be overridden by either a revised form or by your spoken word (when conscious and mentally competent). The person you appoint as your proxy is only called upon if and when important healthcare decisions need to be made and you are unable to do so for yourself. This means anytime you are being anesthetized for surgery, are unconscious briefly or for an extended period of time, or are declared mentally incompetent.

There is a clause in the Healthcare Proxy that refers to anatomical gifts. Here you are given the opportunity to document your wishes regarding the donation of your entire body or designated body parts at the time of your death. You can also specify whether this gift is for the purposes of transplantation, therapy, advancement of medical or dental science, research, or education pursuant to the Uniform Anatomical Gift Act. In support of your Anatomical Gift wishes, you may also have to file forms with the specific medical or research facility you have chosen to be the recipient of your anatomical gifts. These documents should be kept together with your Healthcare Proxy, and both documents need to be in agreement with one another.

When selecting a Healthcare Proxy and Alternate Proxy, your obvious choice is often not the right one. Don't worry about offending anyone for not choosing them but be sure to explain to them why you made another choice. For example, my brother was my obvious choice, but when I reflected on how hard it was for him to be around our mother when she was dying, I realized how hard it would be for him to serve me in that way. I chose someone else who I have instructed to make sure my brother will be well-informed and able to just focus on being my loving brother. Other than the legal criteria spelled out by state laws, consider the following in choosing a proxy. Pick someone who:

- Knows you well and will respect your wishes and needs, even if they would make different personal choices
- Can provide a safe emotional space to share your thoughts and feelings without imposing theirs on you
- Will be able to take care of his/herself while serving you in this capacity.
- Will support your needs even when the going gets tough
- Will be able to handle potential conflicts between your family, friends, doctors, and caregivers to ensure your wishes are honored
- Will stay informed of your condition and be available to make important decisions
- Is likely to be available in the future. For example, does he/she live close by? If not, will they come if needed?

• A Living Will is not always considered a legal document. However, its purpose is to provide clear and convincing evidence of your wishes regarding care and treatment in the event that you are deemed to have no reasonable expectation of recovery. The purpose of having a Living Will is to exercise your right to instruct your doctors and caregivers to withhold or withdraw treatments that would simply prolong your life under such conditions and to focus instead on keeping you comfortable and pain-free. Specific treatments sometimes withheld or withdrawn include:

- Cardiac Resuscitation (CPR) is a group of treatments

used when someone's heart and/or breathing ceases. CPR attempts to restart the heart and breathing through mouth-to-mouth breathing, pressing on the chest to circulate the blood, electric shock, and/ or drugs to stimulate the heart. When used quickly in response to a sudden event like a heart attack or drowning, CPR can be life-saving. However, if some-one has stopped breathing for more than four to six minutes, lack of oxygen to the brain may lead to brain damage. It is important to realize that the suc-cess rate for CPR is extremely low for people at the end of a terminal disease process—especially for the elderly, for whom successful CPR, if achieved at all, is seldom sustainable and often results in broken ribs.

- Mechanical respiration involves inserting a tube through the nose or mouth and into the windpipe, forcing air into the lungs. For the dying patient, mechanical ventilation often merely prolongs the dying process until some other body system fails. It can supply oxygen, but it cannot improve the under-lying condition.

- Artificial nutrition and hydration can save one's life by supplementing or replacing ordinary eating and drinking when used while the body is healing. It can also be used long-term for those with serious intesti-nal disorders or irreversible and end-stage conditions. Withdrawing artificial nutrition and hydration does not cause starvation or pain to the patient, and no legal or ethical issues exist when done in accordance with the patient's wishes. It is the underlying dis-ease, *not* the withdrawal of treatment, that causes death.

- Antibiotics are often used in hospitals and other healthcare facilities where elderly and terminally ill patients are vulnerable to contagious and opportunistic infections. Antibiotics tend to weaken the immune system and make the patient susceptible to other infections in a downward spiral of one infection and antibiotic after another.

- Maximum pain relief, including the use of narcotic medications for the terminally ill patient, is considered by many to be truly compassionate and humane. It is for this purpose that these medications exist because they enable doctors to effectively treat most pain and keep the patient comfortable.

2. Fill out your forms. Once you have educated yourself about choosing a Healthcare Proxy and the decisions that he/she could be called upon to make on your behalf, filling out your forms should be straightforward. Remember, you need to speak to both your Proxy and Alternate Proxy to get their consent before appointing them. There are lots of wonderful websites to consult about the ins and outs of Advance Healthcare Planning that provide downloadable forms for every state.

Exercise 34: Filling Out My Forms

Go to caringinfo.org and download your state-specific Advance Directive forms. Not all states use the same terminology for these forms. For example, in Kansas the Healthcare Proxy is called a Durable Power of Attorney for Health Care Decisions and the Living Will is called the Kansas Declaration. Referencing the information above, your own research, and the state form instructions:

• Fill out your forms.

- Discuss your wishes with your primary and alternate proxies.
- Copy and distribute your forms.
- Schedule your annual review date of your forms on your calendar for the next five years.

---

3. Communicate effectively. Talk to your healthcare proxy, family, loved ones, and doctors about the specifics of your wishes regarding end-of-life care. Don't be surprised if they resist or insist that they don't want to talk about things like that. Ask them to listen because it is important to you and because you do not want any squabbling or misunderstanding over your wishes. Be sure to have a thorough conversation with your appointed proxy and alternate proxy about what you are asking them to do. Before you appoint them, make sure they understand your wishes and are capable and willing to honor them.

4. Distribute and enforce. Plain and simple—what good are our forms if no one knows where they are or what they say? Know where your forms are located; make copies and distribute them to your doctors, proxy, and alternate proxy; keep a copy in your wallet; and bring a copy when being admitted to the hospital or having same-day surgery—in other words, anytime you might be put under anesthesia. Also, keep a copy of your Healthcare Proxy and Living Will in the glove compartment of your car and bring them with you whenever traveling, especially overseas.

5. Review your decisions at least annually. When looking over your forms each year, be sure to check online to find out if there have been any changes in your state's laws regarding AHP. If so, review those to be sure your forms and understanding of the laws are up to date. If needed, redo your forms and redistribute them as discussed in #4 above. Review your Healthcare Proxy and Living

Will each year to be sure they remain an accurate reflection of your wishes. Also, review your forms whenever there is a major change in the law, when there is a new medical treatment option that might affect your choices, or if you receive a terminal diagnosis, have a change of marital status, or want to change your proxy or alternate proxy. Relationships change and maybe you need to rethink who your primary and alternate healthcare proxies are.

Advance healthcare planning is your right, but it is also your responsibility to get in the driver's seat and exercise that right. It's not a one-time thing. Circumstances change and so do our minds. Pay attention and take care of your precious self so others can take care of you according to your wishes.

other healthcare considerations

• The MOLST (Medical Orders for Life-Sustaining Treatments) or the POLST (Portable or AKA Physician Orders for Life-Sustaining Treatment) form is filled out by a doctor and defines the goals for care of a seriously ill patient. It serves the purpose of ensuring that these end-of-life care instructions are effectively communicated and will be honored by all healthcare personnel. In essence it translates the patient's wishes into doctor's orders. This is especially important as a MOLST is a doctor's order, which holds more weight in a medical setting because it is precise and can easily be interpreted in an emergency. A MOLST is most helpful for patients with serious health conditions who might be transported by EMS back-and-forth between their home or a long-term-care facility and hospital.

The MOLST form goes from one place to another with the patient so that all medical personnel will know what the doctor has ordered, per the patient's wishes, in terms of life sustaining treatments, future hospitalization and transfer, antibiotics, treatment guidelines, and other instructions.

Unlike the Healthcare Proxy and Living Will, which only take effect in the event that an individual can no longer make decisions for him or herself due to diminished mental capacity, the MOLST takes effect immediately and is not contingent upon the patient losing the capacity to make complex medical decisions.

The MOLST form is bright pink, so it is easily recognizable and is typically placed in the very front of a patient resident's file. As with all directives, the MOLST should be reviewed periodically, including whenever the patient is transferred from one care facility to another, when there is a substantive change in the patient's condition, or if the patient's preferences change.

• A Do Not Resuscitate order (DNR) requests that you not be given cardiopulmonary resuscitation (CPR) if your heart stops or if you stop breathing. In the absence of a DNR, medical and EMS personnel are legally bound to try to resuscitate any patient whose heart has stopped or who has stopped breathing. The choice to have a DNR or not is a direct reflection of the patient's personal beliefs regarding death. Some people say, "Do everything you can to save me." Others, taking into consideration the relative probability of success of CPR-based on the patient's condition, may choose to post a DNR. For example, if the patient is elderly and infirm, medical intervention may be perceived as invasive rather than helpful.

A DNR can be part of your advance directives form or you can obtain a DNR Order from your state department of health or the hospital or long-term care facility where you will be located. Some facilities have their own preferred form, so be sure to ask and use their form if available. Also ask your doctor to put your DNR Order in your medical chart. DNR orders are accepted by doctors and hospitals in all states. There is also a nonhospital DNR that can be kept visible in the home or bedside in a nonhospital setting. This is very important because, in the event that emergency personnel are called to care for you, they are also required to do what is necessary to stabilize a person for transfer to a hospital, both from accident sites and from a home or nonhospital facility. However, if EMS personnel are presented with a valid DNR form signed by your doctor, or they see that you have a standard DNR bracelet on, they must comply with the DNR order.

Unfortunately, the reverse can be true as well. Many studies have shown that even when a DNR exists, it is not unusual that concern for a patient's safety by medical and emergency personnel can get confused with the intent of these documents, resulting in unwanted life-saving treatments being administered.

legal, financial, and personal end-of-life planning made really easy

The material in this section is accurate to the best of my knowledge. However, I am not a lawyer, accountant, or financial advisor. Also, laws and rules vary from state to state and evolve over time. So, please seek confirmation from professionals when putting your own legal and financial affairs in order.

minimizing professional fees

Here you will find many helpful ideas that are often overlooked. However, it is no substitute for professional input from your financial, legal, and tax advisors. There are really three dimensions to all of this: educating yourself about your options, making choices, and then having the professionals make your decisions legal.

If your personal information is well organized and easy to find and you have appointed a competent person to serve as Executor of your estate, then things are likely to go smoothly. However, if this is not the case, large sums of money will likely be diverted to lawyers and accountants to collect the information needed to finalize your affairs, not to mention the emotional drama this may cause for your loved ones. No one wants to see the estate of a loved one ravaged by professional service fees. Too often, the deceased is the only one who knew the answers to many essential questions that must be answered after death. The more you anticipate and document what will be needed, the less others will have to figure out at the expense of your estate. There are numerous workbooks on the market to gather your information. Some of them go into so much detail, I find them discouraging by virtue of the sheer amount of information that must be collected. What you need depends on how complicated your financial life is and whether or not you have professionals already guiding you. To give you a sense of what you will need to do, I have provided highlights below. Just keep in mind that legal fees for a simple will are several hundred to a thousand dollars. The legal fees associated with finalizing an estate where there is no will or a poorly written one will run thousands of dollars and potentially deplete or significantly diminish the estate.

filing a death certificate

Before any legal matters can be tended to when someone has died, the Executor of his or her estate needs to file a death certificate. If you have been appointed Executor of someone's estate, be sure to secure the following information from them before they die:

- His or her full legal name and marital status
- Other names by which he/she has been known
- Date and place of birth
- Social Security number
- Veteran's Serial Number if applicable
- Military service—which branch and what years
- Occupation, employer, and years in the field
- Full legal name of spouse (living or dead) and his or her date and place of birth and Social Security number

- Location of marriage certificate
- Name of his or her father and his place of birth
- Maiden name of his or her mother and her place of birth
- Country of citizenship
- A list of his or her remaining blood relatives
- Proof of military service if a veteran
- Education and employment history
- List of organizations in which membership is held
- Names of organizations to which donations should be made

wills and trusts

Wills and Trusts are legal instruments that allow us to plan ahead for the disposition of our possessions according to our expressed wishes. The terms of a will legally dictate the disposition of one's property. A will is a legal document that goes into effect only when you die. It directs who will receive your property at your death and identifies someone to act as your Executor to carry out your wishes. Probate is the court-supervised legal process by which this is accomplished. In contrast, a trust is a legal instrument to which you transfer your assets and it does not require probate. A trust goes into effect as soon as you sign it.

The need for a will or a trust has far less to do with how much stuff you have and far more to do with whether or not you want to have any choice in the matter of what happens to your money and belongings. Married individuals and those in committed relationships should each have separate wills. If you have young children, you can use your will to name a guardian for them. If you have pets, be sure to state who you would like to care for them—but ask their permission first. Many people think wills and trusts are only for the wealthy. Not so. They are for the smart, regardless of the modesty or magnitude of one's material and financial wealth. If you have no will, you have no voice.

Regardless of how much or how little you have, death in the absence of a will means that the law of the state in which you reside will direct the disposition of your property. Legally, this is referred to as intestate succession. This may upset a lot of people who may come forward insisting that you had promised something to them. No matter how strongly loved ones feel about what they think you wanted, the law makes no exceptions, even when it is known what you intended or to accommodate special needs or circumstances if there is no legal will. Creating even the simplest legal will is well worth the expense of one visit to an attorney to state your intensions and to spare your loved ones the distress of not knowing your wishes and having to surrender the situation to state law.

While state laws differ, there is a fairly consistent pattern of awarding the property of the deceased to spouses and blood relatives. For some reason, there are a lot of misconceptions about the typical patterns of distribution. For example, many people assume that if someone dies without a will, then all their estate will go to their surviving spouse, if they have one. Actually, most states only award about a third to half of an estate to the spouse with the remainder going to surviving children, parents, or siblings. If the deceased has children, but no spouse, usually the property goes entirely to the children. If someone has neither a spouse nor children, then property usually passes to surviving parents or siblings.

Some people tell themselves they do not need a will because everyone already knows who is to get what. While your loved ones might know your wishes, unless you have a will, they don't have the legal authority to distribute your property! A will not only expresses your wishes but grants the authority to enforce those wishes. There are too many horror stories of families torn apart over who gets Auntie Dorothy's filigreed vase. Rather than tempting fate with the possibility of your family members jockeying for position over the disposition of your assets, legally document your wishes.

Generally speaking, in order for a document to be recognized as the last will and testament of an individual, it must appear to the court to be intended to be one's final will as expressed by the wording contained in the statement. Therefore, a simple list of property and beneficiaries would not qualify. It also needs to indicate that the individual is of sound mind and be signed by two witnesses in each other's presence, along with the presence of the person whose will it is. In essence, the witnesses are testifying to the fact that the person knows what he or she is doing and that the document is intended to be his or her last will and testament.

where to begin

It is important to pace yourself and not let end-of-life planning become overwhelming. I find setting monthly doable goals helps, and as each segment gets organized, it's easy to subsequently update and revise information as needed. If you are someone who tells yourself you don't need a will because you don't have anything of value, you are wrong. Running to an attorney to draw up your will is not the first step. Giving yourself a basic education and organizing your thoughts and information first will allow you to make a list of specific aspects of your affairs that you want carefully addressed. It will also save time and, therefore, money.

If you want to save some money, before you go to an attorney, gather the following information so the attorney can advise you and create your will or trust:

- Some basic information about you that will be needed by the Executor of your estate
- An inventory of your possessions
- A list of all accounts and assets held in your name or as joint accounts
- Instructions about what can be found where, including legal documents, keys, access codes, and your electronic life

- Your wishes concerning the distribution of your money and possessions

Once you have your will or trust legally documented, review it annually along with your Advance Healthcare Planning documents.

Depending upon your heirs and the complexity and value of your financial assets and possessions, your lawyer will advise you whether a will or a trust is more appropriate for your needs. Either way, you will need to spend some time figuring out what you have and what you want to have happen with it. Having well-organized information makes the actual creation of your legal documents much easier and therefore less expensive. A good place to start is to create an inventory of what you have. The more thorough you are with this, the less time, aggravation, and money it will cost in professional fees for someone else to do so without your input. Expect this to be one of those projects you break down into smaller goals and do over time.

Exercise 35: My Inventory of Belongings

Make a list of all your valuable possessions, including real estate and tangible personal property such as vehicles, equipment, heirlooms, antiques, jewelry, art, collections, equipment, and other valuables. Take a picture of each item on your list. Provide a sufficient description of each item to indicate its location, value, and if any appraisals have been done.

- For each item, indicate whether you own it in whole or in part. If the latter, identify other owner(s) and your respective portions of ownership.
- For each item, indicate its location as well as the location of any files or documents pertaining to that item.

- In anticipation of creating or updating your will or trust, designate for each item to whom you would like it to go after your death. This may be a person or organization. If there is to be more than one recipient, specify how the ownership is to be divided. Then, in the event that the named beneficiary predeceases you, name a second and third level of recipients.
- Make a second list of any additional items you own that you would like to designate to go to a particular person(s) after your death. These might include things of sentimental value or significance to the designated recipient. For each item, note its location, take a picture of it, and indicate the person you would like to receive it as well as an alternate in the event that the first designee predeceases you.
- Make a list of all potential beneficiaries named in your list, along with their contact information.

This next exercise is the most cumbersome as it involves identifying, recording, and organizing all your financial and business records. Take your time, as there is a lot to do here, and being thorough, accurate, and well organized is important.

Exercise 36: The Location of My Financial and Business Records

List the account information and locations for all of the following, noting if these are individual or joint accounts, if there are any assigned beneficiaries, and where any relevant records are stored:

- Income Tax Records for the current or previous year
- Banking Records (including checking, savings, credit unions, and safe deposit boxes)

- Contracts
- Insurance Policies (including life, homeowners, mortgage, vehicle, liability, health, and long-term policies)
- Employment Records
- Credit Cards, Debit Cards, and ATM Cards
- Online Paperless Billing Accounts
- Automatic Bill Payment Accounts
- Paper Billing Accounts
- Mortgage(s)
- Loans Payable
- Loans Receivable
- Retirement Accounts (including pensions, Keogh plans, 401k plans, securities, stocks, bonds, commodities, mutual funds, savings bonds, CDs, Treasury notes, annuities)
- Patents, copyrights, trademarks, or royalty agreements

Be sure that your beneficiary designations on retirement plans, bank and brokerage accounts, and insurance policies match those stated in your will. If there is a discrepancy, then the person named in the policy or account records as the beneficiary will get the money.

Exercise 37: My Electronic Life

Make a list of all electronic communications equipment you own such as cellphones and computers and any passwords required for access to the device itself or to your applications and/or accounts on the device. Indicate whether they are owned or leased and the location of any contracts. Taking pictures of these devices helps as well.

Include all online accounts (financial, retail, medical, social media) and list what email address is associated with that account as well as your password, user name, and any codes and security questions and answers that might be required to access your account. It can be overwhelming how many accounts we have. I have a ten-page list!

---

the executor of your estate

The Executor you choose is responsible for carrying out your wishes in accordance with the laws of your state. If you have not designated an Executor, then the state court will choose an administrator to finalize your affairs. You will need to appoint both an Executor and an alternate in the event that your Executor is unable to serve in this capacity when the time comes. Do not appoint Co-Executors as someone has to have final say. You will want to familiarize your Executor with all relevant information, records, accounts, and trusted advisors (attorney, accountant, financial advisor, etc.). They will also need access to contact information for beneficiaries and others who need to be contacted. It is wise to provide your Executor with written instructions and review them annually just to be sure they are comprehensive and clearly understood. The less time your Executor needs to spend personally to wrap up your affairs and the fewer professionals he or she needs to hire to assist with this work, the less money will be required to be withdrawn from your estate to pay these individuals. Plain and simple—time is money. It can also be very stressful to have to search through your papers without knowing what one is looking for or where things are located.

The duties of the Executor include the following:

- Before the will is probated (approved by the court), the Executor will need to pay for your end-of-life ritual expenses and maintain and take care of estate property, including any businesses run by the deceased.

- After the will has been probated, the Executor will need to:
  - Publish a legal notice in the newspaper that the estate is in probate.
  - Take an inventory of Estate assets. If the assets are valuable, an item-by-item professional appraisal may be required. If the estate is modest and asset values are fairly straightforward, then the Executor's assessment will probably be sufficient.
  - Go through the personal files of the deceased to gather all account and policy information needed.
  - Make designated distributions to beneficiaries and dispose of the remainder of your belongings.

probate

Probate is the legal process of proving that a will is valid: it has been drawn, signed, and witnessed in accordance with state law. The probate process evolved as a way to minimize conflicting claims of entitlement or ownership of property left after a death.

Here's how the probate process works. The Executor files the will in probate court along with proof that he or she has been legally appointed as Executor. A challenge at this level may result in a genealogical search to identify all blood relatives of the deceased to verify that there are no other alleged Executors of the estate. Once the Executor or administrator of the estate has been recognized, letters go out to the heirs and relatives and notices go in newspapers, so creditors can make their claims. Then the Executor has to determine which bills, claims, expenses, taxes, and fees are valid claims against the estate and which are not. Valid claims are paid, and the Executor distributes what is left to the heirs named in the will. If there is no will, the state names the heirs (usually relatives of the deceased). The big deal about probate is the amount of time, money, and aggravation this process is going to take. And that primarily depends upon how well your affairs have been put in order ahead of time.

Even the simplest of estates can take about a year to distribute. What can you do to minimize the cost of the probate process? Create well-organized records of relevant information, get a professional will or trust set up, and distribute assets in ways that are exempt from probate. These include life insurance, property in a trust, holding property jointly with the right of survivorship, and creating payable-on-death accounts which are all payable directly to the named beneficiaries without probate. While even these forms of distribution may require some attorney and accounting fees, the expense is often less than those required by the probate process.

granting power of attorney

A Power of Attorney is a legal document that allows you to give someone the authority to handle your finances for you if and when you are unable to do so for yourself. Just as a Healthcare Proxy has the authority to make healthcare decisions on your behalf when you are unable to do so for yourself, someone who has legal Power of Attorney for you can pay your bills, deposit checks, and make all financial and investment decisions for you.

There are two kinds of Power of Attorney. The first is a General Power of Attorney in which the authority granted ends when you are deemed to no longer be mentally capable of handling your finances yourself. In contrast, a Durable Power of Attorney extends this authority beyond your loss of capacity. Both kinds expire at the time of your death, and responsibility for your financial affairs will be handled according to the directions in your will or according to state law in the event that you do not have a will.

payable-on-death accounts

By setting up your bank, brokerage, or other type of account as a Payable-on-Death (POD) account, you can name a beneficiary to receive all the money in that account directly when you die. In other words, that money does not become part of your estate that will go through probate. Those funds are paid immediately and directly to your designated beneficiary, whether a person or an organization. They cannot get money from your account while you are alive. POD accounts, which also are called Transfer-on-Death (TOD) accounts, generally are easy to set up at banks, brokerage firms, and other financial institutions.

naming a guardian for minor children

When a parent dies, someone else becomes the guardian of any minor children. In most situations, a surviving spouse living in the same household is recognized as the guardian, unless proved to be unfit. In the case of a divorce, the death of the custodial parent will most likely result in the noncustodial parent being named guardian if they wish to be, even if the custodial parent had named someone else to be guardian to the children. While state laws may override someone's stated wishes in a will, it is still very important to designate a guardian and at least one alternate to influence the decision of the court and to make your wishes clearly known to family members.

A guardian is legally responsible for the person and property of the children. In some cases, it might be appropriate to appoint different people for these functions, especially if the child has significant assets or if the person deemed to be the best person to nurture them is either unskilled, unwilling, or unable to tend to their financial and legal affairs. Due to the cumbersome legal requirements for periodic reporting and the limitations on how the money left to a child can be spent, many people choose not to leave money directly to a minor child. An alternative is to leave the money or property to the child when he or she comes of age (usually age eighteen or twenty-one) and is recognized by the law to have exclusive control over his or her own property. To avoid some of these issues, many people with minor children choose to establish a trust instead of a will.

pets

Some of us have pets that we treasure and want to make sure will be well cared for after we are gone. Be sure to identify at least one or two people who agree to either personally care for your pets or will find them a home.

where to keep your records

A copy of your Advance Healthcare Planning documents should be kept together and be located visibly. The first place the EMTs will look for your records if they are called to your home is on your refrigerator. Either put your documents there or a note to the EMTs directing them to your documents. I also keep a copy of my medical history with my documents, so they are well informed about my physical health.

The other key documents, such as your will, power of attorney, and information pertaining to your end-of-life ritual preferences, should be clearly marked in your files, and your Executor should know where this information is. Although a safe deposit box sounds like a good place to keep these important documents, it has two big drawbacks: The box is only available when the bank is open and only to people who are signers on the box with you. Consider keeping originals in your box for safekeeping and copies at home that indicate the location of the original documents.

end-of-life ritual decisions made really easy

It is enormously helpful to your loved ones if you take the time to express your preferences for any end-of-life rituals that are important to you. This includes both spiritual and religious rituals you want performed before your death, as well as your thoughts on a funeral or memorial service or other gathering on your behalf after your death. While there are two basic schools of thought about whether these rituals are for the deceased or for his or her loved ones, I believe that the more input given by the individual, the less stressful it will be for those planning the ritual when the time comes.

Exercise 38: Important Names and Contacts

Make a list of key people who will need to be contacted in the event of your death. Be sure to include the name, organization, address, phone, email, and fax numbers for each of the following:

- Executor
- Attorney
- Financial Durable Power of Attorney
- Healthcare Proxy and Alternate Proxy

- Primary Care Physician
- Dentist
- Funeral Home
- Clergy
- Religious Organizations/Affiliations
- Accountant
- Financial Manager
- Stockbroker
- Tax Preparer
- Insurance agent
- Home Security Company
- Property Manager (if renting)
- Clubs/Organizations you are affiliated with

Make two additional lists—one of people you want contacted in the event that you are near death and a second of people to be notified of your death. If you want to do this on your computer as two groups, be sure to label them clearly and to let your Executor know they are there.

---

end-of-life ritual options

There are two primary kinds of end-of-life rituals—those performed before death and those after. While you might not be particularly fond of funeral or memorial services, it is important to remember that there is something universal about these ceremonial acts that gives a fuller understanding of our common humanity. Regardless of the form that they take, death rituals are an important part of the process of grieving, both in terms of letting go of the deceased and carrying forward our love for him or her. With the exception of the disposition of the body through either burial or cremation, all other services and rituals are optional by law but may be required to comply with religious or ethnic traditions.

• Before-Death Rituals

Most before-death rituals relate to spiritual or religious beliefs and practices of the dying. For example, in my spiritual community, prayer groups come to our deathbed and serve at a distance as well in support of our soul's journey out of the body. If you have any rituals that would be important to you, be sure to include instructions and contact information with your Advance Healthcare Directives. If you are the loved one of a dying person, be sure to ask if there are any rituals that would be important to them.

• After-Death Rituals

Essentially, after-death rituals typically involve a funeral or a memorial service. A funeral might be prescribed by the deceased's religious or spiritual tradition or may be a nonreligious service performed at a funeral home or elsewhere. If a religious or spiritual service is to be held, the appropriate clergy and funeral director can provide guidance on what is involved. The primary difference between a funeral and a memorial service is that a funeral tends to focus upon tradition, grief, and loss while a memorial is typically a customized celebration of the life lived by the deceased along with an acknowledgment of loss.

- A Traditional Funeral: A traditional funeral tends to put more emphasis on the body of the deceased—preserving and beautifying it for a last look and the transporting and burial or cremation of the body. As noted earlier, the National Funeral Directors Association estimates the average funeral in the US, excluding a cemetery plot and grave, to be about $9,000.

Funeral directors are being called upon to revolutionize their approach to stay relevant as many of us are rethinking our priorities for after-death rituals and are finding alternative approaches that are less costly and, for some, more heartfelt. Demand is growing for memorial services and celebrations, cremation, and green funerals. Some people are even choosing to host an end-of-life party before they die to say their final farewells to friends and family. New choices bring with them the opportunity, challenge, and increasing importance of figuring out ahead of time what is meaningful to us.

Exploring what is right for you in terms of end-of-life rituals may or may not involve actual preplanning with a funeral home and prepayment for services. However, it is a kindness to your loved ones if you leave instructions about your wishes regarding a service in your honor, cremation versus burial, and any other pertinent instructions or information.

Making arrangements for end-of-life rituals is no longer simply a matter of going to the funeral home to be guided through their process of making choices after someone has died. Many are seeking services in locations other than funeral homes, which are often considered too somber. It is more common for people to think through what is and is not meaningful to them and to document their preferences ahead of time.

- Memorials to Grieve Loss and Celebrate Life: An effective memorial gives solace to the bereaved, dignity to the departed, and heartfelt memories to the assembled mourners. It may be a small and intimate gathering of loved ones or a gala, multimedia event in honor of the deceased. Some people are creating memorial videos or memory books to be shared at their services, allowing loved ones to have greater insight into the life, beliefs, and wisdom of the deceased from his or her point of view. Some are choosing to hold memorial services at home or a favorite place in nature, a restaurant, auditorium, or some location other than a funeral home that holds special meaning. In some states, this trend is in part driven by state laws that prohibit the serving of food and beverages in the funeral home. While funerals almost always take place near the time of death, a memorial may be done weeks or months later, allowing loved ones to move past their initial stage of mourning first. Typically, memorials are held within a year after the death.

The question of who will officiate at a memorial is a matter of personal choice, as there are no rules. You might prefer a member of the clergy of a particular religion but not want to have a traditional funeral service. Or a non-dogmatic interfaith or ecumenical minister might be appropriate—one who can set a spiritual-but-not-religious tone. Most funeral directors are now available to perform a brief tribute in the funeral home, but many only offer a standardized format. The celebrant movement has created a new kind of officiant. A celebrant is a funeral director or lay person who has attended a workshop or online program to learn how to officiate at memorials. Celebrants are not ordained clergy members. Finally, you might prefer to have a relative or friend officiate. Each type of officiant, as well as the individuals in each category, brings their own unique set of skills and capabilities. It is important to choose carefully as some officiants are able to give you much more support than others.

- Green Funerals: Environmentally conscious funerals are a new trend that includes any or all of the following: no embalming; the use of biodegradable clothing, shroud, and/or casket; and burial in a green cemetery or the spreading of ashes for those who have been cremated.

Many people do not realize that embalming, expensive sealed caskets, and burial vaults are not required by law. However, traditional cemeteries may require them. In contrast, a green cemetery or memorial nature preserve does not. A green cemetery is designed to let nature take its course by promoting a natural habitat through the growth of native trees, shrubs, and wildflowers, which bring birds and other wildlife to the area. No pesticides and herbicides are used in an attempt to control nature. A green burial is an alternative to cremation for those who are environmentally conscious, for the carbon footprint of a green burial is significantly less than that of cremation. Green funerals are now considered the most environmentally friendly alternative for the disposition of human remains. Typically, it is far less costly than a traditional burial as well.

ways to reduce costs of end-of-life rituals

Since end-of-life rituals are among the most expensive purchases many consumers will ever make, it is wise to pay attention to what you are paying for and to find ways to reduce expenditures. Remember, spending more money does not equate to having greater love and respect for the deceased. Here are some ways to reduce your expenses:

- Cremation instead of burial or green burial eliminates the expense of a casket, vault, or burial plot. A green burial reduces costs even further.
- Renting a casket or selecting the lowest cost container available for cremation
- Opting out of expensive urns and memorial walls in favor of dispersing the ashes in accordance with state laws

- Choosing direct burial or immediate cremation to save the expense of embalming, body preparation, and funeral home and staff expenses associated with having a viewing

home funerals

Just as home births and home schooling have found renewed appeal, so have home funerals, which enable families and loved ones to take charge personally of the end-of-life rituals surrounding the death of a loved one. Home funerals are legal in most states. If interested in a home funeral, check with the Funeral Consumer Alliance (funerals.org) to determine what is legal in your state. This non-profit organization seeks to protect the right of consumers to choose a meaningful, dignified, affordable funeral. In addition to providing educational materials and monitoring funeral industry trends and practices, they also serve as a consumer advocate for legal and regulatory reforms in the industry. There are also numerous websites available that provide home funeral guidelines in different states that can show you how to have a dignified and loving home funeral for less than $1,000.

joining a memorial society

Memorial societies provide members with the guarantee of a low-cost cremation or funeral in exchange for a one-time modest fee of approximately $25 to $50. Many are associated with the Funeral Consumers Alliance. Local memorial societies are also nonsectarian, not-for-profit organizations that help people who desire simplicity, dignity, and economy in funeral arrangements. Through alliances with local licensed funeral directors, these societies can assure members a selection of plans for cremation, burial, and other services, ranging in cost from approximately $800 to $2,500 and at no cost if a member chooses to donate his or her body to a medical school.

prepaid funerals and Totten trusts

The motivation to prepay for one's funeral with a particular funeral home is not only logical and financially astute, but it is an act of loving kindness as well. Very simply, it allows us to free our loved ones of the burden of having to plan and bear the expense of our end-of-life rituals. Furthermore, paying at today's prices for a hopefully distant future need is a hedge against inflation.

While some people have had positive experiences with prepaid funerals, the general wisdom is that, while it pays to plan ahead, it is not necessarily beneficial to pay in advance. Unfortunately, the reality is that millions of dollars of prepayment funds are misspent or misappropriated every year. In rare cases, funeral providers sell virtually worthless policies or mishandle, mismanage, or embezzle funds. Also, some funeral homes go out of business before the need for one's prepaid funeral arises. In 1984, the Funeral Rule was enacted by the Federal Trade Commission, requiring funeral providers to give consumers accurate, itemized price information and specifications about their goods and services. Unfortunately, this law does not cover many aspects of prepayment contracts that are governed solely by state laws. Most states have preneed contract laws; however, they vary widely from state to state.

A safer alternative is to set up a Totten Trust which is a payable-on-death (POD) account. This is a trust fund that you set up with a bank and can deposit whatever amount you wish. The account is portable and remains in your name until death when it is immediately released to the account beneficiary rather than having to go through probate. It is suggested that you appoint the person you wish to handle your end-of-life arrangements as the trust beneficiary.

There are two final considerations about preneed contracts. First is the fact that an increasing number of people are choosing to design their own services outside of the funeral home setting. The second is that more important than prepaying for your end of life rituals is discussing your preferences with your family or the one person you would like to have carry out your wishes.

documenting personal preferences

With so many choices to be made at such a tender-hearted time, it behooves us to give our loved ones the gift of documenting our preferences or lack thereof ahead of time, so they are not left with the task of trying to figure out what we would have wanted. Imagine if you no longer feared death and had all your affairs in order, you could simply be free to enjoy living your life.

Exercise 39: Preferences for My End-of-Life Rituals
and Body Disposition

This exercise helps you to articulate and organize information and thoughts about your obituary, end-of-life ritual, and body disposition.

1. Obituary:
    • What, if any, input would you like to give for your obituary?
    • What newspapers/websites should your obituary appear in?
    • Are there any organizations you would like a copy sent to?
2. Memorial and/or Funeral:

- Indicate in your own words whether or not you have preferences about your end-of-life rituals or if you would like someone else to take charge of arrangements at the time of your death. If so, identify that person(s) and provide contact information.
- Have you made prearrangements for your funeral/memorial? If so, with whom/what funeral home? If you have prepaid, indicate where the contract is located.
- Which of the following do you prefer?
  - A traditional religious funeral service (specify which spiritual or religious tradition)
  - A nonreligious funeral or memorial service/celebration of life
  - Would you like both a funeral and a memorial service?
  - Would you prefer that no service be held?
- If you want either a funeral or memorial:
  - Do you want it to be public or private?
  - Where would you like your service to be held?
  - Do you have a preferred officiant? Is so, provide contact information.
  - Indicate any specific preferences you have regarding the content of your service.

3. Body Disposition:
- If you prefer to be buried:
  - Do you want a green funeral or eco-burial?
  - Have you purchased a plot? If so, where is it and where is your contract located?
  - Do you have any specific preferences about your burial?
- If you prefer to be cremated:
  - What would you like done with your cremated remains?
  - Do you have any specific preferences about your cremation?

Exercise 40: Moving Forward and Thank You

And here comes your final exercise.

1. Make a list of any end-of-life planning that you have not yet completed. Decide when you want to complete this and book appointments with yourself on your calendar to follow through.
2. Ask yourself if there is anyone among your family and friends who you would like to help or encourage to get his/her end-of-life planning competed. Decide how you are going to do this and act accordingly.
3. Stand in front of the mirror and make eye contact with yourself. Thank yourself for doing your part to break through the Death Taboo. Say, "I'm proud of myself for lightening up about death so I can enjoy my life even more."

chapter 15

the end?

*"*Goodbyes are only for those who love with their eyes.
Because for those who love with heart and soul, there is no
such thing as separation.*"*

—Jalāl ad-Dīn Rumi

D EATH PUNCTUATES LIFE. IF LIFE did not end with death—
the end of the physical existence—if we just went on and on
and on for eons in our current identities, how would our lives be
different? Would we keep aging forever? Would life matter quite so
much if we did not die? The inescapability of death challenges us
regarding what we hold dear. Ironically, with all our focus on the
physical—how we look and what we accumulate—in the end it is
love and our very breath which we hold most precious, and even
those must be let go.

It is death that makes life so very precious and profound. Those
who deny death and pretend it doesn't exist take life for granted and
are lulled into a kind of unconsciousness that forfeits the opportunity to live boldly, deeply, and profoundly connected to ourselves
and each other. Have you ever watched someone with a terminal
diagnosis embrace the sweetness and beauty of life and the tenderness of loving with a heightened sense of participation and appreciation that escapes many of the rest of us? What great teachers
they are for us. Given the inevitability of death, it seems bizarre
to pretend we can make it go away by denying it and that we are so

insulted, shocked, and surprised when it is our turn. Far better, we have the option to live as though any moment could be our last.

Accepting the reality of death and dying is not a resignation or some kind of approval of the idea but rather a surrender into the mystery of living and dying—of the fact that life and death do, in fact, stand side by side, harbingers each to the other abiding. For some, this surrendering of what we hold onto and what we try to push away from us is an acknowledgment of God or a power or force that is greater than our individual will. It is a matter of tapping into an inherent wisdom of the full cycle of life and death as experienced throughout the natural world. An old Yiddish adage says: "Man plans, and God laughs." This captures the reality of our earthly existence. Whether we believe in God or not, clearly there are forces beyond our illusion of control that impact the course and quality of our lives. Spiritual literature is filled with advice that we must "let go and let God." That sounds good, but in reality, most of us find more comfort in attempting to exercise some semblance of control over our lives. Then life happens, appointments are canceled or rescheduled, the weather doesn't cooperate with our plans, marriages and friendships end, and all sorts of surprises—including death—come out of left field, throwing a wrench into our best-laid plans.

Somehow, we must cope with the fact that we are not gods with complete control over our lives. We live, we hope, we plan, and we discover that time reveals what the truth will be. This is one of the great cosmic jokes of this universe we live in.

Each of us is entitled to our own beliefs about death. Whether you believe that death is the end and nothing happens after that, or that we have nonphysical identities that continue on, your beliefs will inform how you live your life and how you relate to death. In my opinion, inherited beliefs deserve to be challenged or explored by an individual rather than taken on blind faith. Challenging our beliefs gives us the opportunity to strengthen them or to evolve them. I remember in college when I was first introduced to the concept of reincarnation and later to our identities as souls, my personal beliefs about life and death were profoundly altered to this day.

The following poem by Henry Scott-Holland (1847-1918), "Death Is Nothing at All," is often read at funerals. Scott-Holland was a priest at St. Paul's Cathedral of London and did not intend this writing to be a poem. It was actually delivered as part of a sermon entitled "Death, the King of Terrors" in 1910 while the body of King Edward VII was lying in state at Westminster. My mother asked me to read it at her funeral.

Death is nothing at all.
It does not count.
I have only slipped away into the next room.
Nothing has happened.
Everything remains exactly as it was.
I am I, and you are you,
and the old life that we lived so fondly together is
untouched, unchanged.
Whatever we were to each other, that we are still.

Call me by the old familiar name.
Speak of me in the easy way which you always used.
Put no difference into your tone.
Wear no forced air of solemnity or sorrow.

Laugh as we always laughed at the little jokes that we
enjoyed together.
Play, smile, think of me, pray for me.
Let my name be ever the household word that it
always was.
Let it be spoken without an effort, without the ghost
of a shadow upon it.

Life means all that it ever meant.

It is the same as it ever was.
There is absolute and unbroken continuity.
What is this death but a negligible accident?

Why should I be out of mind because I am out of
sight?
I am but waiting for you, for an interval,
somewhere very near,
just round the corner.

All is well.
Nothing is hurt; nothing is lost.
One brief moment and all will be as it was before.
How we shall laugh at the trouble of parting when we
meet again!

This poem reminds me of all the ways that my dear mother Cake lives on in my heart and in my daily life. Soon after her death, I stoically brought a carload of her things to the thrift shop. The last bag contained winter hats, and on the very top was my mother's favorite. As I turned to go, my hand reached behind me and grabbed that hat. Ever since, it has lived on the headrest of the front passenger's seat of my car. I just needed to keep that little piece of her—her love for that hat and my memories of her in it—alive. Every time I look at it, I feel her with me, and I smile.

works cited

Arntz, A., L. Dreesen, and H. Merckelbach. 1991. "Attention, Not Anxiety, Influences Pain." *Behavior Research and Therapy,* no. 29: 41–50. doi.org/10.1016/S0005-7967(09)8006-5.

AXA Equitable. 2006. "Aging Parents and Common Sense: A Practical Guide for You and Your Parents." *Consumer Insight Series*, 5th ed. caregiving.org/wp-content/uploads/2020/05/Aging-Parent-Guide_5thed.pdf.

Bourgeault, Cynthia. 2005. "Jesus as Tantric Master." Audio CD disc 2, track 3. *Encountering the Wisdom Jesus.* Louisville, CO: Sounds True.

———. 2005. "The Kingdom of Heaven is Within." Audio CD disc 2, track 3. *Encountering the Wisdom Jesus.* Louisville, CO: Sounds True.

Brach, Tara. 2014. "Transforming Pain into Joy." *Writing to Heal Webinar: Interview with Mark Matousek.*

Brayne, Sue, and Peter Fenwick. 2008. *Nearing the End of Life: A Guide for Relatives and Friends of the Dying.* Highfield-Southampton, UK: University of Southampton/Clinical Neuroscience Division.

Brayne, Sue. 2020. *Living Fully, Dying Consciously: The Path to Spiritual Wellbeing.* Guildford-Surrey, UK: White Crow Books.

Brierley, John. 2014. *A Pilgrim's Guide to the Camino de Santiago,* 10th ed. Ashland, OR: Camino Guides, Kaminn Media Ltd.

Byock, Ira, MD. 2014. *The Four Things That Matter Most.* New York: Atria Books-Simon & Schuster.

California Health Foundation. 2012. "Final Chapter: Californians' Attitudes and Experiences with Death and Dying." chcf.org/wp-content/uploads/2017/12/PDF-FinalChapterDeathDying.pdf.

Callanan, Maggie. 2009. *Final Journeys: A Practical Guide for Bringing Care and Comfort at the End of Life*. New York: Bantam-Random House.

Caring.com. 2020. "Estate Planning and Wills Survey." caring.com/caregivers/estate-planning/wills-survey.

Carver, Raymond. 1996. *All of Us: The Collected Poems*. New York: Vintage Books.

Chödrön, Pema. 2007. *Practicing Peace in Times of War*. Berkeley, CA: Shambhala Publications.

——— . 2019. *Taking the Leap: Freeing Ourselves from Old Habits and Fears*. Berkeley, CA: Shambhala Publications.

Clary, Patrick. 2006. *Dying for Beginners*. Owens Valley, CA: Lost Borders Press.

DeSpelder, Lynne Ann, and Albert Lee Strickland. 2009. *The Last Dance: Encountering Death and Dying*. 8th ed. New York: McGraw-Hill Higher Education.

Duke, Marshall P. 2013. "The Stories That Bind Us: What Are the Twenty Questions?" *Huffington Post* (March 23, 2013). huffingtonpost.com/marshall-p-duke/the-stories-that-bind-us-_b_2918975.html.

Ecclesiastes 3:1–2 (KJV).

Eisenberg, Richard. 2014. "Americans' Ostrich Approach to Estate Planning." *Forbes/Personal Finance* (April 4, 2014). forbes.com/sites/nextavenue/2014/04/09/americans-ostrich-approach-to-estate-planning/?sh=788c6d81521.7.

Emerson, Ralph Waldo. 1995. *Emerson's Essays*. New York: Harper Perennial.

Ertz, Susan. 1943. *Anger in the Sky*. 1st ed. London: Hodder & Stoughton.

Fairleader, Philip. 2007. *The Late Middle Ages*. Chantilly, VA: The Teaching Company.

Feifel, Herman, ed. 1983. *The Meaning of Death*. New York: McGraw-Hill.

Fenwick, Peter, and Elizabeth Fenwick. 2008. *The Art of Dying*. New York: Bloomsbury Continuum.

Firestone, Lisa. 2015. "The Value of Sadness." *Psychology Today* (July 2015). psychologytoday.com/us/blog/compassion-matters/201507/the-value-sadness.

Gawande, Atul. 2014. *Being Mortal: Medicine and What Matters in the End*. New York: Metropolitan Books.

Hayes, Temple. "When Did You Die?" *OM Times Magazine* (December 2014): 23–24.

He-Ru-Ka, Gtsan-Smyon, W. Y. Evans-Wentz, Zia-Ba-Bsam-'Grub, and Donald S. Lopez Jr. 2000. *Tibet's Great Yogi: Milarepa*. Oxford, UK: Oxford University Press.

Huffington, Arianna. 2014. An Interview with Oprah Winfrey. OWN: Super Soul Sunday (May 10, 2014).

James, John W., Russell Friedman, and Eric Cline. 2003. *Grief Index: the "hidden" annual costs of grief in America's workplace: 2003 Report*. Sherman Oaks, CA: Grief Recovery Institute Educational Foundation.

John-Roger. 1976. *The Power Within You*. Los Angeles: Baraka Books.

———. 1984. *Passage into Spirit*. Los Angeles: Baraka Books.

———, 2004. with Pauli Sanderson. *When Are You Coming Home?* Los Angeles: Mandeville Press.

Johnson, Judith. 2008. *Life as a Trust Walk*. PhD diss., Peace Theological Seminary and College of Philosophy, Los Angeles.

———. 2013. *The Wedding Ceremony Planner*. 2nd ed. Naperville, IL: Sourcebooks Casablanca.

Kabat-Zinn, J. 2015. An Interview with Oprah Winfrey. OWN: Super Soul Sunday, (April 12, 2015).

Kabir. 2007. *Kabir: Ecstatic Poems*. Translated by Robert Bly. Boston: Beacon Press.

Karnes, Barbara. 2012. *End of Life Guideline Series: A Compilation of Barbara Karnes Booklets*. Oakland, CA: Berrett-Koehler Publishers/BK Books.

Keyssar, Judith Redwing. 2010. *Last Acts of Kindness.* Scotts Valley, CA: CreateSpace Independent Publishing Platform.

Kierkegaard, Søren. 1986. *Fear and Trembling.* Translated by Alastair Hannay. New York: Penguin Classics.

Kochanek, Kenneth D., Sherry L. Murphy, Jiaquan Xu, and Elizabeth Arias. 2017. *Mortality in the United States, 2016.* Centers for Disease Control and Prevention: National Center for Health Statistics.

Kübler-Ross, Elisabeth. 2014. *On Death and Dying.* New York: Scribner.

Kübler-Ross, Elisabeth and Todd Gold. 1998. *The Wheel of Life: A Memoir of Living and Dying.* New York: Touchstone/Scribner.

Langer, Gary. 2002. "Poll: Americans Not Planning for the Future." *ABC News,* (August 26, 2002).

Lewis, C. S. 2001. *A Grief Observed.* C. S. Lewis Signature Classics Series. New York: Harperone.

Lipka, Michael and Claire Gecewicz. 2017. "More Americans Now Say They're Spiritual but Not Religious." Pew Research Center/Fact Tank. pewresearch.org/fact-tank/2017/09/06/more-americans-now-say-theyre-spiritual-but-not-religious/.

Lipton, Bruce H., and Steve Bhaerman. 2010. *Spontaneous Evolution.* Audio CD. Louisville, CO: Sounds True.

Lucy's Love Bus (2006). lucyslovebus.org/who-we-are/about-lucy.html.

Manns, Mary Lynn, and Samantha Little. 2011. "Grief and Compassion in the Workplace." University of North Carolina at Asheville. cs.unca.edu/~manns/GriefAndCompassionInTheWorkplace.pdf.

Marion, Jim. 2011. *Putting on the Mind of Christ: The Inner Work of Christian Spirituality.* Newburyport, MA: Hampton Roads Publishing.

Masters, Robert Agustus. 2013. *Knowing Your Shadow.* Audio CD. Louisville, CO: Sounds True.

Matousek, Mark. 2008. *When You're Falling, Dive.* 2nd ed. Scotts Valley, CA: CreateSpace Independent Publishing Platform.

Mehrabian, Albert. 1981. *Silent Messages: Implicit Communication of Emotions and Attitudes*. Belmont, CA: Wadsworth.

Merton, Thomas. 1999. *The Silent Life*. 1st ed. New York: Farrar, Straus and Giroux.

MetLife Mature Market Institute and National Alliance for Caregiving. 2006. *The MetLife Caregiving Cost Study: Productivity Losses to U.S. Business*. caregiving.org/wp-content/uploads/2020/05/Caregiver-Cost-Study.pdf.

Miller, Andrea. 2014. *Buddha's Daughters: Teachings from Women Who Are Shaping Buddhism in the West*. Boulder, CO: Shambhala Publications.

Miller, B. J. 2015. "What Really Matters at the End of Life." March 2015. TED Talk. ted.com/talks/bj_miller_what_really_matters_at_the_end_of_life?language=en.

Moeller, Stephen. 2017. "Complicated Grief." *The Grief Recovery Method* (blog). Grief Recovery Institute, February 22, 2017. griefrecoverymethod.com/blog/2017/02/complicated-grief.

Moore, Thomas. 1994. *Care of the Soul: A Guide for Cultivating Depth and Sacredness in Everyday Life*. New York: HarperCollins.

Morton, John. 2003. "Loving Each Day." *Movement of Spiritual Inner Awareness* (July 30, 2003). msia.org/quotes/search?qs=When+we+are+not+aware+of+God%27s+constant+love+and+blessing&lang=en.

Moyers, Bill. 2000. *On Our Own Terms: Moyers on Dying*. September 10, 2000. New York: Public Broadcasting System (PBS).

Murphy, Sherry L., Jiaquan Zu, and Kenneth D. Kochanek. 2013. "Deaths: Final Data for 2010." *National Vital Statistics Reports*. *The Center for Disease Control*.

National Alliance for Caregiving and AARP. 2009. "Caregiving in the U.S. 2009." (November 2009). assets.aarp.org/rgcenter/il/caregiving_09_fr.pdf.

National Funeral Directors Association. 2019. "2019 NFDA General Price List Study Shows Funeral Costs Not Rising As Fast As Rate of Inflation." (December 19, 2019). nfda.org/news/

media-center/nfda-news-releases/id/4797/2019-nfda-general-price-list-study-shows-funeral-costs-not-rising-as-fast-as-rate-of-inflation/.

National Hospice and Palliative Care Organization. 2018. "History of Hospice Care." nhpco.org/hospice-care-overview/history-of-hospice/.

Ostaseski, Frank. 2017. *The Five Invitations: Discovering What Death Can Teach Us About Living Fully*. New York: Flatiron Books.

Phifer, Nan. 2001. *Memoirs of the Soul*. Toronto: Walking Stick Press/Penguin Random House, Canada.

Pollard, Kelvin M., and Paola Scommegna. 2014. "Just How Many Baby Boomers Are There?" *Population Reference Bureau* (April 16, 2014). *prb.org/justhowmanybabyboomersarethere/*.

Proverbs 23:7 (KJV).

Ram Dass, and Stephen Levine. 1995. *Grist for the Mill*. Berkeley: Celestial Arts-Ten Speed Press.

———. Ram Dass Audio Collection. 2006. Audio CD: "Conscious Aging." Tracks 4 and 5. Louisville, CO: Sounds True.

Randall, Rhonda. 2015. "America's Health Rankings 2015 Senior Report: Successes and Challenges in Senior Health." *United Health Foundation*. americashealthrankings.org/learn/news/americas-health-rankings-2015-senior-report-successes-challenges-senior-health.

Réa, Rashani. 1991. "The Unbroken." rashani.com/arts/poems/poems-by-rashani/the-unbroken/.

Revelation 3:20 (KJV).

Rilke, Rainer Maria. 1993. *Letters to a Young Poet*. rev. ed. New York: W. W. Norton.

Rogers, Everett M. 2003. *Diffusion of Innovations*. New York: Free Press/Simon & Schuster.

Rumi, Jalāl ad-Dīn. 1995. *The Essential Rumi*. "The Guest House." Translated by Coleman Barks with John Moyne. San Francisco: Harper.

———. 2004. *Rumi: Selected Poems*. Translated by Coleman Barks with John Moyne, A. J. Arberry, and Reynold Nicholson. London: Penguin Books.

Russett, Tim, host. 1997. *Before I Die: Medical Care and Personal Choices*. New York: Public Broadcasting System (PBS).

Sacks, Oliver. 2015. "My Own Life." *New York Times* (February 2, 2015): Op Ed, A25.

Searight, H. Russell, and Jennifer Gafford. 2005. "Cultural Diversity at the End of Life: Issues and Guidelines for Family Physicians." *American Family Physician, Forest Park Hospital Family Medicine Residency Program* (February 1, 2005): Vol. 71, 3.

Sogyal Rinpoche. 1993. *The Tibetan Book of Living and Dying*. San Francisco: Harper.

———. 1996. *Reflecting on Death*. Audio CD. London: Terton Sogyal Trust.

———. 2003. *Living and Dying Today*. Audio CD. London: Terton Sogyal Trust.

———. 2005. *Impermanence*. Audio CD. London: Terton Sogyal Trust.

———. 2011. *The Essence of The Tibetan Book of Living and Dying*. Audio CD. Part One: Contemplating Death and Impermanence. London: Terton Sogyal Trust.

———. 2011. *The Essence of The Tibetan Book of Living and Dying*. Audio CD. Part Two: Preparing for Transformation at Death. London: Terton Sogyal Trust.

———. 2014. *Transcending All Fear of Death*. Audio CD. London: Terton Sogyal Trust.

Teno, Joan, and Pedro Gozalo, et al. 2018. "Site of Death, Place of Care, and Health Care Transitions Among US Medicare Beneficiaries, 2000–2015." *Journal of the American Medical Association* (2018).

The Baltimore Catechism. 1941. *CatholiCity*. rev. ed. catholicity.com/baltimore-catechism/.

"The Cost of Dying." 2010. CBS: *60 Minutes* (August 8, 2010).

Thompson, Hunter S. 1998. *The Proud Highway: Saga of a Desperate Southern Gentleman, 1955–1967*. New York: Ballantine Books.

Tolle, Eckhart. 2004. *The Power of Now*. Vancouver: Namaste Publishing.

Turner, Johanna, and Sharon Lerner. 2012. "Grief at Work: A Guide for Employees and Managers." *American Hospice Foundation*. americanhospice.org/grief-at-work/.

United Health Foundation. 2019. *America's Health Rankings Senior Report*. americashealthrankings.org/learn/reports/2019-senior-report.

Wilson, E. O. 2008. *On Human Nature*. 2nd ed. Cambridge, MA: Harvard University Press.

Wittgenstein, Ludwig. 1966. *Tractatus Logico-Philosophicus*. London: Routledge & Kegan Paul.

Worden, J. William. 2008. *Grief Counseling and Grief Therapy, Fourth Edition: A Handbook for the Mental Health Practitioner*. New York: Springer.

Zaslow, Jeffrey. 2002. "New Index Aims to Calculate the Annual Cost of Despair." November 20, 2002. wsj.com/articles/SB103773937895627388.

acknowledgments

My deepest thanks go to you, my readers, for your part in deconstructing the American Death Taboo. As a result, each day more people are finding peace and greater wisdom in death's presence.

This book has been a fourteen-year birthing process which began with a deathbed promise to my dear mother, Grace Mundy. Fulfillment feels fabulous!

My heart is full for having so many people buoying me along this journey by believing in me and this book. My gratitude to all who have read this manuscript in its many incarnations.

A special thank you to Jeffrey Davis, founder of Tracking Wonder, for showing me how to endure the process of finding my voice and the deeper truth I wanted to speak about in this book . . . again and again and again until I found it.

Thank you to Paul Cohen, Susan Piperato, and Colin Rolfe of Monkfish Book Publishing Company for being such a pleasure to work with and for the true spirit of cooperation with which they have engaged with me as an author.

My gratitude to Ann Hutton, my editor, who polishes my writings and always takes great joy in finding every misplaced comma and my myriad other grammatical errors.

My thanks to Bill Corsa, whose belief in me and the importance of this book kept me going through the most discouraging of times.

And thank you to the EAC (Esteemed Association of Creatives) for providing me a safe place month after month to have them bear witness to my journey. They are always encouraging me and nudging me along with next steps—sometimes crawling and sometimes shooting for the moon. Thank you, Mike Haller, Will Nixon, Ann Hutton, and Adam Hocek.

about the author

 Judith Johnson is an author, mentor, and educator whose work focuses on developing the ability to consciously thrive and evolve into one's best self. Whether writing, mentoring, leading workshops, or speaking to groups, her focus is to help others to live their lives as a true reflection of their most treasured truth and inner wisdom.

A lifelong curiosity has focused Judith's attention on how our beliefs inform our thoughts, feelings, and behaviors. Her work draws upon personal life lessons, her spiritual journey, doctoral degrees in social psychology and spiritual science, wisdom teachings from around the world, and experience in mentoring since 1983.

Ordained as an interfaith minister in 1985, Judith serves as a chaplain at her local hospital and counsels the grieving. She is also the author of *The Wedding Ceremony Planner: The Essential Guide to the Most Important Part of Your Wedding Day* and *Writing Meaningful Wedding Vows*.

Her numerous articles, published online about consciousness, relationships, and the end of life, can be accessed at judithjohnson.com/blogs. To learn more about Judith and her work, visit her website and follow her on Facebook and Instagram as The Thriving Studio.